1999 BEST TRAVEL DEALS

THE EDITORS OF
CONSUMER REPORTS TRAVEL LETTER

Consumers Union • Yonkers, New York

A SPECIAL PUBLICATION FROM CONSUMER REPORTS

Director, Special Publications Andrea Scott
Project Editor Linda Coyner
Designer Susi Oberhelman
Page Composition Jennifer Dixon
Special Publications Staff Robert Markovich, Michael Quincy, Pauline Piekarz, Joyce Childs

CONSUMER REPORTS TRAVEL LETTER

Editor Laurie Berger
Production Associate Richard Schwartz
Research Associates Josef Aukee, Emmitt Graham
Research Assistant Laurie Amat

CONSUMER REPORTS

Editorial Director Jackie Leo
Editor Julia Kagan
Executive Editor/Director, Editorial Operations Eileen Denver
Design Director George Arthur
Managing Art Director Timothy LaPalme
Director, Publishing Operations Maggie Brenner
Retail Sales & Marketing Will Michalopoulos
Manufacturing Coordinator Steven Schiavone

CONSUMERS UNION

President Rhoda H. Karpatkin
Executive Vice President Joel Gurin

Copyright © 1999 by Consumers Union of United States, Inc., Yonkers, New York 10703.

Published by Consumers Union of United States, Inc., Yonkers, New York 10703.

All rights reserved, including the right of reproduction in whole or in part in any form.

ISBN: 0-89043-916-8

ISSN: 1091-6288

First printing, January 1999

Manufactured in the United States of America

Consumer Reports Best Travel Deals is published by Consumers Union, the nonprofit organization that publishes CONSUMER REPORTS, the monthly magazine of test reports, product Ratings, and buying guidance. Established in 1936, Consumers Union is chartered under the Not-for-Profit Corporation Law of the State of New York.

CONTENTS

Preface 5

INTRODUCTION

Why travel deals cost more 9
This year's best travel deals 11

PART I — TRAVEL BASICS

Chapter 1 — Travel ABCs 15
Chapter 2 — Package tours and cruises 27

PART II — AIRFARE KNOW-HOW

Chapter 3 — Deals on airfares 41
Chapter 4 — Deals on the Internet 57
Chapter 5 — Consolidators 65
Chapter 6 — Frequent fliers 73
Chapter 7 — Charters 83
Chapter 8 — Bad seats 89
Chapter 9 — Special fares 97
Chapter 10 — Flying overseas 107

PART III — BY CAR OR TRAIN

Chapter 11 — Good deals on car rentals 111
Chapter 12 — Cars and trains in Europe 127
Chapter 13 — Maps from your computer 151

PART IV — HOTELS

Chapter 14 — How to get the best deals 165
Chapter 15 — Hotels at half price 181
Chapter 16 — Budget hotels 189
Chapter 17 — Extended-stay hotels 195
Chapter 18 — Deals for frequent stayers 203
Chapter 19 — Hotel deals abroad 213
Chapter 20 — Villas, condos, and other rentals 221

PART V — TRAVEL SAVVY

Chapter 21 — Overseas travel strategist 233
Chapter 22 — Travel insurance 245
Chapter 23 — Phoning home 255
Chapter 24 — Staying healthy 261

RESOURCE GUIDE   283

PREFACE

Consumer Reports Best Travel Deals is an annual publication from *Consumer Reports Travel Letter,* a newsletter published by CONSUMER REPORTS, the monthly magazine best known for test reports, product Ratings, and buying guidance. CONSUMER REPORTS is also a comprehensive source of unbiased advice about services, personal finance, health and nutrition, and other consumer concerns. Since 1936, the mission of Consumers Union, the parent organization, has been to test products, inform the public, and protect consumers. Our income is derived solely from the sale of CONSUMER REPORTS magazine and our other publications and services, and from nonrestrictive, noncommercial contributions, grants, and fees. We buy all the products we test, and accept no free samples. We take no advertising from outside entities, and we do not let any company use our reports or Ratings for commercial purposes.

Our information services include:

CONSUMER REPORTS. When you subscribe to the magazine, you get 12 monthly issues plus the annual Buying Guide. Write us at P.O. Box 53029, Boulder, Colo. 80322-3029. Subscriptions are $26 for one year.

CONSUMER REPORTS TRAVEL LETTER. Our monthly newsletter with money-saving travel information and travel deals. To subscribe (12 issues, $39), write us at P.O. Box 53629, Boulder, Colo. 80322-3629.

CONSUMER REPORTS SPECIAL PUBLICATIONS. We publish a series of specialty buying guides sold on newsstands and in bookstores, as well as books on personal finance, health, and other consumer issues.

CONSUMER REPORTS ONLINE. The CONSUMER REPORTS web site can be found at *www.ConsumerReports.org*. Free areas of the site give general buying guidance, a comprehensive list of product recalls, manufacturers' phone numbers, and other useful information. Members-only sections provide searchable Ratings of electronics, appliances, cars, and more, along with the current issue of CONSUMER REPORTS and participation in message boards. Membership is $2.95 per month or $24 a year ($19 for CONSUMER REPORTS subscribers).

CONSUMER REPORTS BY REQUEST. Specially edited reports from CONSUMER REPORTS are available by fax or mail. Call 800 789-3715 for an index of what's available. The index costs $1.

CONSUMER REPORTS ON HEALTH. Our monthly newsletter devoted to your health and well-being covers fitness, nutrition, medication, and more. To subscribe (12 issues, $24), write us at P.O. Box 56356, Boulder, Colo. 80322-6356.

ZILLIONS. Our bimonthly magazine for kids ages 8 and up, featuring toy tests, games, and "money smarts." To subscribe (6 issues, $16), write us at P.O. Box 54861, Boulder, Colo. 80322-4861.

CONSUMER REPORTS NEW CAR PRICE SERVICE. Our comprehensive reports compare sticker price to dealer's invoice for car light trucks, and for factory installed options. Call 800 651-4636. Reports cost $12.

CONSUMER REPORTS USED CAR PRICE SERVICE. Find the market value and reliability data for most 1983 to 1997 used cars and light trucks. Call 800 422-1079. Reports cost $10.

CONSUMER REPORTS AUTO INSURANCE PRICE SERVICE. Compare the cost of insurance for the coverage you need; find the best price. Now available in Ariz., Calif., Colo., Conn., Fla., Ga., Idaho, Ill., La., Mich., Mo., Miss., N.C., Nev., N.J., N.Y., Ohio, Pa., Tenn., Texas, Utah, Va., Wash., and Wis. Call 800 944-4104. Reports cost $12.

CONSUMER REPORTS TELEVISION. Produces our nationally syndicated consumer news service, Consumer Reports TV News.

INTRODUCTION

TRAVEL IN '99

Why travel deals cost more.....................9

This year's best deals 11

WHY TRAVEL DEALS COST MORE

Travel services are perishable. Unsold airline seats, hotel rooms, and cruise cabins can't be held in inventory. Once a plane takes off or a liner sails, unfilled seats or cabins are a dead loss. That's why getting a deal on an airline ticket, a cruise, or a hotel room is more complicated than finding one on a TV set, a sweater, or a bank loan.

The age-old way for suppliers to move unsold goods or services is to cut prices; travel is no exception. But travel suppliers don't just cut prices across the board. They rely on computer projections to tell them what will sell at list price and what will have to be discounted. Result: You can often find deep discounts at the same time that suppliers are still trying to sell the same services—for the same time periods—at full, list price. That's why travel deals are so full of seemingly arbitrary restrictions and limitations, why the travel marketplace is full of unconventional, anonymous outlets, and why consumers need a guide through the maze.

Each segment of the travel industry deals with perishability in different ways:

AIRLINES. Business travelers need the flexibility to book trips at the last minute and to make last-minute changes in any itineraries they booked early. Accordingly, airlines tag tickets that provide such flexibility with astronomical, full-fare prices that few leisure travelers will pay. The airlines then court price-sensitive consumers with fares that are less than half the business rates—for tickets with restrictions that make them unattractive to most business travelers. Where even those deals don't do the job, airlines sell other seats through "outlet" stores called consolidators—either at below-list prices or at list prices but without the usual restrictions (advance purchase, Saturday-night stay, blackout dates, and the like).

If you can live with the restrictions, the airlines' asking prices for promotional and sale airfares are often as good a deal as you're likely to find. If not, Part II, Airfare Know-How, will help you find alternatives.

HOTELS. They, too, fish for price-sensitive travelers. Their bait is a mix of advertised promotions, selective discounts to senior travelers and through half-price programs, and back-door deals through brokers (the hotel parallel to airline consolidators). Some advertised rates—hotel chains' own promotions and regular rates at budget hotels—are good deals. But to get the best deals, you must often deal through alternative, low-profile sources. Part IV, Hotels, will steer you to your best options.

CRUISE LINES. They give the best deals to travelers who book very early or very late. Chapter 2 will show you how and where you're likely to find the best prices.

CAR-RENTAL AGENCIES. Rates are chaotic; there's no real substitute for comparison shopping on each individual rental. And when you do that, you'll find that rental companies often advertise attractive rates, then try to sock you with add-on charges—mandatory fees or charges for overpriced options—at the counter. Chapter 11 tells how to avoid or minimize those hidden extras.

Even within a single segment, no one buying strategy works best in all circumstances. This handbook outlines strategies for getting the best deals on just about any travel service, names the suppliers that offer the best services and prices, and tells how to avoid rip-offs and scams. Its reports are based on articles that appeared in *Consumer Reports Travel Letter,* but web addresses and phone numbers have been updated.

THIS YEAR'S BEST TRAVEL DEALS

BUYING AIRPLANE TICKETS ONLINE. If 1998 put weekend internet fare specials on the map, 1999 will be the year of the big online discount. American led the way in late 1998 with the debut of Daily FAAres, discount fares posted each day on its web site. Big online agencies—Travelocity, Preview Travel, and MSN Expedia—are becoming equally aggressive.

Airlines will also will make it worth your while to book online. Last year's 500-mile bonus per booking wasn't rich enough to lure technophobic travelers online. By the end of the year, many carriers had upped the ante to a more enticing 1,000 miles round-trip. Some also threw in extra miles for selecting an e-ticket, using a kiosk, or making repeat online bookings.

If you're not surfing the web this year, you'll miss out on some big fare bargains. For consumers, this means a broader selection of discounts. But buyer beware. Airlines might begin looking like online agencies, but they won't necessarily give you a complete selection of flight and travel options. A new way to find the best deals online: Visit sites like Smarter Living (*www.smarterliving.com*) that aggregate fare and rate information.

LOW-FARE AIRLINES. Low-fare entrants are experiencing a renaissance of sorts, after a year without safety incidents and support from some unlikely sources. After last summer's Northwest strike stranded the upper Midwest, carriers like ProAir and Kiwi stepped in to provide essential service. Late last year, two new start-ups—Access Air and Shuttle America—launched service. Recent newborns ProAir and Spirit were granted precious slots in New York. And the biggest news to date: Southwest plans to start up service this spring from Long Island's Islip MacArthur Airport, just 40 miles east of slot-locked LaGuardia. The carrier tested a $99 round-trip transcontinental flight from Baltimore/Washington International to Oakland during Thanksgiving, a taste of things to come. Vanguard and AirTran have also been successful in entering more markets. As we went to press, one low-fare airline bit the dust: Reno Air was acquired by American Airlines.

HOLIDAYS IN ASIA. Asia's financial woes aren't expected to disappear anytime soon, and while that's bad news for most, it's good news for travelers. Much of Asia should remain a great travel bargain for the coming year. The dollar will remain strong, and hotels and airlines will continue to shave prices as they scramble to fill the rooms and seats left empty by disappearing business travelers and strapped Asian tourists staying home. Four- and five-star hotels that were going for as much as $400 a night are down to $80, says Linda Hoffman, director of leisure markets for travel agency network Carlson Leisure Group of Minneapolis.

Best deal destinations: Bali, Singapore, Jakarta, Bangkok, and Kuala Lumpur. But the same economic conditions that make Asia a bargain for travelers exact a hardship on the locals—with potentially violent consequences. Jakarta was rocked in November by deadly pro-democracy protests sparked by high unemployment.

HOLIDAYS IN MEXICO. One of the best deals, as usual, can be found south of the border in Mexico. Though it offers the same kind of sun and sand of a Caribbean vacation, it can cost half as much. Bargain hunters would do well to avoid Cancun; it's one of the few places in Mexico with American prices.

TOP U.S. TOURIST DESTINATIONS. Asia's economic crisis, combined with an oversupply of rooms, will bring consumers some relief from sky-high U.S. hotel prices this year. Rates will increase a moderate 4 percent across the board in 1999, predicts Smith

Travel Research, a consulting firm that tracks the hotel industry. That's almost double inflation but half the hike of 1996, when rate increases hit a record high of nearly 8 percent.

Some of the best bargains will be found in the country's top tourist destinations. Hawaii, for example, is reeling from the disappearance of Asian visitors, Florida is recovering from a string of natural disasters, and Las Vegas is expecting more than 20,000 new hotels rooms to open for business within the next 18 months. Each has seen their occupancies and room rates decrease in 1998, prompting a slew of hotel promotions. Four Hawaii hoteliers are slashing rates by 50 percent for seven-night stays all year long. We expect this type of discounting to continue throughout the year.

COMFORTABLE PLANE SEATS. Linking the words "comfort" and "airline seat" should be a crime. But times are changing. You just might find a modicum of comfort this year.

The business traveler is the new pampered pet of the airlines, hungry for their tickets. International business travelers enjoyed free limo travel to the airport, gourmet meals, and wider, more comfortable seats. British Airways even has them snoozing on their "minisleeper" seats. Top-of-the line treatment for business class will continue as airlines compete to fill their seats, especially in the wake of the Asian recession and the subsequent dip in business travelers.

What's good for the business traveler is good for the tourist, because we like to use our frequent-flier miles to step up a class to more comfort. But some of the perks are filtering down to lowly coach. In an apparent bid to keep pace with archrival Virgin Atlantic, British Airways has launched a "New World Traveller Economy class," with more comfortable seats, individual video screens, double-decker meal trays, and toys for kids on its long-haul flights.

On long haul flights, United offers an "S" back contour seat in coach and adjustable "ears" to stop the sleep-destroying jolt of a falling head. American is also offering headrests and a newly designed coach seat design in coach on its international flights.

PART ONE

TRAVEL BASICS

1 Travel ABCs 15

2 Package tours and cruises 27

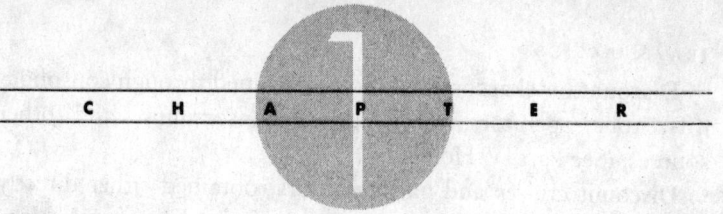

C H A P T E R 1

TRAVEL ABCs

Why pay full price? In this book, we'll introduce you to valuable discount sources—consolidators, travel clubs, half-price and preferred-rate hotel programs, and cruise discounters—that help you get the vacation you want for less.

But let's begin with some basics: how to find a good travel agent; how to save with off-season travel; and special deals for senior and single travelers.

THE RIGHT TRAVEL AGENT

You may choose to plan and book your own trip. But a capable travel agent can often find better bargains; answer questions about currency exchange, visa service, and so on; and, even if only as an order processor, make trip preparation easier.

Using a travel agency doesn't relieve you of the responsibility of doing your homework: The more you know, the better a consumer you'll be. But a good agent can relieve you of a lot of drudge work.

To help customers cut costs, a good travel agent will be willing and able to find or arrange for:

Discount airline tickets, secured from wholesale brokers known as consolidators and sold to travelers at substantially lower prices than the airlines charge. (See Chapter 5.)

Discount hotel accommodations, obtained through consolidators, tour operators, travel-agency consortiums, and other sources. (See Part IV, Hotels.)

Discount cruises and package tours, obtained either directly from the tour and cruise operators or from discount clearinghouses. (See Chapter 2.)

Reallocation of airline seats from expensive to inexpensive categories and selective waiver of restrictions on ticket purchases. Those rule-bending adjustments are offered in various ways by some airlines to some travel agencies.

Not every agency can take advantage of all these tools. Large agencies in major metropolitan areas generally have the broadest access. Some discounts are more readily available to agencies that specialize in business travel. Some—especially airline seat reallocation and waiver of restrictions—are often limited to certain markets or applied only in limited circumstances.

WHAT CREDENTIALS MATTER? Many certificates on an agent's wall may merely indicate membership in trade- and professional-organizations. But one credential has real meaning: a certificate recognizing a certified travel counselor, awarded by the Institute of Certified Travel Agents (ICTA). It attests to five years of professional experience as well as the completion of a five-part course covering sources of information beyond those found in the computer-reservation systems used by travel agencies.

PAY BY THE HOUR? When the agent acts as your consultant, you pay a per-hour fee

---

FIND AN AGENT ONLINE

The American Society of Travel Agents can help you find a travel agent in your area. Use their web site (www.astanet.com) to fill out a Trip Request Service form. One or more ASTA agencies will respond to your request. Other features of the site include daily travel-news headlines, information on filing a consumer complaint if you have a problem with an ASTA agency, scam warnings, and links to other travel-information sources.

Travel ABCs **17**

for services; the agent arranges all services at the lowest available net price and rebates all commissions. This system removes the inherent agency conflict between maximum income and client service. Unfortunately, very few agencies work that way.

PAY A FEE? Several years ago, the main U.S. domestic airlines imposed a cap on commissions paid to travel agencies. To offset the loss of revenue, many agencies started adding a fee (up to $25 or so) to issue an airline ticket.

SIZING UP AN AGENCY

Pick your travel agent carefully. Begin with recommendations from friends and associates. Then interview agency managers and assess each establishment.

SERVICE AND CONVENIENCE COUNT. Here are some features to consider: an accessible location with parking; a 24-hour, 7-day-a-week phone service; client record-keeping; acceptance of your charge cards; fast and efficient ticket delivery; and branches or affiliated offices in other cities to assist with trip changes.

THE RIGHT CONNECTIONS. Does the agency belong to a consortium or hotel-booking service that offers preferred discounted corporate hotel rates? Does it have an arrangement with a consolidator to supply discount tickets? If so, you may get a better price. However, a financial incentive from specific hotel chains or airlines for client bookings may keep the agency from looking for the best deal. Also determine if they're willing to scout the computer system—or go outside the system—to make reservations.

TRAVEL RESOURCES. The agency needs sufficient resources to plan the best trip at the best price. Here are key indicators:

• An adequate guidebook and video library and wide selection of brochures available for loan; at least books from one of these annual series: Birnbaum Guides, Michelin Red or Green Guides, Frommer's Budget Travel Guides, the Let's Go Budget

18 TRAVEL BASICS

Guides, Fodor's Travel Guides, and good U.S. and world atlases.

• Industry references such as print copies of both the domestic and international Official Airline Guide editions; the Thomas Cook worldwide rail and shipping guides; Star Service, the leading trade source for evaluating hotels and cruises; and Special Travel Index, the semiannual directory of special-interest tours.

• An Apollo, Worldspan, Sabre, or System One terminal at the desks of all or most of the agents—and in use.

REBATING TRAVEL AGENCIES

Rebating agencies refund about half (or more) of their commission. Your discount is typically 4 to 5 percent of the standard list price (but it can run higher on some purchases). On many travel purchases, that doesn't add up to much. You're often better off paying full commission to an agency, especially one that's adept at finding the best discounts that suppliers offer. But on some services—especially those that aren't usually discounted—a small rebate is the best you're likely to do.

The size of a discount isn't the only significant factor in a travel purchase. As a rule, the larger the discount, the more restrictions it entails—or the smaller the likelihood that it will be available when you want it. While an agency rebate is small, it's available anytime.

Rebating agencies are no-frills operations. They expect you to do your own homework checking for the best airfare, cruise, or tour deal and deciding exactly what you want to buy. Then they'll make reservations and (where required) issue tickets or vouchers.

OTHER REBATERS. Some full-service travel agencies rebate part of their commission (usually well under 5 percent) to large business clients. Employees of those clients may be able to take advantage of those rebates for personal travel.

Travel ABCs 19

Hundreds of banks package travel-agency services (including rebates) with their MasterCard and Visa cards or other customer services. Some include that service with their ordinary cards or service packages; others limit it to Gold versions.

Several rebating agencies now maintain sites on the Internet, where travelers can check on the specific discounts offered and buy tickets either by e-mail or by phone.

JOIN A TRAVEL CLUB?

A few decades ago, really cheap airline tickets were available only through travel clubs—complete with membership cards, "dues," and other clublike features. But today, you needn't sign up with a club to take advantage of consolidator airfares, hotel-broker room discounts, cruise discounts, last-minute tour discounts, and modest rebates on agency travel purchases. You'll find plenty of sources happy to provide those services whenever you're ready to buy.

On the other hand, some key travel-club services are available *only* if you sign up for them on some sort of a membership basis. If you want any one of those services, you'll have to pay about as much as you'd pay for a full-service club, so getting access to several services through a single membership fee may make sense for you.

Annual dues range from moderate (for some American Automobile Association affiliates, say) to stiff (for Players Club, which targets gamblers). Some clubs' dues cover an entire family or household, others cover just one individual.

INTERNET CLUBS. Dozens of travel clubs have recently cropped up on the Internet.

FULL-SERVICE CLUBS. These offer at least three of six major services: Hotel discounts. Half-price hotel programs are offered by most of the listed full-service clubs (see Chapter 15). You get a discount off-rack rate (standard price) at 3,000 or more participating

20   TRAVEL BASICS

hotels whenever they expect to be less than about 80 percent full. Anyone serious about keeping travel costs down should have access to a half-price program.

Many full-service clubs also promote smaller discounts at several large hotel chains. Several full-service clubs (and some of the special-interest clubs discussed later) claim to offer additional hotel discounts, "up to 65 percent off" regular rates. But all they really do is refer members to Hotel Reservations Network (HRN), a large hotel broker that requires no dues and sells to anybody, club member or not (see Chapter 15).

Airfare discounts. A few clubs include one or more discount airline coupons with their annual membership packet. With a coupon, you can knock up to $125 off the cost of a ticket, depending on the ticket price. However, these coupons are usually heavily restricted.

A few other clubs sell discounted, consolidator air tickets. Being able to buy them through a full-service travel club may be convenient, but it's hardly a reason to join: Chapter 3 lists other sources that don't require yearly fees.

The Air Courier Association focuses on courier travel (although it offers enough other features to warrant "full-service" listing). Courier travel can—at least sometimes—cut airfares by more than half, but it's practical for only a minority of travelers. Relatively few courier seats are available for sale; couples can't travel together, you're often tied to a fixed return flight, and you may not be able to check baggage. With its periodic newsletters and bulletins, the club is a good way to keep on top of courier options, but you don't need to join anything to take advantage of courier flights.

Dining discounts. A dining program is a feature of most of the travel clubs. The discounts are usually a mix of percent-off (25 percent off a total check, up to 50 percent off a single item) and two-for-one deals when you eat at participating restaurants.

Travel ABCs **21**

BASICS

Last-minute cruise and tour deals. Several clubs include participation in the Travel Alert program, which provides last-minute deals on tours, cruises, and airline tickets through travel agencies. A few clubs run their own last-minute programs.

Just about every club promises big cruise discounts. But cruise discounting is so widespread that you can find a deal through almost any full-service or discount agency (see Chapter 2). If you join a club for other reasons, by all means check out its cruise options. But if you just want a good price on a cruise, you don't need to pay any dues to get it.

Travel-agency rebates. Most clubs run an in-house travel agency that rebates some of its commission on any travel service you buy there. Typically, the rebate amounts to 5 to 10 percent of the total price. You get your rebate either as a refund check or a credit to your charge card.

Emergency road service. Clubs with a focus on motorists feature emergency assistance or towing when members break down on the highway. Anyone who drives extensively should belong to such a program. If it provides additional travel benefits, so much the better.

Clubs often promote a long list of further benefits, too:

Vacation rentals. Several clubs provide a separate discount program focused on condos, villas, and resorts. However, it often isn't clear what the rack rate is for privately owned lodgings—and therefore whether any given price is really a discount.

Car-rental discounts. Almost all the clubs claim to provide modest car-rental discounts, but most give you certificates with so many conditions that they're not very valuable. Moreover, comparable car-rental discounts are readily available elsewhere —through frequent-flier programs, charge-card bill stuffers, and a wide range of other sources.

Grab bag offers. Under this heading fall discounts on tourist attractions, merchandise, car washes, and movie admissions; travel accident insurance; overseas emergency-referral services; and such.

In general, such minor extras aren't worth a lot. But if you join a club for a bigger benefit, you may find them useful occasionally.

SPECIAL-INTEREST CLUBS. Dozens of clubs cater to narrower interests. For example, there are clubs that cater to those looking for expensive hotels and resorts, upscale vacation-rentals, singles-matching organizations, deals at golf courses, and to gamblers.

OFF-SEASON TRAVEL

Many of the world's vacationers want to travel in the same few months. As a result, airfares and hotel rates tend to rise and fall with the seasons. If you can schedule your travel at times when most visitors are at home, you can often enjoy substantially lower prices and less crowding than in peak touring season.

BY AIR. Intercontinental routes linking the U.S. with Asia, Europe, South America, and the South Pacific have at least two seasonal price levels, usually called high and low. On all those routes, seasonal changes are limited to Economy Excursion fares. Some routes have only one seasonal fluctuation each year; others may have several.

Several U.S.–Europe and U.S.–South Pacific fares have an intermediate, "shoulder" level. Shoulder fares usually cover a period of several weeks between the other two seasons.

In most instances, the round-trip fare you pay is determined by the date on which you start your trip. The return can be at any time permitted by the ticket's length-of-stay restrictions. In a few cases, however, the price of the round-trip varies by the date of your return flight as well.

Fares within North America are generally not called seasonal, but they often do vary through seasonal promotions. Airlines also adjust the number of seats assigned to various price categories to change their yield without changing advertised fare levels. And some low fares can be blacked out during periods of highest

Travel ABCs　　**23**

demand. (On many routes, fares vary by hour, day, or week.)

BY RAIL. Amtrak, the private U.S. intercity rail passenger system, uses multiple rates for each route in its system; some of them vary seasonally. VIA Rail, Canada's passenger rail system, also offers off-peak rates on many of its routes.

BY RENTED CAR. In some countries, several of the major car-rental companies adjust rates seasonally. They also offer special U.S. promotions during slow seasons.

ROOMS. Hotel prices are seasonally adjusted in most resort areas and in some major cities. Seasonal price changes are common in the Caribbean, the main European beach destinations (French and Italian rivieras, Greek islands, Spanish coasts), Hong Kong (most big tourist hotels), the major South American vacation areas (Bariloche, Rio), the prime U.S. winter vacation areas (Arizona, Florida and adjacent states, and Hawaii), and in many U.S. summer-vacation areas (lakes, mountains, coasts). Low-season rates may be less than half the peak rates.

Seasonal adjustments in hotel rates vary greatly according to destination. Some areas have only one high and one low season a year, while others have several. (Special local festivals or conventions always push up rates.)

Hotels in major cities rarely adjust their prices by season, but some manage to make seasonal adjustments by promoting special rates or airline packages. Tour operators often offer reduced-rate promotions at major European city hotels in July and August, when most business activity grinds to a halt.

Seasonal variations can be found through discount sources, but there are no hard-and-fast rules. Some half-price coupon and club rates are available only during the off-season. Preferred rates, on the other hand, are apt to remain constant throughout the year.

HIGH-VALUE SEASONS. In many destinations, spring and fall shoulder seasons provide the best mix of weather and cost.

Those seasons can be relatively short (Quebec) or quite long (Greek islands). In Ft. Lauderdale, moderate weather and low rates overlap for only a few weeks in early December. The low costs and mild climate make Australia's winter (our summer) a good time to visit.

Low-season travel provides benefits that often go beyond lower prices and good weather. Major tourist areas that may be mobbed in high season are uncrowded and far more accessible. You can even enjoy weather-dependent activities, with reasonable luck, in the shoulder season. But check guidebooks or call tourist offices before you schedule a trip. In some places, there are so few off-season visitors that key attractions and visitor services may be closed or may operate only on reduced hours.

RESOURCES FOR SENIORS

Travelers who reach their fiftieth birthday can join the American Association of Retired Persons (AARP). It costs only $8 per year (including free membership for a spouse) and brings many benefits, including some discounts on hotel and car rentals.

Currently, a number of big hotel chains participate, giving discounts of 10 to 50 percent to AARP members. (See Chapter 14.) Several car-rental companies and one bus-tour firm participate as well. Other firms also give discounts to AARP members, even though they have no contractual arrangement with AARP.

Other seniors' organizations also offer travel benefits, including discounts, to their members. Examples include Catholic Golden Age, Mature Outlook (a travel club), National Alliance of Senior Citizens, National Association of Retired Federal Employees, and several airline clubs (see "Senior Clubs," Chapter 9). The smart policy is to mention the organizations to which you belong when you make your airline, hotel, or car-rental reservation, and ask if you're eligible for any deals.

SINGLES TAKE A HIT

Traveling solo can be expensive. Anyone who's read a travel brochure knows about the high extra charge a single traveler on a package tour or cruise must pay for sole occupancy of a double hotel room or cabin. The single supplement typically runs some 25 to 75 percent of the "land" portion of a tour or cruise — sometimes almost 100 percent. Such outrageous surcharges are tough, but not impossible, to beat.

The travel industry aggressively courts singles. But when you take a closer look, you find that most tours and cruises promoted for singles really aren't aimed at people who want to travel alone for privacy or flexibility. Instead, the tour operators are usually offering a matching service: They'll find some other single to share accommodations and costs with you.

If you really want a room or cabin to yourself instead of a traveler's blind date, you do have some choices:

Cruises. Solo cruisers are a bit better off than solo package-tour travelers. Most cruise ships have some single-berth cabins (though they often cost as much as a bottom-of-the-line double cabin with the single supplement added). Cruise lines sometimes offer promotional rates for single occupancy.

Some cruise lines reduce or eliminate the single supplement for last-minute single-occupancy bookings on cruises that aren't filled. Many are sold through travel clubs and discount cruise brokers.

Package tours. Conventional sightseeing or resort tours that target travelers who don't want to share are few and far between. Your best bet (if you're up to the physical demands) is an adventure tour.

Those limited options aside, the preferable option is to travel independently, not on a package tour. Arrange your own single-rate hotel accommodations. Several of the business-oriented preferred-rate hotel programs specialize in single-rate hotel discounts (see Chapter 14). In many parts of the world, older hotels often have some small single rooms at rates well below the double rate. Solo travelers can save by traveling by train rather than renting a car.

FOR DISABLED TRAVELERS. Persons with disabilities will want to make a pretrip stop at *www.projectaction.org,* a web site run by Project Action of National Easter Seals. An important part of that site is an accessible traveler's database that provides information on handicapped-accessible transportation services nationwide.

You select the state and the city you're planning to visit. That brings you a list of resources, including public transit, taxis, van rentals, airport shuttles, and travel agencies, that cater to persons with disabilities, and hotels with shuttle services for the disabled. Links are provided to entries that have their own web sites.

Though the site was well organized and easy to use, the listings were incomplete when we checked in mid-1998. The San Francisco page, for example, listed Golden Gate Transit (a service running from the city to its northern suburbs) but not BART (the regional rapid-transit system) or MUNI, the primary system serving the city—both of which provide handicapped access. The New York listing included PATH (a rail line connecting New York with New Jersey) but didn't cover the city's subway and bus system or the commuter rail lines that serve the northern and eastern suburbs.

C H A P T E R

BUYING PACKAGE TOURS AND CRUISES

One of the main appeals of cruises and package tours is the possibility of hassle-free travel with an all-in-one price. You can find cruises and tours in a range that should suit just about any travel taste, temperament, and pocketbook. But neither should be bought blindly: Careful shopping yields hefty savings.

PACKAGE-TOUR ABCS

When you buy a package tour, you get two or more travel elements—air transportation, lodgings, meals, ground transportation, entertainment, car rental, airport transfers, sightseeing, and so on—for a single price. Put together by organizations known as wholesalers or tour operators, such tours are available for every conceivable interest and destination, from golfing in Scotland to bicycling through Asia.

Basic packages to city or sun-sand-surf locations (e.g., Florida, Hawaii, the Caribbean, or Mexico) are often good deals. You get a price break from the packager's ability to buy airfare, hotel, ground transfers, and sightseeing in bulk. Long available from tour operators, packages are also available from major hotel chains, airlines, and other providers.

Escorted tours handle virtually everything for you, including what you see, eat, and do once you reach your destination. Most local touring is by bus, with either a local guide or an escort who accompanies you throughout your trip.

Such tours have several disadvantages. A lot depends on the quality of your tour guide and the personalities of your fellow travelers; both factors are out of your control. Some people find the regimented schedules unpleasant. The pace of activities is generally only as fast as the pace of the slowest person on the tour. And the whole thing is prepaid, pretty well locking you in even if the tour turns out to be unsatisfactory.

The advantages include minimal effort and fuss (unless you get a bad tour), camaraderie, and, in some cases, lower prices, particularly at hotels. Sometimes an escorted tour is the only way to take part in activities or get to places that are otherwise inaccessible to tourists. You also benefit because the facilities and itinerary on a quality tour have been carefully selected and prescreened.

Travel on your own. To suit people who don't need hand-holding when they travel, many tour operators provide à la carte options that let you travel independently once you reach your destination. And, of course, you can always have a travel agent or tour operator tailor a trip to your specifications—though that's the most expensive way to travel.

Choosing a tour. A travel agent or the advertisements in newspaper travel sections can lead you to attractive tours. If you already know where you want to travel, you might also check your travel agent's copy of the "Official Tour Directory." Some tour operators offer a range of choices for different budgets. Cosmos and Trafalgar specialize in low-cost, no-frills travel.

Buying package tours and cruises **29**

You usually won't find big discounts on tours (except perhaps cruises); margins are thin. At best, you can get a rebate of 5 percent or so by buying through a discount travel agency (see Chapter 1).

With careful shopping, you can sometimes discover a smaller tour operator that's a real gem. Small firms may specialize in a particular destination, run offbeat tours, or find interesting lodgings that don't accept large groups.

ZINGERS IN FINE PRINT. The specifics of a tour package are found not in the tour brochure's color pictures and colorful prose but in its fine print. Don't skip that tiny, boring type—what you don't know can hurt you. Some tour operators aren't completely frank about what they're offering.

The brochure's fine print normally applies to all the tours listed. Necessarily, some of it deals with boilerplate (official corporate names, tour numbers) and purchase conditions (minimum time for paperwork, cancellation provisions, possible children's reductions). Beyond those basics, the fine print seems designed mainly to protect the operator in case things go wrong. Some of the fine print from the more consumer-oriented tour operators also tries to inform the traveler of potential problems. (You can tell a lot about a tour operator's concern for its customers by whether the fine print is even readable.)

Here's what to look for:

How much? Brochure prices are often subject to change—reasonable enough, since prices are set far in advance. But a traveler should be informed of the actual price and conditions before buying. The fine print may also reserve the operator's right to increase the price or modify what a tour provides after a traveler has paid a deposit or even paid in full (with such changes specifically ruled out as grounds for a full refund). Avoid such tours if you can. Some operators guarantee the price in the brochure.

Some brochures quote a package price with a firm airfare component. Others list the lowest airfare available at the time of printing (usually a regular coach/economy excursion, or a tour-based fare available only for a tour package), adding that it's subject to change if the airline raises fares. Most never list an airfare.

U.S. regulations are stricter for charter flights (and tours based on charter flights) than for those using scheduled airlines. A traveler must be given a full refund if, before departure, the operator imposes any major change—a price increase of 10 percent or more, say, or a switch in departure or arrival dates. But many important changes don't qualify as major: A price increase of less than 10 percent, a change in departure time, or a rerouting to pick up extra passengers at another city, for example, don't entitle you to an automatic refund on a charter-based tour.

The airline you'll fly. If an airline sponsors a tour, it generally provides the transportation. Independent tour operators may list several airlines (any of which could be used on a given tour) or a single airline (with a provision that it's subject to change). Whenever you're not promised a specific airline or if the airline is subject to change, you may wind up with below-average economy service and have to put up with cramped seating or inconvenient routing.

Cancellation/change. Brochures should spell out specifics on cancellations and itinerary changes. Typically, travelers who cancel well in advance are eligible for full refunds (minus a fee). After a cutoff date (15 to 60 days before departure), there's commonly a sliding scale of penalties or even, on many tours, no refund at all.

Many operators let you change travel dates or accommodations, subject to availability, for an additional $20 to $100 per change; a few waive the fee for the first change. A few operators impose especially stringent cancellation provisions for tours during seasonal events at popular destinations—Carnival in Rio, say, or Christmas in Hawaii.

Complaints. Some operators specify a maximum period in

Buying package tours and cruises 31

which to file complaints and refund requests; they may also specify the method for resolving conflicts and complaints. Those provisions may not be legally binding, but they're often intimidating.

Documents. A few operators state how many days before the tour they will send tickets or vouchers to you. You may incur an additional delivery charge if you make a reservation within the final month before travel. Some operators include a section that describes the documents you must have to participate in the trip (visas, passport, medical certificates, and so forth) and disavow any responsibility for conditions that result from your failure to have the appropriate paperwork with you during the tour.

Inclusions and exclusions. Most tour brochures list inclusions and exclusions—specifics about charges that might be subject to question. Some package prices include services you might not consider obvious: for example, tips to airport and hotel porters for handling your bags. Other things being equal, the more inclusions the better.

Most exclusions are unsurprising—charges for excess baggage, telephone calls, room service, laundry, and so on. Ski-tour operators may disclaim responsibility for lack of snow. Some brochures commit operators to refunds for services that were promised and not delivered. But others allow the operator to make minor changes without refund—and the operator is the judge of what's minor.

Accommodations. Tour operators generally reserve the right to substitute "comparable" or "equivalent" hotels for those featured in the brochure. Some make specific promises—for instance, limiting substitutions to hotels of at least the same rating as those featured in the brochure. The basis for the rating may also be stated (a government system in Europe, for example). If not, the rating is often taken from the "Official Hotel Guide," a standard industry reference. (See Chapter 14.) Other brochures promise not only comparable quality but also similar

32   TRAVEL BASICS

location within or near a city center or close to a major attraction—a useful protection.

Note what else the brochure promises—or doesn't promise—about room quality and location. If nothing is said, you're usually assigned a run-of-the-house room, which can be anything with the promised number of beds and bath facilities. Be prepared for the worst room in the hotel if you're not guaranteed anything better.

Food. Typically, the fine print sets forth a meal policy. Interpret "Continental breakfast" to mean bread and coffee or tea laid out for self-service. Unless a brochure specifically promises lunch and dinner choices from a menu, you may end up with assembly-line, dollop-it-out meals. A few premium operators include alcoholic beverages on some occasions, but most don't.

Itineraries. The fine print usually doesn't say anything more about routings than the tour description in the front of the brochure. A few brochures, however, add some specific disclaimers. Several operators reserve the right to make minor adjustments in sightseeing itineraries and to vary the order of cities or attractions visited in a multistop tour.

No-smoking tours. If you want to avoid secondhand smoke, choose a tour with a ban on smoking. Omission of such a ban in the fine print may mean there will be a smoking section on the bus. Ask in advance to be sure.

Consumer protection. Several trade associations offer consumer protection plans. The U.S. Tour Operators Association (USTOA), to which a few of the larger tour operators belong, requires its members to post a surety of $1 million—a useful protection but not enough to make good on all claims if a big operator fails.

The National Tour Association (NTA) maintains a consumer-protection fund to cover traveler claims if a member tour operator defaults because of bankruptcy. The American Society of Travel Agents (ASTA) offers several forms of consumer protec-

Buying package tours and cruises 33

tion, but they're all voluntary. It operates an escrow account that tour operators can use to safeguard clients' deposits. It lists tour operators that offer consumer protection through USTOA or NTA. And it has arranged for umbrella insurance that individual travel agencies can buy to protect clients against supplier default of any kind.

Most operators recommend trip-interruption insurance (see Chapter 22) as a way of hedging your risk and sell it as a tour add-on. If you decide you need coverage, we recommend you buy it directly from an independent insurance provider. If you do buy from the tour operator, watch out for unexpected insurance charges added in with other elements of the tour.

DEALING WITH PROBLEMS. Try to resolve any tour problems as they crop up. Complain early to your tour guide or other company representative (if you're on an escorted tour), or to the tour operator's headquarters or your travel agency back home. Keep your cool, and be specific about the problem and what resolution you desire.

If no resolution is possible, it may be best to bail out. That might be expensive, but it may also prevent further grief, and it may strengthen your case for a refund or a chargeback (a credit from the charge-card issuer for the disputed charge). You'll then have to pursue your complaint with care, patience,

CRUISE CLEANLINESS

The U.S. Public Health Service regularly inspects the sanitation of cruise ships. Most ships pass, but a few don't. Check the *Consumer Reports Travel Letter* for the latest scores, or check *www.cdc.gov/ nceh/programs/sanit/ vsp/scores/scores. htm.* For a fax-back copy, call (don't fax) 404 332-4565, and ask for Document 510051. To request a full inspection report for an individual vessel, write Chief, Vessel Sanitation Program, National Center for Environmental Health, 1015 North America Way, Room 107, Miami, Fla. 33132.

34 TRAVEL BASICS

and a series of letters setting forth your problem and the resolution you expect. As a last resort, consider filing a formal complaint with USTOA or NTA (for tour operators) or ASTA (for travel agencies).

CRUISING FOR DISCOUNTS

The cruise market is booming, and it's easy to see why: Hotel prices have ballooned, but you can still buy a week-long cruise for under $200 a day per couple—not much more than you'd have paid 10 years ago. Cruise lines openly promote price cuts for customers who book early, and they push backdoor discounts through a variety of discount agencies. That can provide good values for careful shoppers who know how the system works.

Think of a cruise as a seagoing package tour with the works thrown in. The price of a cruise covers almost all your costs: transportation, accommodations, food, entertainment, and sometimes even wine with meals.

If you're picking your first cruise, don't choose solely for price. Lines and ships have different personalities that cater to different vacation styles. First-time cruisers who buy the cheapest cruise, disregarding cruising area, shipboard facilities, or clientele, may be in for some unpleasant surprises.

Your main choices are where to cruise, when to go, and which ship to take. Probably the most popular areas are the Caribbean and the Alaska Inside Passage. But you can also cruise the U.S./Canadian east coast, Hawaii, Mexico's Pacific coast, the Mediterranean and Aegean, the Norwegian coast, various European rivers, the Orient, and the South Pacific. Occasional longer cruises may cross the Pacific or circumnavigate South America.

Many ship and barge cruises sail the Mississippi/Ohio river system in the U.S.; the Danube, Elbe, Moselle, Rhine, and Volga

Buying package tours and cruises **35**

rivers in Europe; and the canal systems of Britain and France.

What sort of cabin should you select? Ignore the brochure pictures, which are taken with a wide-angle lens. Budget cabins usually measure 9 by 12 or 10 by 13 feet. On most ships, they're inside, with no portholes or windows.

Some expensive cabins have windows facing a deck. They're like motel rooms on an outside corridor: You can enjoy either your privacy or the view, but not both at the same time. Not many cabins have double beds.

For more information, ask friends with cruise experience for recommendations. Get advice from a travel agent. Some agents specialize in cruises, but they may also have contracts with preferred suppliers who give them commissions in return for steering you to their ships.

WHICH AGENCY? The first rule of cruise buying, especially for first-timers, is to deal with someone who has been around the industry long enough to have firsthand knowledge of individual ships, lines, and popular destinations and ports. A good price on an inappropriate ship or uninteresting itinerary is not a good deal.

Cruising remains one of the few travel services that you can usually buy only through a travel agent (though some cruise lines are reportedly considering direct consumer sales). Several kinds of agencies sell cruises:

A **cruise-only agency** concentrates on one aspect of the travel business, so it can give real advice rather than just take orders. Many cruise-only agencies promote themselves as discounters. Though just about any cruise-only agency has access to the cruise lines' major promotions, the big discounters sometimes beat their competition.

A few big cruise discounters have gone bust in recent years, leaving customers with neither their prepayment nor their cruise. If you deal with a discounter, check its credentials before you buy. A cruise-only agency should, at a minimum, be affiliated with the Cruise Lines International Association (CLIA) or the National Association of Cruise-Only Agencies (NACOA). Neither organization has a consumer-protection program, but members must fulfill modest training and financial requirements. It's also a good idea to check the Better Business Bureau in the agency's home location for complaints or problems.

Many **full-service agencies** book cruises as well as other travel services. The big, multibranch chains often have discount deals as good as those available through cruise-only agencies. Even a small, independent agency should have at least one agent who keeps up with the cruise industry or has an arrangement with a cruise discounter.

If you get a mere order-taker on the line when you inquire about a cruise, try another agency or ask to speak to someone who knows about a particular cruise that interests you.

WHEN TO BOOK. The best deals, cabins, and dates go to early-bird buyers. Early-booking prices and deadlines are listed in the cruise brochures. Early typically means four to six months before departure date. All the big lines guarantee to refund customers the difference if they later undercut their early-booking rates.

Instead of giving cash discounts to early buyers, some lines offer credit for shipboard purchases or free hotel accommodations before or after the cruise. In addition to their published advance-purchase fares, many lines offer two-for-one specials, kids-free programs, or unpublicized reductions for prior customers.

In addition to the price reduction, advance-purchase travelers have the best selection of cabins. Early booking may also be the only way to get a discount on very popular cruises.

LAST-MINUTE DEALS. Still, you don't necessarily need to book early to get a good price, especially if you're flexible. Last-minute bargains, at least for passengers from certain regions, are often available one month before sailing for some ships that aren't full. Among the best bets for bargain rates are repositioning cruises,

Buying package tours and cruises **37**

between-season trips on which a ship moves from one region to another—from a summer in Alaska to a winter in the Caribbean, for example.

UPGRADING YOUR CABIN. The discount market offers another attraction: the chance to combine a discount price with a free upgrade. Upgrades become available when a cruise ship sells a higher percentage of inexpensive than expensive cabins—a fairly common occurrence. Upgrades can be used either as rewards for repeat customers or for travelers who book early or as incentives to attract first-time cruisers.

It's no longer true that you're necessarily more likely to be offered an upgrade as an incentive for buying late. Today, when a line decides to cut prices, it may upgrade early bookers and sell the freed-up cabins at lowered rates.

However, cruise lines know that a good number of travelers who book early are seeking a specific cabin or location. Many of those early bookers wouldn't consider a change, even to a larger cabin, an upgrade. Accordingly, a cruise line may hesitate to reassign a traveler who booked early unless it's sure that the traveler really wants an upgrade.

If you book early but would welcome an upgrade, make sure your agent adds a specific notation in your reservation file that you are interested in upgrading if offered.

ALMOST ALL-INCLUSIVE. Cruise prices, despite their hype, aren't really all-inclusive. Here are the main extras you'll face:

• Tipping can easily add as much as $10 a day per person to the cost of a cruise.

• Shore excursions are almost always extra, easily adding $30 to $40 a person for each stop. We recommend you shun the cruise lines' tours and arrange your own after you arrive in port. Rent a car or hire a taxi and go where you want, when you want.

• Liquor is excluded from most cruise rates.

• On-board expenses for shopping or gambling are extra.

38   TRAVEL BASICS

Some ship lines offer "shipboard credits" toward such expenses as an added booking incentive for some sailings.

• Port charges can add as much as $200 to the price of a cruise. The cruise line may well add a bigger port charge than the port actually charges them and pocket the difference.

In 1997, however, six of the biggest cruise lines (Carnival, Celebrity, Dolphin, Majesty, Norwegian, and Royal Caribbean) agreed to include port charges in their advertised prices. The agreements were reached with the Florida attorney general's office. Most other big lines later adopted the Florida rules.

One caveat: Discount agencies and other resellers—especially those outside the reach of Florida's enforcement powers—may continue to split the real cost of a cruise between a lowball advertised figure and an additional figure disclosed in fine print—or later, at the time of sale. Anyone checking cruise prices with a reseller should determine whether port charges are included and, if not, how much they add to the advertised price.

PART TWO

AIRFARE KNOW-HOW

3 How to get deals on airfares 41

4 Airfare deals on the Internet.........57

5 Airfare deals from consolidators ..65

6 Frequent fliers..............................73

7 Charter flights.............................83

8 Bad seats.....................................89

9 Special fares 97

10 Flying overseas...........................107

CHAPTER 3

HOW TO GET DEALS ON AIRFARES

For many travelers, getting the best airfare is more than just an exercise in smart shopping: It's a challenge to beat a system they perceive as unfair and capricious. This chapter provides a kit of fare-cutting tools. The Resource Guide at the end of this book tells where to call for bookings.

RECOGNIZING BARGAINS IN COACH

These days, only a tiny fraction of travelers pay full coach fare. Yet airlines continue to use that standard as a basis for their discount claims.

To recognize a bargain, compare any domestic fare you're considering with the coach excursion fare on a major airline. Those fares, known by such trade names as Super Saver and Max Saver, are the lowest the big lines offer except during true fare sales. For international flights, the equivalent is the cheapest economy excursion, usually called Apex or Super Apex.

42 AIRFARE KNOW-HOW

The big airlines call these low-end prices discount fares, but that's a misnomer—they're list prices for highly restricted tickets. Those tickets are nonrefundable but usually exchangeable—you can't get a cash refund, but you can generally apply their dollar value toward the purchase of another ticket, minus a processing fee (currently $50 on big lines). A few tickets are still truly non-refundable: If you don't use them as originally issued, they become worthless.

Coach/economy excursion seats are limited. An airline may offer no more than 10 percent of its seats (or none at all, on some flights) at the lowest advertised prices.

SALE FARES: HARD TO BEAT

American travelers have enjoyed an almost steady stream of domestic airfare sales over the past few years. Typically, the purchase window is quite small—some sales last just one day—but buyers usually have several months to complete travel at the sale prices. Domestic sale fares can run as much as 50 percent below regular coach-excursion fare levels (though 30 to 40 percent reductions are more common). Typical transcontinental sale fares hover around the $400 mark.

You'll have a tough time beating a sale airfare on a major line. Such promotions may offer straight fare reductions, free or low-cost companion tickets, or free tickets to one area if you buy a ticket to another.

Even the cheapest regular coach excursions can also be a good buy, especially for longer trips. But you may find it hard to get seats at the lowest fares.

The restrictions and buying limitations on all these attractive list-price tickets are designed to make them difficult for business travelers to use. But the limits often prevent vacation travelers from using them, too: You must usually make reservations and

How to get deals on airfares **43**

buy tickets long before departure. Travel may be limited to certain days or dates or require a Saturday-night stay, and seats may not be available when you want them.

Sale fares are usually advertised early in the week in major newspapers. But you can get a head start by having a travel agent check the computer reservation system over the weekend. All new fares, including some that aren't advertised in the papers, show up there first.

If your preferred airline doesn't have a seat when you want it, check another carrier. Competitors almost always match sale fares, even if they don't advertise the fact. However, the airline that started the fare war will most likely have more sale seats than its competitors.

It also pays to be flexible. Flights at nonpeak times—midday, late at night, or midweek—will have far more sale seats available. If the flight or day you want is sold out, there's still hope. Try calling the reservation number in the late evening or early morning. That's when airlines reevaluate their pricing and release some high-priced seats at lower prices. After about 10 p.m. Eastern time, you may be able find a cheap seat on a flight that had none earlier in the day.

What if you've just missed an advertised sale's midnight deadline? Try calling directory assistance in a city in an earlier time zone. Ask for the local reservation number—not the 800 number—of the airline, then call it to reserve your seat. If it's not midnight yet in Honolulu, the sale is still on there.

Once you've paid, watch for even better fares. Nonrefundable tickets can almost always be reissued for a lower, sale price. Despite the $50 or so per ticket that the airlines charge for the reissue, the price difference could still make the switch worth the effort.

If you cannot accept the restrictions that apply to most sale fares, try other strategies.

LOW-FARE AIRLINES

As another way to save, try a low-cost carrier. Low-cost lines, in fact, often make it possible to combine two short-haul flights for less than it costs to fly direct. That "split-ticket" method has limitations, though: You'll have to stop and change planes. If your carrier doesn't automatically switch your bags to another carrier, you'll have to recheck them yourself. And you may have to wait a long time for your connecting flight at the intermediate airport—the separate low-fare lines don't coordinate schedules.

There has been quite a bit of come and go in recent years, but a few of the new lines, such as ProAir, AirTran, and Vanguard, seem to be showing some staying power. They offer low unrestricted fares, and several offer even lower fares if you reserve in advance, fly at off-peak times, or buy a round-trip ticket. Most provide only very tight coach/economy seating. Except as noted, none has a frequent-flier program. None charge extra for advance reservations, and all accept major charge cards.

Most of these lines don't "interline"—that is, exchange baggage or offer through fares with any other line. (If you want to connect to another line, you must claim your bags and recheck them.) On ticketless airlines, you book with a charge card by phone and receive a confirmation number that you give to an airline agent at the boarding gate. Ticketless lines can also be booked through travel agents, although some aren't listed in the computer reservation systems (CRSs) that travel agents use.

CHECK OUT CHARTERS

Charter flights also offer savings opportunities over the cheapest coach/economy fares on a major line (see Chapter 7). Domestic charters fly mainly from large cities to popular tourist and gam-

How to get deals on airfares **45**

bling destinations: Las Vegas, Florida, Hawaii, and the Caribbean, plus ski centers in the winter and Europe in the summer.

REDUCTIONS FOR HUBBING

On a few long-haul routes, some lines offer travelers a lower fare for a connecting flight through one of the line's hubs than for a nonstop flight. (On the other hand, hubbing makes each one-way trip take about two hours longer than a nonstop flight and increases the risk of missing a connection and losing baggage.)

In addition to providing a fare saving, a hubbing connection sometimes lets you use an airport that's handier to your origin or destination point than a major airport. The airlines don't fly transcontinental nonstops to or from such airports as Burbank, LaGuardia, Long Island/MacArthur, Oakland, or National, but they fly frequently between those airports and one or more mid-country hubs. A hub connection to or from one of those secondary fields can save you a bit extra (in ground-transportation cost) and partially offset the extra travel time.

DISCOUNT TICKETS

Airlines often unload some tickets through consolidators—outlets that sell those tickets to the public for less than the airlines' posted price (see Chapter 5). The most consistent consolidator deals are for travel across the Pacific, where they're available most of the year at prices as much as $300 below the cheapest advertised economy excursions. Similar reductions are available across the Atlantic during the summer, when advertised fares are high. During the winter, the airlines' advertised low-season fares are hard to beat.

Consolidator tickets are rare for travel within the U.S. Even when available, they seldom cost less than the cheapest advertised coach excursions, though they often carry less onerous restrictions.

The biggest risk with consolidator tickets is in buying them: All too many discount agencies are slow to deliver tickets and reluctant to provide any assistance once they've made the sale. Your best protection is to buy with a charge card. Other problems are minor but worth noting: The cheapest ticket may entail extra connections or layovers. If something goes wrong, the airline on which you're ticketed isn't likely to transfer you to another line. You may not earn frequent-flier mileage. And you may not have a choice of seats or meals.

DISCOUNT COUPONS

Airlines frequently offer dollars-off coupons, with the amount of reduction usually keyed to the price of the ticket. You can get those coupons from a variety of sources—many Entertainment half-price books have them, for example (see Chapter 15). You also see them in promotions from such sources as retail stores, banks, and charge cards.

Airlines sometimes even accept coupons issued by a competing line. When planning a trip, check the acceptance of any airline discount coupon you happen to have (except one for a frequent-flier promotion, which typically isn't transferable). If you prefer to use a line other than the issuer—for a better schedule, perhaps, or to concentrate your frequent-flier benefits—ask the competitor if it will match the discount.

There's no risk to coupons, but they often impose restrictions on where or when you can travel, and you may not be able to combine them with sale fares. Use them if you can accept the limitations.

TWOFERS

Airlines often offer free or cut-price companion tickets. One traveler pays the full price, and a companion traveling on an

How to get deals on airfares **47**

identical itinerary gets a free or discounted ticket. Southwest's ongoing "Friends Fly Free" promotion is the most prominent example, but it changes fairly frequently, so check with the airline.

There's certainly no risk to twofers. The biggest problem is that the purchased ticket must usually be at full fare. That makes twofers a good deal in business or first class, where other reductions are rare. But you can often buy a ticket for coach/economy for less than half the base fare required for a twofer.

REBATES

All airlines pay travel agents a commission. The standard rates are 10 percent on domestic tickets, 8 percent on international. However, most big U.S. lines have recently capped commissions on international tickets, domestic tickets continue to be capped at $25 for a one-way ticket, $50 for a round-trip. So far, several smaller lines have not adopted the cap.

Cap or no cap, airlines continue to offer commission overrides for agents who meet sales quotas. Overrides run 1 to 5 percent of the ticket price for domestic flights and can be as much as 40 percent or so on international tickets. Some agencies pass on part of their commissions to travelers in the form of rebates. You can save 7 to 10 percent on just about any domestic ticket by buying from one of these agencies. (See Chapter 1.)

Many bank charge cards and travel clubs also offer a ticketing service that rebates 4 to 5 percent of the ticket price—about half the usual commission.

STATUS FARES

Special fares for groups—known as status fares—provide discounts, though not necessarily impressive ones. Discounted fares for meetings and conventions, for instance, are minor: usually 5

48   AIRFARE KNOW-HOW

percent off the lowest regular excursion fare. Most airlines also give an underwhelming 10 percent discount to seniors for domestic or international travel.

On the other hand, the senior coupon affords some great bargains. Certain status fares provide some savings for youngsters. Compassionate fares—discounted fares for travelers going to a funeral or the bedside of a gravely ill relative—also are helpful for last-minute travel in an emergency. (See Chapter 9.)

OTHER COST CUTTERS

Adroit use of loopholes in ticket-buying rules can also cut your costs substantially. The following strategies are popular, but they're risky and invite cancellation of your ticket if you're caught:

Back-to-back tickets. Sometimes called "nested" tickets, these let travelers avoid the Saturday-night stay that the cheapest coach excursions normally require. (They must, however, comply with all the other restrictions—advance-purchase period, seat limitations, and nonrefundability.)

Instead of buying one expensive round-trip ticket that doesn't require a Saturday-night stay, travelers buy two cheap round-trip excursions, each of which does require a stay—one from their home city to their destination and back, the other from their destination to their home city and back. They use the "going" portion of the first ticket to start their trip and the "going" portion of the second ticket to return. The two tickets are separate, so the airline presumably can't tell how long they stay at their destination.

Back-to-back tickets save money whenever the cheapest coach excursion is less than half the unrestricted round-trip fare. If coach excursion tickets are bought during a fare war, the savings can be even larger.

In the simplest version of the strategy, a traveler actually takes just one round-trip, throwing away the "return" portion of both

How to get deals on airfares **49**

round-trips. But of course back-to-back tickets can save far more if used for two trips (the "return" coupons of the tickets provide the second trip). As the major limitation, the traveler must typically take both trips within 30 days, the maximum stay allowed on many of the cheap excursions.

Airlines say that back-to-back tickets violate their rules. For a while, they tried to police their use through ticket audits. But passengers quickly figured out how to get around that barrier (by buying each of the two tickets on different airlines or from different travel agencies), and some airlines have apparently stopped trying to collect.

Continental is, as far as we know, the first airline to threaten action against individual travelers who "abuse" airline rules that prohibit back-to-back ticketing. Continental has claimed, among other things, to go after the frequent-flier accounts of travelers caught using back-to-back tickets.

Even if a traveler buys the two round-trip tickets on two different airlines, they can easily detect a violation, even on just one ticket: Not showing up for the return portion of a round-trip could be viewed as evidence of an intent to bypass airline ticket rules, and such no-shows would be easy to track.

So far, we haven't seen any comparable moves from other airlines. But you can be sure they're watching closely. Rather than using the risky back-to-back maneuver, fly a low-fare line that doesn't apply the onerous Saturday-night-stay requirement.

Hidden-city ploys. Now and then, you can save by overshooting your mark: A traveler headed from A to B buys a cheaper ticket from A to C by way of B, and gets off the plane (or doesn't get on the connecting flight) at B, the real destination. You can't check baggage to the intermediate city where you plan to get off. If your ticket says you're going through to New York, say, your bags would have to be checked through to there, too.

This trick works best on one-way tickets. While you might use the "going" portion of a round-trip ticket to New York for a trip from San Francisco to Cincinnati, you'd run a big risk on the return trip. These days, airlines typically issue boarding passes for both flights of a connecting itinerary when you check in for the first flight. Showing up at the departure gate in Cincinnati with a ticket to San Francisco (rather than a boarding pass) for what is supposed to be a connecting flight will immediately arouse the agent's suspicion.

Airlines have been checking for hidden-city ticketing, a violation of their rules. If you're detected, you or your travel agency may receive a bill for the difference between what you paid and what you should have paid for the shorter flight.

On round-trip tickets, your return space may also be canceled. And if you check in for the final destination of a through flight and get off at an intermediate stop, you could delay the flight several hours while the airline investigates the "loss" of one passenger.

Frequent-flier coupons. An entire underground industry has developed to broker frequent-flier awards, which are primarily used for upgrades. A broker pays a frequent flier to obtain an award, then sells it to someone else at a profit. If you see a discount agency's newspaper ad for "Business and First Class, up to 70 percent off," it's probably selling frequent-flier awards.

Buying such an award isn't illegal, but it's risky. Airlines are scrutinizing frequent-flier awards more carefully; if a carrier thinks you bought your ticket from a broker, the carrier may not honor it. Furthermore, airlines allot so few premium-class seats for free frequent-flier travel that, even if you buy a coupon, you'll have a tough time using it. Don't buy someone else's coupons unless you enjoy taking big-time financial risks.

PREMIUM-TRIP AWARDS

On all the big U.S. lines, you can exchange frequent-flier credit for free business or first-class tickets to most parts of the world.

How to get deals on airfares **51**

Here's what the big lines require for an off-peak, round-trip ticket in a premium class—first class on two-class planes, business class on three-class ones:

• For trips within the lower 48 states, you typically trade in 35,000 to 45,000 miles. That award normally is also good to nearby cities in Canada and the Caribbean. Figuring credit at 2 cents a mile, a premium domestic trip costs about $800—passing our reasonableness tests for most long-haul flights.

• For a trip to Hawaii, you usually surrender 50,000 to 60,000 miles. But 60,000 miles of credit is worth $1,200; using it that way makes sense mainly for travelers from the East Coast, Midwest, or South. West Coast travelers can buy first-class seats for about the same money.

COUPON WARNING

Watch out for any agency that promises you premium-class discounts of 70 percent or so. Chances are it's a coupon broker, selling frequent-flier awards bought from travelers. Individuals sometimes sell their own awards, as well. Either way, you run a big risk. The airlines don't allow the selling of frequent-flier awards, and they enforce the ban vigorously. If they catch you, they may not honor your tickets.

• To Europe or South America, the typical bite is 75,000 to 85,000 miles and to Asia or the South Pacific, 80,000 to 90,000 miles. At about $1,600 in credit, a premium round-trip to Europe effectively costs many travelers over twice as much as a cheap economy excursion. Still, it's less than double the cost of a peak-season round-trip from many cities in the South and West, and less than half the big lines' business class fares on most routes.

The major problem with premium frequent-flier trips is wangling a reservation. While close to 70 percent of the respondents to our surveys get the premium trips they request, a sizable minority (about 20 percent) tell us that they can get seats for premium-class trips only "a few of the times" they request them or

52   AIRFARE KNOW-HOW

"never." Anecdotes about the scarcity of seats abound, too. When seats are available, however, frequent-flier credit probably provides the best way to escape coach at a reasonable cost.

MOVING UP WITH UPGRADES

Frequent fliers can also use their credit to upgrade a purchased coach/economy excursion ticket:

• Most big domestic lines require 20,000 miles to upgrade a domestic coach excursion ticket to the next higher class of service. In effect, you pay $400, a reasonable figure for a round-trip upgrade on a typical long-haul flight. Several lines let you upgrade a full-fare coach ticket for even less mileage.

• U.S. Airways follows a different formula. For 2,500 miles of credit each, you can get upgrade certificates that you "spend" in increments of one-way flight distance—one certificate for a flight up to 799 miles, two for 800–1,599 miles, three for 1,600 miles or more. That's a good deal: You need only six certificates (15,000 miles of credit) to upgrade even the longest domestic round-trip, and the credit required for shorter trips is much less.

• Upgrading economy excursions to Europe requires 40,000 miles, worth $800, on most lines. That can more than double the cost of many trips, but you'd still pay well under half the asking price for a business-class ticket. It's an especially good deal for travelers from the West Coast. Offsetting its domestic advantage, U.S. Airways doesn't provide mileage upgrades on excursion fares to Europe at all.

• American and TWA let you use mileage upgrades with even the cheapest sale tickets, Continental doesn't upgrade any sale fares, and Northwest doesn't upgrade international sale fares. Other lines allow upgrades with "selected" excursion fares, giving them the freedom to adjust the minimum upgradable fare as

How to get deals on airfares **53**

they see fit. Only Continental and TWA allow travelers on senior coupons to use mileage upgrades.

BARGAIN PREMIUM CLASS

A few small lines offer business or first class tickets at a lot less than the big lines charge:

• Airlines that fly along the West Coast offer first-class seats at much lower prices than they charge on comparable routes elsewhere. Low-fare Reno Air initiated low first-class fares in that area, which have been copied by the big lines on routes where they compete with Reno.

• Two lines offer low first- or business-class fares on some or all scheduled domestic and international flights: ProAir, operating from Detroit, and Tower, which flies from New York.

• AirTran has added business-class seats to its DC9s, with fares pegged at only a modest premium over its unrestricted coach fares.

• On El Al flights from the U.S. to Tel Aviv, you can upgrade from any economy ticket, including the cheapest excursions, to business class for a surcharge that makes the total trip cost less than double the economy excursion price and about half the regular business-class fares.

CHECK PREMIUM CHARTERS

Several European-based charter lines (and scheduled lines, such as Martinair, that operate like charters) offer premium seating at reasonable prices. They fly from as many as a dozen major North American cities to home bases in Europe. Their flights take off all year from Florida; otherwise, routes on most lines are seasonal, operating in spring, summer, and fall from a few major gateways in the Northeast, Midwest, South, and West Coast.

You'll find low-cost premium-charter seats from the U.S. on

CityBird to Brussels, Condor to Cologne and Frankfurt, Corsair to Paris and Papeete, and Martinair to Amsterdam. SkyService offers premium seating on charters from Canada to Europe and Las Vegas. (Tickets are sold only through participating tour operators; call a travel agency.) As usual with charter and charter-like lines, flights from each North American gateway generally operate only once or twice a week.

Seating is generally on a par with big-line domestic first-class or transatlantic business class. Premium-charter fares are typically 75 to 150 percent higher than charter economy fares. Only some pass one of our reasonableness tests—that of charging less than double big-line economy fares—but all charge well under half the business-class fares on major lines.

The other charter lines we checked don't offer a premium option. For some flights, however, tour operators may charter planes with a premium-class cabin. Whenever you consider a charter, ask your travel agent or the tour operator about any premium options.

PLATINUM TWOFERS

With an American Express Platinum card on certain airlines, you can get twofers in business or first class—buy one ticket at the regular fare and get a free second ticket for a companion. On most twofer deals, both travelers must follow identical itineraries, although separate return schedules are sometimes permitted. As of late 1998, AmEx offered this deal for travelers who buy business- or, in some cases, first-class tickets on Aeromexico, Air Canada, Air New Zealand, Alitalia, Asiana, China, Continental, Iberia, LanChile, Lufthansa, Sabena, SAS, Swissair, and U.S. Airways. (Fares are subject to limitations on dates, routes, and seat allocations.)

Twofers in premium classes are most attractive for flights across the Pacific, where a list-price business-class ticket often

How to get deals on airfares 55

costs about the same as two economy excursion tickets. But business-class fares to Europe—and especially to London—are so high that, even at half price, a business-class seat can cost more than three times as much as an economy excursion.

The Platinum deal is subject to annual renewal in early spring, so the list of participating airlines may change. Even so, the twofer deal alone is attractive enough to justify the $300 annual cost of a Platinum card for travelers who charge enough to qualify. (If you already have a regular or Gold AmEx card, call the customer-service number to ask if you can qualify for a Platinum card.)

SHORT-TERM OFFERS

Other premium-class options are a sometime thing. American, for example, usually lists a few first class flights every week in its Internet-based weekend-travel program. And Cathay Pacific's Internet-only ticket auctions have included premium-class trips.

Airlines sometimes push premium-class twofers, usually in frequent-flier mailings. Some air-sea cruise packages offer bargain-priced upgrades from economy to business class.

There's no way to predict where or when such offers will crop up. Keep an eye on airline ads and mailers from your frequent-flier program—they'll often be your only chance to fly in comfort without paying a gouge price.

C H A P T E R

AIRFARE DEALS ON THE INTERNET

How would you like to fly from Los Angeles or New York to Hong Kong, spend 7 to 30 days, and take side trips to as many as 17 other Far Eastern cities, all for $999 in airfare? Or take a companion to Hong Kong and stay there five days, at the same $999 for both travelers? You could have, had you accepted one of the short-term offers Cathay Pacific promoted a while back on its web site—and only there.

True, those deals were by no means typical; most web promotions were far less generous. Nonetheless, they show that travelers who aren't on the web miss out on some terrific deals these days.

There are far too many travel and travel-related sites, with more cropping up every day, to let us survey Internet travel comprehensively. Even link pages (such as Travel Weekly's at *www.travelweek.com*), set up to compile all the airline sites on a single list, are often seriously behind the times. We can, however, provide an overview of airline sites and point you toward some that may prove rewarding when you're hunting for good deals.

58 AIRFARE KNOW-HOW

WHAT'S AVAILABLE

The Resource Guide in the back of the book lists all the large domestic and Canadian lines, most U.S. low-fare lines, and quite a few foreign-based lines. In addition to giving most airlines' web site addresses, it gives toll-free numbers as well.

SHORT-NOTICE WEEKEND DEALS. Most Internet-only airfare deals are for last-minute domestic weekend trips, often with associated hotel and car-rental offers. The airlines typically post fares on Wednesday for trips that started the following Saturday and returned the following Sunday through Tuesday. Those weekend airfares are often less than half the lowest sale fares. Typically, the hotel and car-rental deals are coordinated with airline destinations and time limits.

A few lines also offer quickie international trips. The lead time and maximum stay for those trips are usually somewhat more generous.

Some lines post fares and destinations directly on their web sites. Others enroll prospects through the web, then send them weekly bulletins by e-mail. Both methods are about equally convenient.

OTHER AIRFARE PROMOTIONS. Quite a few lines list promotions other than weekend deals. Most are occasional or one-shot offers —discounts, visitor tickets, twofers, sweepstakes, and such. Many of those listings simply provide online notice of deals that are also available through non-web channels, but more and more are exclusive to the web.

At the time we were checking, several low-fare lines had attractive web promotions, typically with far less rigid restrictions than the big lines' Internet deals. A few sites made provision for alerting you to promotional deals (a "Click here for special deals" button or some such) but showed no postings at the time we were checking.

Airfare deals on the Internet **59**

PURCHASING TICKETS ONLINE. Many lines let you reserve a flight and buy tickets online through their web site (although you may first have to enroll in the line's frequent-flier program). Most did that directly, a few via links to other ticket-booking sites. However, none of the airline sites lets you make a rigorous fare search of the sort many travelers would want to make before buying a ticket. For that, you'd have had to go to one of the online booking services, such as Expedia (*www.expedia.com*) or Travelocity *(www.travelocity.com)*.

United offers online booking through a separate program. You require special software, but it's free for the asking for United frequent fliers (check program materials for particulars). United's program also allows you to make seat reservations. Typically, though, sites don't let you reserve a specific seat online; you have to call your airline after booking.

FURTHER NET INFO. Most of the sites provide flight schedules. A few show what look like railroad timetables; the rest ask for your origin and destination and then present options.

Several airlines publish seat maps on their sites (though some displays were so small as to be virtually worthless). But neither those sites nor available print media disclose seat width or leg room, which travelers really need to compare lines for seat comfort.

Some of the more elaborate sites provide a wealth of additional data, from news of package tours the airline sold and details on its frequent-flier programs to reports on destinations, weather patterns, and the like. Several sites provide real-time (or close to real-time) flight information. Several have links to other sites—covering destinations, weather, and such—that might be of interest.

THE BEST PLACES TO LOOK

Internet exploration can be seductive—it's all too easy to waste a lot of time nosing around. You might be wise to confine your vis-

AIRFARE KNOW-HOW

its to airlines that you're likely to fly—and within that group, to those whose sites present deals you aren't likely to discover anywhere else. No matter how you organize your web ventures, however, you can be reasonably sure that, over the course of a few weeks, you'll find quite a few attractive airline promotions.

At the time we checked, two airline sites clearly outshone the others:

American had the top airline web program overall. Its last-minute program offered outstanding reductions on domestic and international travel on a wide variety of routes, and it was the only program to provide first class as well as coach travel. In addition to flights, the program included land packages, hotel deals (Hilton), and rental-car offers (Avis).

You enroll on the Internet and receive two weekly bulletins by e-mail. In addition to the last-minute program, American's site also listed current promotions that weren't confined to the Internet, including student fares, opportunities for bonus frequent-flier miles, and a seasonal sale that was going on at the time. American's seat maps were among the best on the web, too.

Cathay Pacific was easily the web champ for one-time promotions, with an ongoing series of CyberTraveler deals, some of which were spectacular. Cathay called its All Asia Pass promotion (the Hong Kong–plus-19-cities deal we mentioned earlier) its "best travel deal ever," and we disagree only because its subse-

---

WEB DEALS ROUNDUP

You can get a quick overview of last-minute airfare deals at *www.webflyer.com.* From the home page, you click on the "deals" button and then enter the first letter of your departure city. The next screen tabulates each last-minute bargain flight from that city and provides a link to the airline sites. You can also find hotel and car-rental deals in a similar way. In addition, the site contains a wealth of information about frequent-flier programs, current special bonuses, and such. As with other umbrella sites, you still have to check with individual airlines to make sure you aren't missing some good offers.

Airfare deals on the Internet 61

quent $999 package for two was probably an even better value.

Other Cathay promotions have included seat auctions (in which travelers submit bids on a specified number of seats and the airline accepts the top ones) and frequent-flier deals.

OTHER SITES TO WATCH

Quite a few other lines had impressive, although more limited, web sites:

Continental, Northwest, and TWA came close to American, with good last-minute deals that included hotels or rental cars. However, each of those programs lagged behind American's in at least one important respect: None provided first-class travel, and Northwest didn't offer international trips.

U.S. Airways offered short-term deals from eight origination points, but the deals were valid only on trips that start at one of those eight points. (You can't start a trip by flying from a destination city to an originating point.) And it provided only air trips—no hotel or car deals.

Air Canada provided a well-rounded site, with short-term fares distributed weekly by e-mail. Up-to-the-minute flight information was a plus.

Canadian listed comparable last-minute weekend fares on its site. In addition, when we checked, the airline was running an auction of frequent-flier trips for less-than-normal mileage.

Alaska and America West were also offering last-minute weekend fares weekly on their Internet sites.

American Trans Air (ATA), Kiwi, Southwest, and Tower, in the low-fare-line category, all had sites that provided special airfare deals. Unlike their larger competitors, they didn't limit their promotions to the following weekend, and they usually permitted you to stay longer at your destination. All are worth checking if they serve your home city.

Delta has occasionally offered twofers and dollars-off deals through its site, although none were offered at the time we checked.

Travelers looking for airfare deals on the Internet might also visit *www.air-fare.com,* which lists a ranking of lowest fares for 40 top U.S. cities. The site manager claims to update the fares daily. For each route, the site shows up to eight different fares: the lowest and second-lowest nonrefundable fare, the lowest 14-day and 7-day advance-purchase fare, the lowest and second-lowest refundable fare, the lowest coach fare that qualifies for a no-cost, confirmed upgrade to first class, and the lowest regular first-class fare. The readout also shows the airline on which each fare is available, the booking class, and the major restrictions.

In addition, the system highlights any major-city pairs on which the fare has dropped 20 percent or more within the previous 24 hours. That's a good way to catch up on the latest fare-war rates. The home page also has links to a few other discount-travel information sources.

As the biggest drawback for many travelers, data are confined to just the routes that link the 40 major cities. In some cases, those will be a reasonably accurate guide to fares to and from nearby smaller cities. But not always: The domestic fare structure is full of inconsistencies, and fares to a big city are often quite different from those to a smaller city nearby.

For travelers seeking overseas discounts, ETN, the worldwide network of discount travel agencies, operates a web site, *www. etn.nl,* where you can list your long-haul trip particulars—dates, origin and destination points, and such—and one of the participating discount agencies will e-mail a "bid" for your trip. The site does not accept requests for trips within Europe or for trips within a single country or between adjacent countries, but it claims to offer a wide range of options for long-haul trips.

If you're looking for sources of discount international airfares

Airfare deals on the Internet   **63**

from U.S. or foreign cities, note that ETN offers another, extensive site (*www.etn.nl/discount.htm#disco*). ETN has assembled a worldwide list of agencies that sell discounted air tickets. The index page gives a brief description of each, along with ETN's rating of the agency (for whatever that's worth) plus a link to the agency's web site. Sources for hotel discounts and other travel deals are also posted.

INTERNET TRAVEL-SCAM WARNING

The Internet has now joined traditional mail, fax, and telemarketing as a channel for familiar travel scams. Here are the ones to watch out for:

The "instant travel agent" program asks a victim to buy his or her own training-plus-ID package. The "new agent" also agrees to sell packages to other consumers and collects a share of their future earnings—a pretty good description of an illegal pyramid scheme.

Bogus vacation-discount certificates are now showing up in mailboxes. "Lucky" recipients are offered a bargain-priced vacation. By the time you add up all the fees, extras, and upgrades, the total cost is higher than a conventional package.

Travel "clubs" ask you to pay as much as $6,000 up front for future use of vacation properties at "bargain" prices. People rarely get their money's worth.

Some promotions promise free air tickets to desirable locales. But you must arrange accommodations through the promoter's travel agency—at an inflated price that more than covers the "free" tickets.

CHAPTER 5

AIRFARE DEALS FROM CONSOLIDATORS

Big airlines frequently tout their lowest prices as "discount" fares. But they really aren't—they're list prices for highly limited tickets. A real discount ticket is one you buy for less than the airline says it should cost. Such tickets can save you several hundred dollars each, almost any time of the year to Asia and Latin America, in the peak summer season to Europe, and occasionally (for travelers who can't accept the restrictions on the airlines' lowest advertised fares) within the U.S.

To get one of those true discounts, you must turn to a consolidator ticket. Consolidator airfares continue to be one of the best travel deals we know of. Any good full-service travel agency can get one for you. Some agencies, however, prefer not to deal with them. In that case, you can buy a consolidator ticket through one of the dozens of discount agencies that specialize in them. You can find their ads in the travel section of your newspaper. Look for small ads with only type listings of discount airfares.

TICKET OUTLETS

Even the lowest advertised fares don't always fill planes. So, rather than offer discounts openly—and invite retaliatory cuts from competitors—many airlines unload some seats discreetly through consolidator tickets.

Consolidators, the airline equivalent of factory-outlet stores, are travel agencies that have contracts with one or more airlines to distribute discount tickets. Some consolidators sell directly to the public (in which case, they also act as discount agencies, discussed below). Others are strictly wholesalers, selling their tickets only through other agencies.

Discount agencies sell consolidator tickets (or other discounted travel services) to the public. Some act as their own consolidators; others buy their discount tickets from wholesale consolidators. Many discount agencies have their own consolidation contracts with some airlines and buy tickets for other lines from wholesalers; many agencies also tend to specialize in just one type of travel service—air trips, cruises, or hotel accommodations.

Full-service travel agencies sell a broad range of travel services to the public. They also counsel clients and provide other customer services. Any full-service agency can (if it chooses) obtain consolidator tickets for clients. However, some agents prefer not to—consolidator tickets aren't in the computer reservation systems that agencies use, they require a bit of extra work, and they may carry a smaller commission than tickets at an advertised fare.

WHAT'S THE FARE?

If frequent-flier benefits (or rock-bottom fares) are important to you, it's useful to know how the airlines price those tickets:

Airfare deals from consolidators **67**

Net fares. Some consolidators contract with an airline to buy tickets at a specified *net* rate for each route. That price remains fixed even when the airline's advertised fares change. Consolidators add their markup, then sell either to the public or to other agencies.

A net-fare ticket normally doesn't show a dollar figure in the "fare" box. In many cases, such tickets don't earn frequent-flier mileage credit, and you can't use frequent-flier mileage to upgrade them. Moreover, the airlines' advertised fares may well drop below net fares during a short-term price war.

Overrides. Other consolidators negotiate an *override* (an extra-large commission) with an airline. When the consolidator sells the ticket, it passes along a big chunk of that commission to the customer. As fares change, prices for those tickets fluctuate. They usually show the airline's advertised fare in the "fare" box. On many airlines, such tickets earn frequent-flier mileage and can be upgraded by using a frequent-flier award.

As with some other sorts of outlet store, consolidators ordinarily don't mention brand names (airlines) in ads or promotions. But you do find out what line you'd fly on when you call to ask about specific fares and schedules.

HOW MUCH DO YOU SAVE?

The amount you'll save depends on where and when you go:

International. You'll probably find the biggest consolidator discounts on tickets to Asia, Europe, and Latin America. Governments must still approve fares on many international routes, so airlines find it easier to discount through consolidators than to change list prices frequently.

Published fares to Europe are seasonal. The best consolidator deals show up in the summer, when advertised fares are close to double the winter ones. Off-season, even the best consolidator prices are no lower than the airliners' regular fares. (In summer, fare wars often slash advertised fares below typical consolidator prices.)

On the other hand, advertised fares to Asia and Latin America don't vary much by season. Consolidator discounts accordingly tend to be consistent year-round.

Domestic. With deregulation, U.S. airlines are free to adjust prices as often and as fast as they want. That pricing freedom eliminated much of the need for back-door discounting through consolidators. As a result, the best advertised fares—the big airlines' cheapest coach excursions and low-fare lines' regular rates—are almost always *below* the best consolidator prices, especially during one of the frequent fare wars. But those advertised fares are usually wrapped in all sorts of restrictions. The main advantage of consolidator tickets to U.S. points is that, while the prices are comparable to the big lines' advertised excursion fares, these tickets do not have the usual 14- or 21-day advance-purchase and minimum-stay restrictions.

FRONT-CABIN DISCOUNTS

The discount market focuses mainly on coach/economy tickets, but some agencies handle business and first class. Even when you find a premium-seat discount, it's seldom a larger percentage of the fare than the discount on coach/economy travel—usually no more than 20 percent, and often less. While that may represent a sizable dollar saving, it seldom brings the cost of a premium ticket down even close to coach/economy prices.

An agency that advertises big business and first-class discounts may actually be a coupon broker that buys frequent-flier awards for resale. That's very different from a discount ticket, and it poses special risks. (For more on that, see "Buying Your Ticket" on page 70.)

LIMITATIONS AND RISKS

Consolidator tickets aren't always your best bet:

• They're inflexible. If your flight is canceled or delayed, the airline isn't obligated to transfer you to another airline (though occasionally they may do so). And you can get a refund only through the discount agency, if at all.

• They often entail trade-offs—an airline you don't like, for example, or an awkward schedule or indirect route with extra stops. You may not receive frequent-flier mileage, be allowed to reserve a seat before you arrive at the airport, or be eligible for special-order meals. Those problems are real: In our consolidator-ticket survey, two-thirds of the respondents reported some degree of inconvenience or disappointment with the arrangements.

• Sometimes you hear that only undesirable airlines sell tickets through consolidators, but that's a myth. Many of the world's top airlines sell that way, at least some of the time. Bottom-dollar transatlantic tickets are sometimes on minor airlines, but you can usually fly on a major line for only a bit more. You can always specify which airlines you prefer (or which you refuse to fly) when you check prices.

Over the years, consolidator tickets have earned a reputation for being risky, but that's too broad an indictment. There's no risk in using a consolidator ticket: Once you have a valid ticket and confirmed reservation, you should have no trouble. The risk is in buying the ticket: Too many discount agencies engage in a variety of practices, ranging from sloppy to dishonest, that can cause trouble:

• Discount agencies may engage in bait-and-switch promotion. Sometimes they can't deliver tickets for the fares promised in their ads—and some agencies highlight fares from some low figure that applies to only a tiny number of the seats.

• Agencies sometimes advertise list-price charter fares as discounts. That's deceptive—charter fares are usually lower than major-airline fares, but they're certainly not discounted. Charter flights are cheaper for good reason: Typically, they're jammed and they fly less frequently than scheduled-line flights. Check-in is also a lot more burdensome, and you usually face huge headaches in the event of a mechanical problem or other major glitch.

• The biggest risks consumers face arise from the fact that consolidators don't own the tickets at the time of sale. According to an ongoing myth, consolidators buy seats cheaply in bulk for resale. In fact, they almost never actually *buy* and take title to a ticket until they have a customer's money in hand.

After getting a customer's money, a consolidator may find that the airline has no more seats at the promised fare. The consolidator must then ask the customer for more money (for a seat at a higher fare), switch airlines, or put the customer on a wait list (perhaps without informing the customer) rather than giving a firm reservation. Or a consolidator who's a bit thin financially may keep the customer's money and wait until the last minute to buy the ticket—at best delaying its delivery, at worst failing to provide the promised flight at the agreed price.

BUYING YOUR TICKET

Those risks needn't pose major problems. In a survey of *Consumer Reports Travel Letter* readers, only about one in 10 respondents reported difficulties. But you do need to be careful.

The safest way to buy a consolidator ticket is through your regular full-service travel agency. If anything goes wrong, you can lean on the agency for a fix.

True, you may save a bit of money if you buy directly from a discount agency, bypassing an extra commission for the full-service agency. If you go that route, take precautions:

• First, determine the major lines' lowest advertised fare to

Airfare deals from consolidators **71**

your destination for your specific dates of travel. Check out list-price charter fares, too. Those are your benchmarks for assessing how good a deal you're getting.

- Next, comparison-shop among several discount agencies. Again, make sure a discounted fare covers your itinerary. For each quote, find out about any limitations—added stops or connections and such.

- If a consolidator ticket doesn't give frequent-flier credit, check to see if the discount is big enough to offset the value of the credit you forgo (about 2 cents a mile, but see also Chapter 10).

- Deal with a discount agency in or near your home city so you can keep track of the process. If something goes wrong, you have convenient access to small-claims court for redress.

- Buy with a charge card. If you don't get your ticket in good time or if something's wrong with it, you can get your money back through a chargeback (bill-cancellation) claim.

- Steer clear of any supposed premium-class "discount" that's actually based on a frequent-flier award purchased from some third party: The risks are much too great. Even though the award ticket is issued in your name, airlines can often sniff out tickets that are based on the sale of awards. Flying on such a ticket violates airline rules; it won't be honored if you're caught. Furthermore, so few premium seats are allocated to frequent-flier awards in peak travel seasons that you'd have a hard time using the ticket after you bought it.

CHAPTER 6

FREQUENT FLIERS AND VERY FREQUENT FLIERS

Businesses ranging from florists to mortgage banks use frequent-flier miles as customer bait these days. When a hotel or some merchant trumpets a "bonus" of 500 frequent-flier miles, you need to know that it's worth no more than about $10 (possibly as little as $5) and act accordingly.

We figure that big-line frequent-flier credit is worth somewhere between 1 and 2 cents a mile—perhaps a bit more if you use it wisely. Here's how we arrived at that range:

Market price. Most big airlines sell frequent-flier credit to other businesses in amounts up to 20,000 miles at 2 cents a mile, for use as customer inducements or employee incentives. Businesses that buy mileage in really big quantities—banks that issue credit-earning charge cards, hotel chains, and car-rental companies—probably pay a bit less.

Free domestic coach trips. We estimate that a domestic frequent-flier award ticket is worth about the same amount of money as a cheap coach excursion ticket for a long-haul flight. Most big

74 AIRFARE KNOW-HOW

lines give you a free round-trip within the U.S. (some include nearby points in Canada and the Caribbean) for 25,000 miles. Those same lines typically charge somewhere between $300 and $600 for their cheapest long-haul round-trips in coach, depending on the distance flown. For a long-haul trip, then, the value of that credit works out to 1.2 to 2.4 cents a mile.

Free economy trips to Europe. Most big U.S. lines ask 50,000 miles for an economy round-trip to Europe. In the winter, you can buy a round-trip from the East Coast to Europe for about $400 and from the West Coast for about $500, putting the value of the frequent-flier credit at about 0.8 to 1 cent a mile. At other times of the year, you'd pay up to $1,000 for the cheapest round-trip from the West Coast to Europe. At that price, credit would be worth 2 cents a mile.

Premium tickets. If you valued credit on the basis of published premium fares, you'd come up with huge numbers—4 cents, 6 cents, or even more than 8 cents a mile. But those figures would be meaningful only if real-world travelers were actually prepared to pay $2,400 for a transcontinental round-trip in first class or $6,790 for a business class seat to London. Few, if any, travelers who buy their own tickets ever pay the airlines' ludicrous asking prices for business or first-class tickets.

Upgrades. Most big lines give a domestic upgrade for 20,000 miles. If the value of the upgrade is equal to the value of a coach ticket, the credit value works out to 1.5 to 3 cents a mile. An upgrade to Europe requires 40,000 miles of credit; by the same formula, that works out to a credit value of 1 to 2.5 cents a mile, depending on the price of economy fares at the time of travel.

USING CREDIT WISELY

Once you've earned the credit, you want to get as much value from it as you can. That means using it in ways that approach or

Frequent fliers and very frequent fliers **75**

even exceed the 2-cent figure and avoiding uses that net you a value of 1 cent or less.

Long trips. You can fly coast-to-coast for the same number of miles as you'd use for even the shortest trip. Clearly, then, you're better off saving your credit for a long trip—one where you'd have to pay up to $600 for the cheapest ticket. Using frequent-flier credit on a trip for which you could buy a cheap ticket for $250 or less just doesn't pay.

If you live in the East or Midwest, save your miles for a trip to

AIRFARE

10 WAYS TO MAXIMIZE MILES

1. Don't think that frequent-flier programs are just for frequent fliers. Over a period of a year or two, you can earn enough miles for a free trip just by repeatedly switching long-distance phone suppliers or by racking up most of your household expenses on a mileage-earning charge card. Among the credit-earning charge cards, Diners Club has the best features (albeit the most-limited earnings opportunities).

2. Concentrate your flying and other earnings on one airline.

3. Miles expire. Use your credit as quickly as feasible.

4. Always save a few miles in your account—you can sometimes "buy" things (such as confirmed seat upgrades) with miles that you can't get any other way.

5. Use your miles for awards that come as close as possible to the higher end of the value range—use 2 cents as a minimum target.

6. Where available, use your credit for upgrades rather than free premium seats—that way, a given amount of mileage can give you good seats on twice as many flights.

7. Be flexible on travel dates and times—sometimes even on your destination. You stand a much better chance of getting the seat you want.

8. Build in a margin of error when you fly on frequent-flier awards—if your flight is delayed or canceled, you usually won't be shifted to another airline.

9. All things being equal, get miles as often as you can. Take the time to apply for mileage on hotels and car rentals, and use a mileage-earning charge card for as much as you can—groceries, office purchases, charitable donations, magazine renewals, and such.

10. But don't overpay just to get miles—on any mileage-earning promotion, calculate the cash value of the miles you get before you buy.

the West or the Southwest. Use them for a short local trip only if the cheapest published fare is exorbitant—as it is on some monopoly markets. And don't use them on a route where you can buy a cheap ticket on a low-fare line—between the Northeast or Chicago and the South, for example, on lines such as AirTran, Delta Express, Kiwi, or Southwest. Similarly, if you live in the West, save your miles for a trip to the East, Midwest, or Southeast. Don't waste them on a short trip for which you could buy a cheap ticket on Alaska, America West, Reno, Southwest, or United Shuttle.

Europe. A frequent-flier ticket to Europe can be a poor use of credit—especially in winter, when your credit is worth as little as 0.6 cents a mile. On the other hand, a frequent-flier ticket to Europe in the summer would be worth a lot more, since summer fares are at least twice as high as the fares offered during a winter airfare sale. But the airlines don't make many frequent-flier seats available for 50,000 miles in the peak summer season—and some lines offer none at all.

Hawaii. A flight to Hawaii may or may not be a good use of frequent-flier credit. The big U.S. lines ask an average of 35,000 miles for a round-trip seat in coach, not a good deal from the West Coast, where discount round-trip tickets to Hawaii regularly run less than $300. But if you're flying from the East, Midwest, or South, where regular fares run upwards of $700, your frequent-flier ticket to Hawaii costs the same 35,000 or so miles West Coast travelers have to use— and that can be a very good deal.

Premium seats and upgrades. For travelers who hate to fly coach/economy, upgrades are a fine way to use frequent-flier miles. Positive-space (confirmed at the time you book) premium seats are available at a reasonable price when you pay with frequent-flier currency, and frequent-flier miles are about the only currency most travelers can use to buy positive-space upgrades.

ELITE FREQUENT-FLIER CLASS

Want to escape the misery of a coach seat? "Elite" status may be your ticket out. And, contrary to popular belief, you don't have to be a 100,000-miler to qualify for that exclusive, very-frequent-flier class.

The major airlines have been quietly loosening restrictions on the kinds of miles that count toward membership in their top-tier programs. In the past, you had to log between 15,000 and 25,000 real miles on sponsoring airlines to reach entry-level elite. But now, flights on partner airlines and commuter carriers, as well as miles from credit-card purchases and bonus promotions, can speed your journey there.

But there's a catch. While the airlines have made it easier to qualify for elite status, they've also made it harder to upgrade, particularly when flying on discounted coach tickets.

Even so, it's worth working toward entry-level elite status. Carriers generally offer a set of 15 or so core privileges to first-floor elite. Most travelers, however, care about only two: front-cabin upgrades and preferred coach seating. While skimpy compared with the perks showered on the highest-ranking members of this class, they can make the difference between pain and pleasure for the average flier.

GETTING TO ELITE

Elite status is an easy target for strategy-minded leisure travelers. The key to success: concentrating all your flights on one airline. Just two trips to Europe plus one domestic flight per year may be all you need to break into the first tier.

In the past, there were only one or two levels of elite; today there may be as many as four. The net effect has been a down-grading of the first-level programs, once the only program for

78 AIRFARE KNOW-HOW

elite fliers. And as this "class" has devolved, so have the requirements for entry.

The elite perks kick in as soon as you earn them. Once you're a member, your status remains valid for a full calendar year or through February of the next year, depending on the airline.

MILEAGE THRESHOLDS. To qualilfy for elite status, you must log lots of miles—between 15,000 and 25,000 annually. This generally includes miles earned on short-haul trips of between 500 and 1,000 miles minimum. If you're a frequent shuttle flier, the biggest airlines will credit flight segments rather than miles. On Delta, for example, 30 segments or 25,000 miles earn elite status. So if you travel frequently to visit a nearby city, you may reach elite status faster—flying fewer miles—than if you take several long-haul trips. The airlines are also bending a bit on another restriction: that only flown miles qualify toward elite status.

CODE SHARES AND PARTNERS. Some airlines allow miles earned by flying code shares and partner airlines to count toward elite status. Most members of the Star Alliance (United, Lufthansa, SAS, Thai and Varig), for example, allow travelers to accrue elite credits, although sometimes those credits are discounted at 50 percent. The number of code shares and partners has tripled since our last survey, as more carriers forge alliances. But beware: Code-share partners will often reduce credit for flights taken by members of an affiliated frequent-flier program. When making reservations, it pays to verify exactly how much credit you'll receive.

> **SETTING YOUR OWN VALUE**
>
> Say a hotel chain gives 1,000 airline miles per stay, but only if you pay the rack (list-price) room rate. Are you better off getting a $20 discount or paying rack rate and taking the credit? To answer that question, set your own value on your frequent-flier credit, based on the ways you prefer to use it. Then do the math for the mileage offer. By our calculations, the value of frequent-flier miles can range from 0.6 cents to as much as 4 cents a mile.

THE MAIN PERKS

For first-level elite members, the benefits outweigh standard-class frequent-flier status, but they aren't as rich as those afforded to the higher tiers.

FLIGHT BENEFITS. Members earn 25 to 50 percent more on each flight than the average frequent flier. That's in addition to bonuses they earn for purchasing or upgrading to front-cabin seating or for limited-time promotions. Many airlines also offer bonus mileage for passing certain milestones. A handful—Continental, Canadian, Delta, and U.S. Airways—give elite members the advantage on getting free seats. The latter three also say they let their elite members bypass blackout dates, a perk usually reserved for higher-level fliers.

UPGRADES. This is the brass ring. But for first-level elites holding discounted coach tickets, the step up can be difficult, if not impossible. Timing is critical. That's because the farther up you go on the elite ladder, the earlier you can call in for an upgrade. Often, the highest elite programs allow fliers to confirm upgrades at the time of booking. For most fliers on cheap tickets, 24 hours is the closest they'll get. In the case of Northwest, you can confirm only on the day of departure. And fliers on Continental are limited to a two-hour preflight window. It pays to call early anyway: Reservation agents will sometimes confirm a low-level elite upgrade when the front cabin is empty.

Upgrade "currency" comes in three forms: mile-based segments, one-way upgrades, and miles. When you qualify in an elite program, the airlines will generally send you a starter kit of upgrades that might get you through one or two trips, depending on how far you're traveling. The airline will reward your continued patronage with free coupons for every 10,000 miles you fly. Of course, you can always buy upgrade coupons before your flight (through city ticket offices, by mail, or online). But be careful:

EARNING MILES ONLINE

Using your computer to earn frequent-flier miles can be easy. If you shop on the Internet, you can earn ClickPoints, which you can convert to credit in the programs of several major airlines or other frequent-traveler programs. There's no set award formula, but you generally get more than one point per dollar spent on your web purchases. (You can earn the usual additional credit by paying with a mileage-earning charge card.)

ClickRewards was launched in March 1998 by Netcentives. Overall, the program seems quite generous. Some of the participating merchants include:

• Barnes and Noble, which gives 1 point per dollar spent over $50 for books, magazines, or software.

• Garden Escape, which gives 150 points for a $50 purchase of garden gifts or supplies, 350 points for a $100 purchase.

• Music Boulevard, which gives 100 points for the purchase of any three CDs.

• Office Max, which gives 200 points when you spend $200 at *OfficeMax.com*.

• SkyMall, which gives 500 points for the purchase of $100 in catalog merchandise.

• 1-800-Flowers, which gives 50 points with the purchase of selected flower arrangements and gifts.

• Club Computer, which gives 1 point for every dollar spent over $50; plus, you can earn 1,000 points when you become a Club Computer member (membership costs $79.95).

Netcentives expects to add additional merchants. You can check current participants through the sponsor's own site or a Yahoo! search site at *clickrewards.yahoo.com*, which displays a ClickRewards logo next to each participant's link.

To earn ClickPoints, you enroll at *www.clickrewards.com,* after which the system tracks your points automatically. You must pay for your purchases over the web, by charge card; Netcentives says it uses state-of-the-art web security. Once earned, ClickPoints are much like points in the American Express Membership Rewards program: They never expire, and you can transfer them, at one mile per point, to any of several accounts in increments of 500 points. Current airline partners are American, British, Continental, Delta, Northwest, United, and U.S. Airways. Alternatively, you can transfer points to the Marriott frequent-stay program or use them for National car-rental discounts.

Despite the program's apparent generosity, however, there's a catch: ClickPoints may be offered instead of a cash discount. You'll sometimes be better off buying at a discounted price and forgetting about the miles.

Frequent fliers and very frequent fliers **81**

At anywhere from $25 to $40 per 500-mile coupon, those upgrades can sometimes be more expensive than the flight itself.

You can also pay for upgrades with miles. For coach tickets you'll need between 10,000 and 20,000 miles, almost as much as it costs for an award ticket. Miles also buy upgrade coupons. On American, for example, a book of eight 500-mile coupons costs 30,000 miles.

If you want to upgrade on international flights, you're in luck this year. Most carriers have made it easier. In the past, moving up to business class on overseas flights meant cashing in miles—some 40,000 at that. Now, as the airlines more aggressively promote their foreign carrier partners, they're also permitting first-level elites to use free and earned coupons toward upgrades.

Most carriers, however, limit the free international upgrades to Canada, Mexico, and the Caribbean. There are several notable exceptions: Continental allows coupon upgrades to Asia and Micronesia; Delta doles out one-way international upgrades for every 20,000 miles flown (on top of the four 800-mile coupons fliers get every 10,000 miles); and TWA dispenses two one-way international upgrades for every two transatlantic segments flown. Those are some of the best values of elite programs to date.

OTHER BENEFITS

Beside upgrades, most major carriers offer a host of benefits for their lowest-level elite members:

Preferred coach seating. Aisle and window seats toward the front of the rear cabin are typically blocked off for elite members of all levels.

Waitlist and standby priority. Every line offers this benefit today. Travelers can waitlist for sold-out flights as well as front-cabin upgrades.

82 AIRFARE KNOW-HOW

Dedicated reservations number. Most airlines today offer special phone numbers for their elite members.

Preferential check-in. Elites generally get a special check-in line at larger airports.

Online account status. Most major carriers have special password-protected areas on their web sites, where elite members can check their mileage balance, redeem miles for awards, purchase upgrade coupons, and carry out other functions.

Lounge access. Canadian lines offer one or two free passes to their membership club lounges.

CHAPTER 7

CHARTER FLIGHTS

A charter can be a cheap, convenient way to fly, but sale prices from major lines and regular prices from low-fare scheduled carriers may well undercut charter prices. Charter schedules can also be peculiar. You need to shop around to identify your best deal.

Scheduled really isn't the antonym of *charter*. Both groups of airlines must operate on schedules, as best they can. It would be more accurate to refer to charter lines as "wholesale" lines and to call those that sell directly to the public (such as American, British Airways, or United Express) "retail" lines. Unfortunately, the industry has used the charter/scheduled terminology for more than 50 years, and it isn't about to change.

To complicate matters further, some small airlines operate what amounts to scheduled service under charter rules. That's because starting up a charter line requires less red tape than launching a scheduled line. On the other hand, although they now hold scheduled-line certificates, a few former charter airlines (such as Germany's LTU) still operate like charters.

84   AIRFARE KNOW-HOW

The main distinction between a charter flight and a flight on a scheduled airline is legal. With a charter, your contract is with a tour operator, not an airline—and the operator is financially responsible for getting you to your destination and back. The operator charters planes and crews from one or more airlines that actually operate the flights.

When things go well, you seldom notice that distinction. But when a problem arises with a charter flight, it's the tour operator that must find a solution. If the airline flying the charter runs into difficulties, the operator is responsible for finding a substitute airline. When travelers have been left stranded at a destination, it's usually because a tour operator failed and couldn't pay an airline for the return trips.

Other charter distinctions can also be important to travelers:

• Many charter trips are flown by specialist charter airlines that don't sell tickets directly to the public and don't list fares, schedules, or available seats in the reservation computers that travel agencies use.

• Charter flights serve very limited routes, generally with neither the benefits nor the inconveniences of hubs or connections. The flights typically go point-to-point between a few major cities and a few major vacation spots.

CHARTER PLUSES

The main reason for choosing a charter over a scheduled airline is that, for any given trip, the charter is usually cheaper. Even when a scheduled line seems to have a price advantage, it may offer only a few seats at the come-on fare. But most charters sell all their seats at the same low price. A charter seat may be your only low-fare alternative when scheduled lines sell out their allotments of seats at their lowest promotional fares.

Price aside, charters have a few advantages:

Charter flights **85**

• Charter tickets are less restricted than the cheapest tickets on a scheduled airline—the minimum advance-purchase period usually depends on how long it takes to complete the paper-work, and the minimum stay depends on how often the charter line flies a particular route, rather than on arbitrary rules. That advantage is often a particular appeal of domestic charters.

A few charter operators, however, do offer restricted fares (advance-purchase or minimum-stay) that are a bit lower than their own walk-up fares. And some charters impose a maximum-stay limit on their lowest fares.

• Charter flights may operate nonstop on routes where sched-uled lines don't. A charter flight may be the only way to fly between some cities without the extra time and hassle of a stop, and possible plane change, at a hub airport.

• A few charter lines offer a premium option, with seats (and often food service) equal to what you expect to find in business class. While a charter's premium seat is considerably more expensive than one of its economy seats, the premium charter seat is a lot less expensive—on average, about 60 percent less—than a business or first-class seat on a scheduled line. A premium charter seat is often the only reasonably priced alternative to a jammed coach/economy seat.

CHARTER MINUSES

Charters aren't always the cheapest way to fly: Within the U.S., more and more scheduled low-fare lines sell seats at prices that match or beat charter prices. Even on the giant scheduled lines, fares may drop below charter levels during fare wars. Moreover, the major lines' advertised fares to Europe in winter are usually low enough to discourage charter competition. Discount tickets from consolidators often undercut charter fares as well.

Charters have other drawbacks, too:

AIRFARE KNOW-HOW

• On any given route, a charter usually operates a lot less frequently than a scheduled line. Many charter programs operate only one weekly "back-to-back" trip: The plane loads with vacationers, ferries them to their destination, and picks up the previous week's group for the trip home. Unless the flight days correspond to the beginning and end of your vacation, a charter could cost you several days of time at your destination. Some programs, however, offer more frequent service. Even on weekly programs, you can usually stay additional weeks (sometimes for an extra charge).

• Most charter airlines have relatively few planes, and they're scheduled tightly. Consequently, flights may arrive or depart at odd hours. And any significant delay of a single flight can throw a charter line's schedule out of whack for days.

• Since charter airlines don't have "interline" agreements with each other or with scheduled lines, a charter line can't sign your ticket over to another line in the event of cancellation or major delay. In those cases, only the tour operator can arrange a substitution; you can't do it yourself.

• Unless you book a premium seat, a charter virtually guarantees an unpleasant trip. Seating on charter flights isn't always worse than on a scheduled line, but it's hardly ever better. Moreover, most charter flights operate close to full: One of the reasons charters are relatively cheap is that close to 100 percent of the seats on each flight are sold, rather than the 70 percent or so you find on scheduled airlines. The result? Extreme crowding.

• Charter airlines normally use other airlines or independent airport-service organizations to handle check-in, boarding, and baggage claim. Many apparently skimp on those services, to judge by the three-hour check-in lines we've often seen for charter flights.

• Some travel agents don't like to sell charter flights, since most aren't listed in the computer reservation systems travel agencies use.

Charter flights **87**

• You may have a tough time getting a refund if you have to cancel a charter flight, and your ticket may not be as easily "exchangeable" (rebookable for a fee) as a coach/economy excursion ticket on a scheduled line. Ask about refunds and exchanges any time you consider a charter. If a ticket isn't exchangeable, you can protect yourself with trip-interruption insurance. But factor in the cost of that insurance—typically $5.50 per $100 of coverage—when you compare ticket prices. Moreover, we suggest you buy insurance either from your retail travel agency or directly from an insurance company: If you buy insurance from a tour operator, you won't be covered if that operator fails.

MAKING YOUR BOOKING

You can buy virtually any charter through your regular travel agency. You can also buy directly from some of the operators, but there's no reason to do so—your flight won't be any cheaper, and you may get a bit less personal service. Several wholesale tour operators sell only through retail travel agencies. Individual travelers shouldn't call those operators, even for general information.

Most charters can also be bought with "land" packages that include hotel accommodations, airport transfers, and sightseeing. Compare prices with the best deal you can get through some other type of hotel-discount program.

Above all, don't buy a charter blindly—there are drawbacks as well as possible advantages. Consider a charter only if it offers a substantially lower fare or much better schedule than a scheduled line, or an attractive premium option.

C H A P T E R

BAD SEATS AND HOW TO AVOID THEM

Airlines have names for their bad seats. American calls them "undesirable." Delta identifies them as "no-recline." Whatever the label, the seats are the airlines' inside secret. Reservation agents usually don't warn fliers about these loser seats. Several airlines claim their computer reservations systems (CRSs) don't even contain the data to make those disclosures. U.S. Airways, for example, identifies a pair of tortuous seats as simply 25B and 25C.

Even the most diligent travel shoppers will find it frustrating—if not impossible—to keep track of the worst coach seats. That's because the airlines constantly rejigger seat layouts—and "floor plans" differ among airlines and aircraft.

Nevertheless, location, location, location—the three most important determinants of real estate value on the ground—are equally important to travelers 35,000 feet in the air. In fact, seat location has become more important than ever, now that airlines are fitting as many seats as possible into their planes and many planes are fully booked.

THE SEAT INVESTIGATION

We conducted an investigation of widebody coach cabins operated by major U.S. and foreign airlines. Why widebody? Because a bad seat on a 6- or 12-hour flight is infinitely worse than the same seat on a short hop.

Our report identified an estimated 77,000 undesirable seats—specifically, non-recliners, middles, and seats near the bathroom —on 800 widebodies of 11 global airlines. That represents 41 percent of coach seats on those aircraft. We also rated the planes on their seat-undesirability quotient. Not surprisingly, the type of aircraft you fly can make the difference between a pleasurable flight and a painful one—even in coach.

Do you hate middle seats? You're nearly three times as likely to get stuck in one on a 747 as you are on a 767. When it comes to avoiding a seat near the restrooms, your best bet is the seat configuration on a DC-10; only 8 percent of its seats, on average, are located too close to a lavatory. On the other hand, up to 18 percent of the seats on some A300-600s,

SEAT ARRANGEMENT

COACH/ECONOMY

Plane	Configuration
A300/310/330/340	2-4-2
A320	3-3
DC9/MD80/MD90	2-3
DC10/MD11	2-5-2; 2-4-3
L1011	2-5-2; 2-4-3
737	3-3
747	3-4-3
757	3-3
767	2-3-2
777	2-5-2

BUSINESS CLASS

Plane	Configuration
A300/310/330/340	2-3-2; 2-2-2
A320	2-2; 2-3
DC9	2-2
DC10/MD11	2-3-2; 2-2-2
L1011	2-3-2
737	2-2
747	2-2; 2-3-2
757	2-2
767	2-2-1; 2-2-2; 2-1-2
777	2-3-2; 2-2-2

Source: *Consumer Reports Travel Letter,*
July 1998 and October 1998

Bad seats and how to avoid them   **91**

and about 23 percent on 767-200s, are too near the bathroom.

Then there are the non-reclining seats, which can account for as much as 10 percent of a plane's coach cabin. While the proportion of these seats is small compared to total coach seats, that's little comfort to the unlucky flier who is sitting in one.

FULL DISCLOSURE

Statistics aside, a seat frozen in the upright position can be downright painful, particularly for passengers with chronic back problems. For this reason, we urge the airlines to advise consumers when they're getting a subpar product. One airline—Continental—actually agreed to change its policy as a result of our investigation. It plans to equip reservations agents with information about seat recline for all wide- and narrow-body jets.

NO RECLINE

Seats that don't fully recline are the airline industry's well-kept secret. Although fliers don't generally ask whether a seat reclines, they should. When a passenger sitting in front drops his seatback into your lap, you become a human sandwich.

We measured the differential on one DC-10 and found, not surprisingly, that non-recliners can lose as much as 20 percent, or five inches, of horizontal space (see page 92). Seats can recline up to eight inches, but few airlines ever reach that maximum.

Unfortunately, getting accurate seat-recline information from reservations agents is more than difficult. Virgin Atlantic is one noteworthy exception. Its agents can access recline information via the CRS, and voluntarily disclose it to passengers at the time of booking rather than waiting for them to ask. We applaud such a disclosure policy and strongly recommend it be adopted by all airlines.

American Airlines is another story. When asked which seats

92   AIRFARE KNOW-HOW

didn't recline, company officials and reservation agents provided conflicting data. The carrier's spokespeople assured us that only one seat in the entire widebody fleet was afflicted with this disorder—19A on the 767-300. The carrier's ticket agents, however, counted 61 seats across five different models and nine seating configurations as non-reclining.

Our own experience shows the ticket agents to be closer to the mark. *Consumer Reports Travel Letter* editor Laurie Berger and her husband got stuck in two no-recline seats (19H and J) on an American 767-200.

LESS SPACE FOR A NON-RECLINER

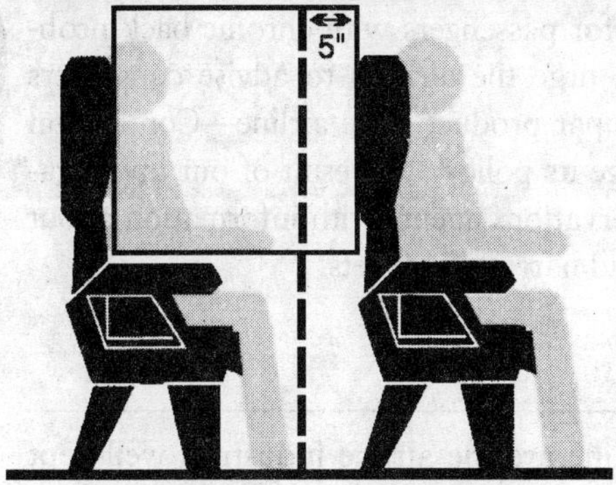

Seatbacks in the upright position

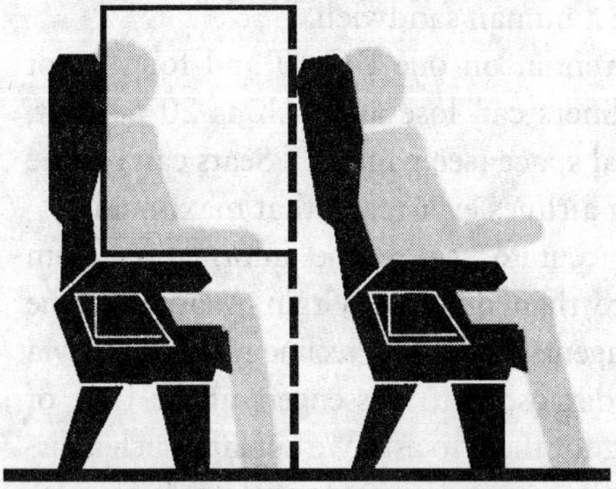

Front seat tilts back 5", reducing clearance for the non-recliner by 20%

They confirmed that all seats located forward of an exit door are frozen. One agent said, "I can promise you that the seats in front of a bulkhead wall don't recline all the way."

Why doesn't a seat recline in the first place? There are two reasons: Its back butts up against a bulkhead wall, giving it little or no space to dip into. Or it's forward of an emergency exit door. Seats directly in front

Bad seats and how to avoid them **93**

of the exit *can* recline —*if* they don't reduce the minimum space required by the Federal Aviation Administration for evacuation.

"Most airlines try to pack on as many seats as possible, so they don't have the room to allow recline," says FAA spokesperson Allison Duquette. Extra seats produce extra revenue, not only per flight but over the lifetime of an aircraft.

Virgin Atlantic's 747 classics, for example, have one more row of seats than their 747-400s, leaving no room for full recline under FAA regulations. That's why seats 65A and 64K on Virgin's 747s are frozen while those same seats on its 747-400s do recline.

Strategy: Always ask the airline to make sure your seat fully reclines. Seats that don't tilt back account for up to 10 percent of a plane's coach cabin. Boeing 747s have the most "stiffbacks"; 777s and L-1011s have the fewest.

To hear the airlines tell it, extra seats are worth money: "Over the lifetime of an aircraft, each extra seat on board can easily generate tens of millions of dollars in additional revenue," says Gary Weissel, customer product manager for Delta.

But Weissel says when business is good in the airline industry, as it is today, carriers compete for customers by offering slightly more comfort, "so there are fewer seats with restricted recline today."

BY THE BATHROOM

Seats located near the lavatories are undesirable for obvious reasons—traffic and congestion tend to build up near the lavatory doors—particularly in the rear of the plane.

Blame it on poor layout. When airlines purchase planes from a manufacturer, they choose one of a variety of possible floor plans. We graded the aircraft models on the proximity of lavatories to seats (see the sample seating chart, page 95).

On aircraft with restrooms in the back of the plane, we counted

94   AIRFARE KNOW-HOW

the aisle seats in the nearest three rows—as well as any aisle seats directly across from a lavatory—as undesirable. Where there is a mid-cabin lavatory directly ahead of or behind a seating section, we deemed only the two seats nearest it undesirable because passengers have other places to line up. And when there is a cluster of toilets in the midsection of the plane, we considered only the aisle seats surrounding the central facility undesirable.

Strategy: Be careful choosing seats on Airbus A300s, Boeing 767s, and MD-11s—they had the largest percentage of these bad seats, with 12 to 13 percent of them located in restroom purgatory, fore and aft. The 747 and 777 families, the DC-10s, and the L-1011s were better, with only 8 to 9 percent of their seats located near the restrooms.

MIDDLE SEATS

Middle seats, cramped and imprisoning, are the easiest to identify. But middles are also hard to escape, because of their sheer numbers. Like lavatory seats, middles are a factor of layout.

Strategy: The 767 is your best bet if you want to avoid these seats. Its seven abreast (2-3-2) configuration means that only 14 percent of coach seats are caught in-between. The Airbus A300, with eight abreast (2-4-2), is your second choice. The 747, with 10 across (3-4-3) configurations in the main cabin, are the worst among airliners. Some 35 to 39 percent of its seats are in the middle. The L-1011, MD-11, and DC-10 improve somewhat on the 747, with their 2-5-2 combination.

THE MOST COMFORTABLE PLANES

We totaled up all three key discomfort factors—no recline, lavatory proximity, and middle seats—and scored each plane on its overall undesirability of seating. The 767 family and A300

Bad seats and how to avoid them **95**

series of planes had the lowest percentage of undesirable seats, averaging 30 and 37 percent, respectively. The 747 family had the most undesirables—48 percent. And the MD-11 was a close second-to-last place, with an average 46 percent of coach seats deemed undesirable.

SEAT ROULETTE: HOW TO PLAY AND WIN

• *Get seat assignments when you book your flight.* Never wait until you arrive at the airport. Even if you already have a seat assignment, check in at the airport an hour or more before departure. If you get to the gate just minutes before takeoff, airlines may reclaim *your* great seats for more-favored cus-

BAD SEATS ON A 767

Boeing 767-300ER

FIRST CLASS | BUSINESS | COACH/ECONOMY

Why they're underable

L **Near a lavatory**

R **Doesn't fully recline**

L R **Near a lavatory and doesn't fully recline**

M **Middle seat**

☐ **OK**

Midcabin

Rear

Seating chart reprinted by special permission from the July 1, 1998, issue of the OAG Desktop Guide–North America. Copyright © 1998, Reed Elsevier Inc. All rights reserved.

tomers, such as high-mileage frequent fliers. The later you check in, the greater your chances of landing a loser seat.

• *Book away from the restrooms and galleys.* Give yourself at least four rows' distance from both.

• *Probe reservation agents on non-recliners.* Keep in mind that seat numbers change when airlines reconfigure the cabin, which they do quite frequently. Airline ticket agents should be able to determine if the recline status of your assigned seat has changed; if they can't, speak to a supervisor. But remember, ticket agents don't always have this information in their systems. The best tactic: Avoid seats in any row forward of an emergency exit door or in the last row of a section.

• *Request an exit row.* If you arrive late and are able-bodied, you may be able to get one of the coveted emergency row seats. They usually offer generous legroom, by coach standards. And airlines cannot assign those seats over the phone; they must see you in person to assess your physical ability to assist in an evacuation.

• *Upgrade.* Escape the misery of coach—and its undesirable seats—by saving your mileage awards for upgrades, not free coach tickets.

If, despite all your efforts, you still get a miserable seat, complain and demand a better one. If a packed plane prevents a change, demand compensation later. You might get compensation along the lines of free upgrade to first class for a future flight.

CHAPTER 9

SPECIAL FARES

Senior airfares are the most widely recognized of "status" fares—deals based on who you are rather than on how you're traveling. There are also status fares for children, youth, and students, and "compassionate" fares for travelers suddenly called to visit a dying relative or attend a funeral.

Status is, in effect, just another restriction that works like advance purchase and Saturday-night stay. They're all designed to give a break to price-sensitive travelers while still charging business travelers top dollar.

You must be prepared to prove your eligibility for a status fare when you buy your ticket and again when you travel. Proof of age is required for senior, children's, and youth fares. You must show an official school ID to get a student fare, and a funeral or death notice or some equivalent documentation to qualify for a compassionate fare. Since status fares are "published," you can buy tickets from an airline or through a travel agency.

98   AIRFARE KNOW-HOW

The table on pages 100–101 summarizes the main status fares for travel within North America. It lists the 10 largest U.S. carriers, the two big Canadian lines, and three smaller lines of particular interest—American Trans Air, the biggest of the minor lines; Midwest Express, consistently top-rated for comfort and service in surveys by CONSUMER REPORTS and others; and Reno Air, a highly rated low-fare line.

As the table shows, some status fares cut a percentage off a fare available to anybody. Others are priced independently; they may or may not be good deals, depending on what alternatives you have.

SPECIAL FARES FOR SENIORS

Airlines offer older travelers a variety of deals. In most cases, the minimum age for eligibility is 62, although it's 65 for some programs.

SENIOR COUPONS. These are one of the best buys in travel. A qualifying senior can buy a round-trip to anywhere within the lower 48 states (some lines include adjacent points in Canada and the Caribbean) for no more than $298. (For a long-haul flight, that's less than even the best sale fares and less than half of the lowest nonsale coach excursion.) You can fly to Alaska or Hawaii for two coupons each way (one coupon to Alaska on United). But no line sells senior coupons for travel to Europe, Asia, or other overseas points.

The table shows the eight major U.S. airlines that sell senior coupons and their prices (as of mid-1998 and subject to change). Each coupon is good for a one-way trip. Connecting flights are permitted on a single coupon, as long as you don't stop over at a connection point. Each traveler must have a separate book—a couple can't use one four-coupon book to take a single round-trip together.

Special fares **99**

The restrictions on all the lines are about the same—and quite liberal. For a confirmed seat, you must book at least 14 days in advance, but you can also travel standby. Round-trip travel isn't required, so there's no minimum-stay requirement. As with most promotional fares, seats are limited.

Senior coupons are valid for a year after they're issued. If you don't take at least two round-trips a year, coupons aren't a good deal. Price variations among the various airlines are small. You'll probably find that your choice of airline depends more on the routes and schedules available from your home city than on differences of a few dollars per trip. On all lines, senior-coupon travel earns frequent-flier credit.

The table highlights differences among the big-line programs:

All eight lines sell four-coupon books. (Continental is the only line that still sells eight-coupon books.) Only TWA sells books of companion coupons, which can be used by a traveler of any age who accompanies a qualifying senior who's using coupons. On U.S. Airways, seniors can use their coupons for one or two accompanying grandchildren, ages 2 to 11, and also get a round-trip within Florida for a single coupon.

Coupons are good deals any time the cheapest alternative round-trip fare is more than $270 to $298 (depending on the airline)—almost always on long-haul routes, often true for shorter trips. But always check the low-fare competition before opting for coupons.

SENIOR CLUBS. Four big airlines run senior clubs:

• United's Silver Wings Plus is open to travelers age 55 or over. Rather than a standard schedule of benefits, it offers a variety of deals. The most consistent bargains in the past few years have been a series of zoned fares, which generally beat even good sale fares and, for all but the longest trips, senior coupons, too.

Membership costs $75 for two years or $225 lifetime. In addition, members must pay an extra fee ($25 to $50) to take advantage of some promotions. Call 214 760-0022 for more information, or check the web site at *www.silverwingsplus.com*.

• Continental's program, Freedom Flight Club, is scheduled to close in November 1998 but will reopen when vacancies occur. Members 62 and over get 15 to 20 percent off any fare. Memberships costs $75 a year for domestic travel, $125 for travel outside the U.S. For information, call 800 441-1135 or check *www.flycontinental.com*.

• Skywise, on Delta, replaces Senior Select Savings Plus. Fares have gone up $10, and there are now blackouts around certain holidays. Like the old program, it offers domestic-zone fares for travelers age 62 or over and up to three companions of any age. Call 800 325-3750 to enroll or check *www.delta-air.com/skywise*.

SPECIAL FARES SUMMARIZED

SPECIAL FARES ON NORTH AMERICAN AIRLINES
Source: *Consumer Reports Travel Letter*, June 1998

Airline	Senior	Youth/student
Air Canada	10% off	Standby on some routes
Alaska	10% off	—
America West	10% off or published discount; $548 for 4 coupons	Published discount on some routes
American	10% off; $596 for 4 coupons	Student fares available on Internet
American Trans Air	10% off	—
Canadian	10% off	—
Continental	10% off; $579 for 4 coupons, $1079 for 8	Published discount on some routes
Delta	10% off; $596 for 4 coupons	$229 for 4, $412 for 8 shuttle coupons
Midwest Express	10% off	Published discount on some routes
Northwest	10% off; $540 for 4 coupons	—
Reno Air	10% off	—
Southwest	Published discount on some routes	—
TWA	10% off; $548 for 4 coupons	—
United	10% off; $548 for 4 coupons	—
USAirways	10% off; $579 for 4 coupons	—

Special fares **101**

• AActive American Traveler Club, on American, offers zoned coach fares (but no premium-class option). It's not open to membership now but is expected to reopen in the spring. To get on a waiting list, call 800 421-5600 or check *www.amrcorp.com*.

SENIOR DISCOUNT. All the lines listed in the table except Southwest (and many unlisted ones, too) give a 10 percent senior discount on virtually any published fare, from the cheapest coach/economy excursions up to first class, for travel in North America. All the listed lines except Midwest Express, Reno, and Southwest give the same reduction to a companion of any age who follows the same itinerary as a qualified senior traveler.

The 10 percent discount is a fallback deal when you can't find anything better. On short-haul coach excursion tickets and sale-

AIRFARE

Senior discount rates on most airlines also apply to companion of any age. Most airlines figure **compassionate rates** from walk-up coach/ economy fares, often required to be round trip; others waive advance-purchase restriction for 7-day excursion fare or make ad hoc adjustments.

Child	Compassionate
Varies by route	50% off
—	50% off
Published discount on some routes	7-day waived on most routes
—	50% off
—	Ad hoc
Reductions from full fare only	50% off
—	50% off
—	50% off
—	50% off
—	70% off
—	Ad hoc
Varies by route	—
$548 for 4 coupons	50% off or waiver
—	7-day waived on most routes
—	Ad hoc

102   AIRFARE KNOW-HOW

priced tickets, that reduction doesn't amount to much money. And coupons are usually a much better deal for a long-haul trip.

Frequent-flier rules are generally the same as those for the any-age fare from which the senior discount is deducted. The discount may not be available on short-term sale fares; you have to check with each airline on each promotion.

Southwest publishes separate fares for seniors age 65 or over, usually with reductions based on the line's unrestricted coach fares. Seniors traveling on Southwest are often better off buying a 21-day advance-purchase ticket at the any-age fare and forgetting about the discount.

Other lines often match Southwest's senior deal on routes where they compete with Southwest. And United's Shuttle allows travelers age 65 or over to buy tickets on nonstop flights for about 15 percent less than the usual 14-day advance-purchase fare, but without the advance-purchase requirement.

NO-BLACKOUT SENIOR FARES

Most airlines make seniors work for their discounts. Continental has taken the opposite approach. Its new Freedom Flight Club for seniors over age 62 is simple: Members get a flat 15 or 20 percent off all fares, all the time.

The lack of restrictions is a big plus. Percentage discounts apply to all fares—even first class—with no program limits above the purchased ticket requirements (such as a 14-day advance purchase and minimum, maximum, or Saturday-night stay). There are no seat limits or blackout dates, even during holidays. And unlike Delta's Skywise, American's AActive American Traveler Club, and United's Silver Wings Plus, Continental's program is not based on zones, so there are no maps or charts to interpret.

But do you pay more for this simplicity? Not when we compared transcontinental fares for midweek coach travel in October

Special fares **103**

1998. Continental's senior club fare was $195.23, beating its own coupon fare of $290 and the other three lines' senior club prices of $298. However, since Continental's program works off published fares, discounts will change as prices fluctuate.

There is one drawback: Freedom Flight Club companion travelers are not discounted. (Continental already offers a 10 percent discount for travelers over age 62, plus one companion, regardless of age, on most flights. But even that companion discount is heavily restricted.)

U.S. membership is $75 per year and covers travel to all 50 states. International membership costs $125 annually and covers travel to all 50 states, Mexico, Canada, Central and South America, the Caribbean, and eight European cities. The program does not include Asia or Australia/New Zealand. All travel Monday through Thursday and Saturday is discounted 20 percent; for Friday and Sunday, the discount is 15 percent. European travel differs slightly: 20 percent off Monday through Thursday and 15 percent off Friday through Sunday. Discounts are on pretax fares.

For seniors fed up with complex programs, Freedom Flight Club is a more flexible, easy-to-use alternative. To apply for membership or book travel, call 800 441-1135.

DEALS FOR JUNIOR TRAVELERS

Young travelers are also eligible for some price breaks:

YOUTH/STUDENTS. TWA's youth coupons are the best of a sparse crop of deals. They're the same price as TWA's senior coupons—with the same conditions but without the companion option. They're a good deal whenever the cheapest alternative round-trip ticket is over $274, which it often is.

American runs an Internet program for college students. Full-time students of any age enroll through American's web site (*www.aa.com/college*); the airline then sends them periodic e-mail bulletins about special fares and other deals.

Other youth/student deals are available from some Canadian and U.S. airlines. Also, airlines run occasional short-term promotions that target young travelers.

INFANTS. Those under age 2 may occupy a half-fare reserved seat on most lines if they're seated in government-approved safety seats provided by their adult traveling companions. Alternatively, an infant can travel free and can occupy an empty seat, if available (on a full plane, an accompanying adult would be required to hold the child throughout the flight). As a third option, an adult without a safety seat can reserve a seat for the infant, but only at an adult fare.

The half-price infant reduction applies to most published adult fares, including the cheapest 21-day advance-purchase excursions; the only exclusions are trips on senior coupons, senior discounts, military fares, tour-package fares, and such. Each traveling adult may purchase up to two half-price infant tickets. Seats for infants are limited and may not be available on all flights.

CHILDREN. Some airlines publish children's fares on a few routes, though they're often based on a reduction from full-fare coach or a premium class and are often more expensive than an any-age coach excursion ticket. Otherwise, children age 2 and over are pretty much stuck with buying adult tickets. Of course, they can take advantage of any-age deals—the 10 percent companion discount when accompanying a qualifying senior or the free-companion promotions that airlines often run.

COMPASSIONATE FARES

Air tickets booked at the last minute are normally very expensive. But most big lines offer compassionate (or bereavement)

Special fares **105**

fares. The most common formula is 50 percent off the lowest last-minute fare (usually that means unrestricted coach). That's often quite a bit higher than the lowest restricted round-trip fare. A few lines differ from that policy, and a few treat compassionate fares as individual cases.

Each line has its own rules about the circumstances that qualify. Typically, all lines grant the fare for attendance at a relative's funeral, but only some do so for severe illness or imminent death. Similarly, the lines differ in how distant a family connection can qualify. If the first line you try turns you down, try another.

Compassionate fares are almost always the best last-minute deal you'll find on a big line. But you may find a better unrestricted fare on a low-fare line.

SPECIAL FARES TO EUROPE AND ASIA

Seniors headed for Europe generally enjoy the same 10 percent reduction they get within North America. However, El Al gives 15 percent (to Israel only). Aer Lingus and Air India have no senior fares. The minimum age is 62 on most lines, but it's 60 on Canadian lines, Air New Zealand, British Airways, El Al, LTU, and Lufthansa. The reduction applies to most fares but may not apply to all sale deals; check with each airline for particulars. Transatlantic airlines may also target seniors for special short-term promotions. But we found no senior reductions to Asia (except through United's club).

On most international flights, infants under age 2 without a seat reservation pay 10 percent of the accompanying adult's fare. Typically, children ages 2 to 11 pay 50 to 75 percent of the adult fare (including economy excursion fares). Travelers who want a confirmed seat for an infant must buy a child's ticket.

Some U.S. and European airlines publish separate youth fares to Europe for travelers aged 12 to 24. Typically, travelers can

106 AIRFARE KNOW-HOW

make reservations only within 72 hours of departure; the return portion of a round-trip is left open, with the same 72-hour reservation limit, but with a maximum stay of up to a year. Seats are restricted and may be blacked out on some dates. Those youth fares may be no cheaper than any-age discount (consolidator) tickets—compare before you buy.

Charters generally charge the same fare to travelers of any age. Even though adult fares may be higher, a scheduled line can often beat a charter for family travel with kids or seniors.

For compassionate fares, several overseas lines, including Aer Lingus, Air France, Austrian, British Airways, Finnair, Lufthansa, Swissair, and Virgin Atlantic, waive the advance-purchase restriction on an economy excursion ticket.

CHAPTER 10

FLYING OVERSEAS

Foreign air travel poses two challenges: getting abroad and getting around once you're there. This chapter will help you on both fronts. The directory of numbers at the end of this book tells where to call for bookings and for information on visitor airfares.

TOURING EUROPE BY AIR

Some tourists find that air travel is the only practical choice for their intra-Europe itinerary. To serve that market, several European airlines and airline partnerships offer special visitor fares that are far below what local travelers must pay.

The general formula is the same for all visitor airfares: You buy a specified number of flight coupons at a set price per coupon. In general, prices are significantly lower than unrestricted economy fares. They're not always lower than the lowest economy excursion fares, but they carry far fewer of the restrictions that often make ordinary excursions impractical for North American visitors. They typically include flights on code-sharing partners and commuter lines affiliated with the major, sponsoring lines. This report will give you an overview of what's available.

SOME NUTS AND BOLTS. True, visitor fares have restrictions of their own, but not the sort of advance-purchase and Saturday-night-stay requirements you find for the typical excursion fare. Instead, you must usually buy the visitor ticket before you leave, showing proof of non-European citizenship or residence (some require U.S. residence, others are also available to Canadians). Some fares also require you to buy an international air ticket to the area where the visitor program is to be used (a "conjunction" ticket, in airline lingo). Some conjunction tickets must be on a line sponsoring the visitor airfare; in most cases, free frequent-flier tickets don't qualify.

All the visitor fares we list limit you to one stop in each destination city. You can, however, usually travel through the sponsoring line's hub or hubs more than once, if you're just changing planes there.

As their most serious limitation, most visitor airfares make you use a coupon for each flight or segment. Except as noted, a trip that entails a connecting flight requires two coupons, doubling the cost of the trip and quickly eroding the potential allure of visitor airfares.

Multiline tickets, introduced in the past few years, help a bit. The problem will ease even more in the next few years as European airlines based in one country start to fly within other countries.

ALL-EUROPE TICKETS. North American visitors are likely to find their best bets among the programs that cover most or all of Europe. Several programs even include nearby points in North Africa and the Middle East. Generally, each airline operates a hub-and-spoke system from one or more home-country cities to important domestic destinations and major cities throughout the rest of Europe.

Flying overseas **109**

NATIONAL AND REGIONAL TICKETS. Most people traveling within a single European country or a small multicountry region are probably better off with a rail pass or a rented car. But even for those trips, flying can sometimes be a good bet.

DEALS ON ONE-WAY FLIGHTS ABROAD

Buying tickets from a consolidator overseas makes particular sense when you need a short-haul ticket to close the gap in an open-jaw flight, when you need a local excursion ticket for a side trip, or when you want a one-way, long-haul ticket as part of your own spur-of-the-moment, around-the-world itinerary. You can sometimes save on a one-way ticket back to the U.S., too (though that's generally possible only when the dollar is strong).

When you shop for airfare discounts abroad, deal with a consolidator that has an office in the country where you plan to buy. Especially with regional tickets, agency margins are too small to cover multiple international fax exchanges and extended phone calls.

Long term, you probably come out ahead by doing business with a good local travel agency overseas. You won't have to deal directly with consolidators. Your retail travel agency can get those discount tickets wholesale and resell them to you at about the same price you'd pay the consolidator.

Find out the cheapest ticket you can buy at an airline's list price before you collect quotes from discounters. If the airlines are having one of their periodic price wars and if you can abide the cheap ticket's restrictions, the airline's advertised price may be your best bet.

No matter what a consolidator's price list says, get a specific quote for any individual ticket. Be prepared to buy a full-fare ticket if the deal falls through.

PART THREE

BY CAR OR TRAIN

11 Good deals on car rentals...........111

12 Cars and trains in Europe 127

13 Maps from your computer.........151

C H A P T E R

11

GOOD DEALS ON CAR RENTALS

Attracted by come-on rates for car rentals that include a weekend or a Saturday night? How about offers of free upgrades to larger models? Watch out for the vanishing-deal effect: You may have to coax the promised rate out of a reluctant reservation agent by quoting an advertisement exactly, or even by citing a code number from an ad.

True, there are fine deals to be had—especially in Florida and California, with their cutthroat competition. But wherever you rent, proceed with caution. Here's how to shop:

PROMOTIONS. A few years ago, we checked to see how easy—or hard—it was for ordinary travelers to get in on advertised bargains. At that time, rental companies were trumpeting deals for the coming month or two.

In a series of calls to the companies' toll-free numbers, we asked for the lowest rates for the dates and car models the advertisements featured. But we didn't mention the ads or ask for discounts unless the agents quoted us rates other than the advertised ones.

Only a handful of reservation agents volunteered the best sale prices. It took gentle quizzing, sometimes nudging, to get other agents to offer the advertised rates. Several agents held firmly to whatever rate they quoted first, even when pressed to check further.

We found that the surest way to get an advertised discount was to quote directly from an ad or to mention the promotion's discount code. That code is usually listed in small print beneath the boldly displayed rate or in the description of the terms and conditions of the rental.

WEEKEND RATES. If your schedule permits you to rent a car over a weekend, you can often get a great deal. There's also the "Saturday-night-keep," a low rate that depends on your keeping the car over a Saturday night.

Weekend rates are usually in effect from noon Thursday through noon the following Monday, and they often include unlimited mileage. But you have to shop carefully. Even on a simple weekend rental, you face a crazy patchwork of rates. The lowest rental rate varies substantially in different cities—and even among companies in a given city. Rates are based on a uniform daily rate, usually with a two- or three-day minimum. Others are flat rates pegged to the length of the rental—generally, the longer the rental, the lower the daily rate. Some locations don't offer weekend rates at all.

You must also be careful to avoid extra charges. Extra-driver charges (see page 115) are sometimes high enough to make a big difference in your total rental bill. In some locations, renting a car at an airport and returning it downtown (or vice versa) costs far more than the advertised weekend price. With some companies, missing the return deadline makes the entire weekend rental revert to the much more expensive weekday rate.

If there's a chance you'll keep a car beyond the usual weekend period, ask about extra-day pricing when you make the reservation, and try to rent from a company that doesn't cancel the

Good deals on car rentals **113**

weekend rate if you miss the return deadline. If you can't find such a deal, you can return the car by the deadline and rerent for the extra day or two at weekday rental rates.

RENT OFF-AIRPORT? Don't automatically decide to pick up a rental car when you arrive at a big airport. We have often found that a company's rental rates in downtown locations are lower than its airport rates.

These days, airport rentals usually don't offer much extra convenience anyway. Most on-airport rental companies now have only a counter inside the terminal. To get to your car, you have to climb into a bus or van and ride to some outlying area.

That being so, consider renting at an airport-area hotel—just take the courtesy van from the baggage claim. (You may have to call for one.) If you arrive late at night, you can book into the hotel and won't need to get your car until the following morning, possibly saving a day's rental—and you won't have to cope with a strange car in a strange city after a long plane trip.

Renting from the hotel may be easier, too. One or more of the larger car-rental companies may well have a desk at your hotel. If not, the rental companies will usually send a van or car to the hotel to pick you up.

SWITCH AIRPORTS? Also, check rental possibilities at alternative airports, where you may find lower rates. Even if rates are the same, a smaller airport—Midway instead of O'Hare, Burbank or Long Beach instead of Los Angeles International, Long Island/MacArthur or Newburgh/Stewart Field instead of New York/ JFK, Oakland instead of San Francisco—saves you big-airport hassle.

SENIOR DISCOUNTS. Some car-rental companies also extend discounts to seniors,

---

CREDIT CARD REQUIRED

You must have a credit card to rent a car easily. Even if a debit card carries the MasterCard or Visa logo, it won't do for a rental because the rental company can't place a hold on a debit card. You can, however, switch to a debit card for payment when you return the vehicle.

CAR OR TRAIN

sometimes tied in to membership in a senior organization such as the American Association of Retired Persons (AARP). However, seniors will generally do better by shopping short-term promotions—rental company discounts are usually only 5 to 10 percent off.

MONTHLY CAR RENTALS. For an extended trip, you're likely to find it cheaper to rent a car by the month, rather than for multiple weeks at a weekly rate—as long as you ferret out one of the good deals. However, a long-term rental requires you to shop around carefully for your specific itinerary—the exact model of car you want, where you plan to drive, and whether you can temporarily return the car and renew your contract after each month.

Check first with local, nonchain car-rental companies in the city where you plan to initiate the rental. Get a copy of that city's Yellow Pages for your search. Make sure to contact some of the renters who are also car dealers—they often have the best rates. Always ask about both monthly and weekly rates—in some cases, weekly rates are significantly lower. On any monthly quote, ask if it covers 28 days or 30 days.

CHECKLIST BEFORE YOU RENT

An ill-maintained rental car raises questions of both hazard and financial exposure. When you sign a rental agreement, you may be agreeing that the car is in good condition. If you spot a defect later, that agreement may limit your recourse. Here's a checklist:

• Check the tires (including the spare) for bulges, cuts, and excessive tread wear. Be sure there's a jack.

• Have obvious body or mechanical damage noted on the contract, so you won't be charged for it later.

• Test the windshield wipers, seat belts, seat adjustments, and all lights, including brake lights.

• Make sure there's an owner's manual. If not, have the agent demonstrate the use of important controls and convenience features (show you how to set the clock and the radio's push buttons, say).

Good deals on car rentals   **115**

HIDDEN EXTRAS

Many car-rental companies won't let you drive away from the lot at low, advertised rates without a struggle. A combination of enticements, threats, and fine print can more than double your rental bill. Here are the main ploys:

ADDITIONAL DRIVERS. Rental companies may add $3 to $15 a day or a flat $20 to $25 a rental for each additional driver in your travel party. Most let your spouse drive at no extra cost, but some may not.

Some companies won't rent to drivers younger than age 21; others require renters to be at least 25 years old. Those with the younger cutoff usually assess an additional charge for drivers aged 21 to 24.

Don't try to save money by not listing additional drivers. If you have an accident, the company could claim you violated your contract and can thus withhold any insurance or service benefits. If you're planning to share driving chores, shop around for a company that has a competitive rate without an extra-driver gouge.

UPGRADE HARD SELLS. Those low advertised rates are usually for a subcompact car. But when you reach the desk, you may be pressured to upgrade to a more powerful vehicle. Many agents try to convince customers that local driving conditions make the subcompact inadequate. That switch—if you fall for it—can balloon your bill. Decide exactly what kind of car you want before you reserve.

COLLISION INSURANCE. Some travelers still find it difficult to rent a car without being gouged for collision-damage waiver or loss-damage waiver (CDW/LDW). That's the quasi-insurance that yields car-rental companies fat daily fees ($7 to $15 a day) for waiving their right to hold you liable if your rental car is damaged or stolen.

Most renters can cover their risk of damage or loss without CDW/LDW. Those risks are often covered by your regular auto policy for driving within the U.S. But a few big auto insurers have backed away from providing complete coverage automatically for rental cars as part of the coverage for your own car. Your own situation depends on your insurance company, the date on which your policy next comes up for renewal, and where you live—some state regulations will require continued coverage. If you rely on your personal insurance for business travel, be sure to check your policy. Have your agent clarify any uncertainties.

CHARGE-CARD INSURANCE. Charge cards and the Gold version of credit cards typically provide CDW/LDW coverage. However, most—though not all—cards offer only secondary coverage, which means you must submit a claim to your own insurance carrier first. In addition, there are many variations and exclusions to be aware of:

• Coverage may vary by rental locations, with different regulations applying to foreign or domestic rentals, and even some state-to-state differences.

• Issuing banks may make their own amendments to standard MasterCard or Visa coverage.

• The length of the rental time also has a bearing on coverage, with some cards offering 30 consecutive days of coverage, others covering only 15 days. If your card allows a 15-day rental only, and you rent on a monthly basis, you may not be covered at all.

• There may also be caps on damage payments.

• A vehicle differing from a standard passenger car—expensive sedans, such as a Mercedes; sports cars; and most vans—may not be covered. Almost universally excluded are trucks, campers, recreational vehicles, sport-utility vehicles, and antique cars.

The variations could make a significant difference to some drivers. If you plan to use your charge-card coverage when you rent, talk to a customer-service representative at your card's toll-free line

Good deals on car rentals **117**

about specifics. If you don't have an up-to-date copy of your card's insurance agreement, ask for one to be mailed or faxed to you.

All cards exclude coverage in some circumstances. Most notable are driving in violation of the rental contract—which means driving off-road, driving outside the permitted rental area (where such a limitation is imposed), use of the vehicle by an unauthorized driver, involvement in illegal activity, and driving while intoxicated. Whenever you rely on charge-card coverage, observe the contract's terms scrupulously.

SALES PRESSURE. Some car-rental agents still use scare tactics, which may include cautioning clients that charge-card coverage is risky or that the car-rental company doesn't have an arrangement with a given charge-card issuer. That's irrelevant—the card-issuer's deal is with *you*.

Alternatively, an agent may tell customers that, without CDW, they won't be allowed to leave the state if they have an accident until the claim is settled. But there's no way a car-rental company can restrict your freedom of movement because you (or your insurance company) owe money for repairs.

Some rental companies would like to keep CDW/LDW alive because it's immensely profitable. It also lets them headline low-ball prices and still profit from the big markup on the insurance. Industry sources estimate the real cost of CDW/LDW at about $2 per day, so a $7 to $15 retail price provides a lot of gravy. Articles in the trade press indicate that individual rental offices and employees are rated, in part, on their success in selling CDW/LDW.

Even if you buy CDW/LDW, the fine print may exclude certain kinds of damage (such as broken or cracked glass) or contain so many loopholes that the car-rental company can charge you for almost any damage.

Damage discovered after a car is returned remains the liability of the renter (who may by then have left the area). However, typical rental contracts have no provision for an agent to inspect and sign off for damages. You're within your rights to insist on a sign-off (but expect an argument).

CDW/LDW ABROAD. You may find it especially tough to avoid CDW/LDW when you rent from a local agency overseas. Many foreign rental companies apparently continue to rely on CDW/LDW for profits, threatening to put a big hold on your card to cover possible damage if you don't. (If you carry more than one card, your countermove is to charge your rental on one card and put day-to-day expenses on the other.)

Your best defense is to prearrange the rental through a U.S. office or agency. Specify when you rent that you intend to use your charge card for collision protection and won't buy CDW/LDW. If you rent abroad, use a major multinational company, which should be accustomed to dealing with Americans who rely on their cards. And if you somehow find yourself about to be denied a car unless you buy CDW/LDW, accept it, note on the contract that you accepted under duress, and demand a full refund as soon as you return home.

LIABILITY COVERAGE. Liability insurance covers damage someone in a rented car might do to other persons or property. Buying CDW/LDW from the rental company does not provide liability coverage, nor do major charge cards provide it as a free extra.

Until fairly recently, car-rental companies normally included enough primary liability coverage in their basic rate to satisfy the legal minimum in the state where a car was rented. With primary coverage, an injured party's first claim is against the rental company's insurance; a renter's personal insurance picks up any excess owed. But in a number of states, large rental companies have switched to secondary coverage, shifting the bulk of accident costs to the driver's own insurance policy. In California, many companies have canceled liability coverage entirely.

If you own a car, you probably carry liability insurance that

Good deals on car rentals **119**

would cover you while driving a rented car. Should there be a claim that exceeds your own coverage, the car-rental company's policy would make up the difference, up to its limit. The switch simply increases the chances of a hit on your own insurance, which would probably increase your rates.

If you don't own a car and therefore don't have automobile insurance, the rental company's secondary insurance becomes de facto primary. (In California, you could be uninsured.) The liability insurance that satisfies most states' requirements is probably enough to cover repair of someone else's car or to fix minor damage to a building. But it's apt to be woefully inadequate to protect your personal assets against a big personal-injury claim. You'd be wise to buy extra liability insurance, no matter where you rent.

Those who frequently rent cars but don't own one (or those who drive cars borrowed from others) should consider a year-round nonowner policy—several auto insurers sell them. If you rent infrequently, you can buy $1 million in additional liability coverage from most car-rental companies for about $7 to $8 a day.

PITFALLS AND POTHOLES

Here are some not-so-obvious problems that may crop up when you rent a car:

Documentation. If you're renting a car at an airport but aren't arriving or departing on a flight, check to make sure that a quoted rate doesn't require you to show a ticket.

Geographic limits. Some companies that specialize in cheap car rentals impose limits on where you can drive. For example, if you rent a car in California, the rental company may prohibit you from driving it into any other state (except for short side trips to Las Vegas or Reno). If you're heading for Arizona or Oregon, you may have to use a more expensive rental—possibly from another company.

Don't assume that the rental company will never know whether you drive out of the permitted areas—if you run into trouble, you've violated the contract. When you're arranging your rental, let the agent know where you plan to drive, and make sure the quoted rate covers your itinerary.

Redlining. Another complication is redlining—marking out certain areas where residents who rent cars locally must pay higher rates or pass extra screening. Ask about surcharges when you reserve.

Mileage limits. Currently, the industry has adopted unlimited mileage as a standard for noncorporate rentals. However, unlimited mileage is not always your best deal. If you're using a rented car mainly for local errands in your destination area, a low daily or weekly rate with 100 or 150 free miles a day may be better than a competitor's unlimited-mileage rate. You have to estimate how far you're going to drive on each rental and compare alternatives.

Fuel charges. A number of companies rent their cars with a "full" tank, requiring it to be returned the same way or demanding a premium price if the rental company fills the tank. But sometimes the tank isn't full, though the checkout slip says it is. Always check before you drive off.

You may also take a hit when returning the car. On many fuel gauges, the needle points to F well before the tank is actually full. If, before returning a car, you fill up to the point at which a gas pump shuts off automatically, you make a gift of about a dollar's worth of gas to the rental company. Try filling up just to the F.

One-way drop-off. With a rental car, "rent it here, leave it there" refers to pickup and return in different cities and may be limited to certain models, seasons, and dates. Some companies allow you to pick up a car from one office and drop it off at another within the same metropolitan area at no extra charge. Many travelers use that provision to rent a car downtown and

Good deals on car rentals **121**

drop it off at the airport. However, for most companies, local one-way drop-off policies vary by location; be sure to check before you reserve.

Franchised locations are often especially reluctant to feature attractive one-way rates. (Second-tier companies have a greater proportion of franchised locations than the Big Four—Avis, Budget, Hertz, and National.) You may find a low one-way rate at one of those locations if you're traveling between two cities with a pattern of heavy one-way rentals (or if the franchisee operates in both cities). But if the company has to send an employee to drive the car back to its original location, you're looking at a hefty drop-off charge.

Locating the least-expensive one-way rental requires well-organized comparison shopping, even more than with ordinary rentals. Decide on the cities in which you plan to rent and return the car, who in the travel party will be driving, and what size car you want. Then get quotes from several rental companies, including extra-driver or underage-driver charges if applicable, and whatever discounts you may qualify for. If you plan to drive for four or five days, get quotes for that period as well as for a full week. The weekly rate may well be better, even if you don't plan on driving for a day or two.

Record checks. A number of rental companies in certain states check driving records before they'll rent you a car. If you plan to rent a car, be sure you know what's in your driving record.

Do you have a clean record? Forget about the screening—at worst, it will extend the rental transaction by a few seconds. Rent from the company with the best deal. Ditto even if you have a questionable record, or if you live in a state that doesn't disclose driving records.

If you have a problem record and live in a state that permits screening, rent from a company that doesn't check records. Ask about it when you call for a reservation.

122 BY CAR OR TRAIN

If you don't know the status of your record, check with your local motor-vehicle department.

Anyone wishing to see exactly what the car-rental companies' computers will pull up can contact TML Information Services, one of the companies that operate the online data services for a driving-record copy. TML charges consumers $9.95 ($7.95 for American Automobile Association members); call 800 388-9099. The company will screen your driving records against the criteria used by the rental companies to bar risky drivers and fax or mail you the resulting report. The service is not available to California or Pennsylvania drivers.

DRIVING IN CANADA

Driving up north is almost like driving from your home to a nearby U.S. state:

DOCUMENTS. To drive, you need only a valid U.S. driver's license, proof of liability insurance, and the vehicle's registration. But to return to the U.S., you must show proof of U.S. citizenship or legal residence. Your driver's license won't do—you need a passport, a green card, or a certified copy of your birth certificate.

LIABILITY INSURANCE. To drive in any Canadian province, whether in your own car or a rental, you must carry coverage against damage you might do to someone else's property or person. The legal minimum is C$200,000 (U.S.$145,000) everywhere but Quebec, where it's C$50,000 (U.S.$37,000). If you're involved in an accident, you'll have to show proof of insurance.

Liability coverage for driving in Canada is probably included in your regular automobile insurance, whether you're in your own car or a rental. But before you leave, check with your insurance representative—if you aren't covered, you'll have to buy a separate add-on policy. If you are covered, ask your company to send you a Canadian Non-Resident Inter-Province Motor Vehicle

Good deals on car rentals **123**

Liability Insurance Card. It certifies that you carry the statutory minimum liability coverage while driving in Canada.

Dollar requires renters who plan to visit Canada to buy supplementary liability insurance, whether or not they need it.

DRIVING A BORROWED CAR. If you drive a car registered to someone who isn't in your travel party, you'll need a letter from the owner granting you permission to take the car into Canada.

DRIVING A U.S. RENTAL CAR. The rental contract serves as the rental-car company's official permission to drive a car into Canada. But many local rental offices establish additional limits of their own. Several Seattle car-rental offices limited Canadian driving just to British Columbia or parts of B.C., we found when we checked for an early-1998 report. And some U.S. renters imposed mileage caps on Canadian driving.

Of course, rental companies have no way to enforce such geographical limits—provided nothing goes wrong. But the limits are part of the rental contract: If you have an accident or a mechanical problem outside the allowable driving area, you'll be liable for towing and repair charges.

We came across an additional, odd restriction. Canadian law prohibits Canadian citizens from renting cars in the U.S. and then driving them into Canada.

RENTING IN CANADA. As with any foreign rental, you'll need a driver's license, a charge card, and an insurance card. The rental company is supposed to give you a card that discloses the liability coverage it provides. But that coverage may be below Canadian requirements, so it's a good idea to get a Non-Resident Inter-Provincial Card from your own insurance company, as well.

Collision insurance, covering damage to the car you're driving, isn't legally required. But unless you drive a junker, it's a good idea. Your own policy's collision coverage probably applies in Canada, but, as with liability, be sure to check before you leave.

Charge-card collision coverage works in Canada in the same

way it does in the U.S. If your own auto insurance includes Canada, the charge card provides additional, secondary coverage. (It will pick up any liability not covered by your car insurance, up to a stated limit.) If your U.S. insurance excludes Canada, your card's coverage becomes primary.

DRIVING IN MEXICO

If you like bureaucracy, you'll love driving into Mexico.

DOCUMENTS. Crossing the border in either direction requires proof of U.S. citizenship or residence. To drive, you need a valid U.S. driver's license and a Spanish translation of it (get an International Driving Permit or an Inter-American Driving Permit, both available through AAA offices).

If you travel beyond the immediate border areas (Tijuana, Tecate, Mexicali, or Baja California) or if you stay in Mexico more than 72 hours, you'll also need a Mexican Tourist Card (*tarjeta de turista,* free at Mexican consulates and tourist offices, border offices, and auto-club offices). The Tourist Card is valid for stays of up to 180 days and must be used within 90 days of its issuance. Visitors must carry it at all times while in Mexico or risk incurring a fine.

INSURANCE. All the auto-insurance companies we contacted told us that their U.S. insurance doesn't cover liability in Mexico. Whether you drive your own car or a rental, you'll probably need to buy separate Mexican liability insurance, widely available from independent agencies in border-crossing areas, through a border-area AAA office, or, if you rent, through a rental agency. Some liability coverage (varying by location and company) is included in Mexican rentals. If the amount isn't close to what you carry in the U.S., buy extra.

Your U.S. insurance probably won't cover you for collision, either. If you don't want to buy the collision-damage waiver

Good deals on car rentals **125**

from the rental company, you can use charge-card coverage if your card provides it. If your own insurance excludes Mexico (as it most likely does), the charge card's coverage will be primary.

DRIVING A PRIVATE CAR. You needn't go through any special formalities if you confine your driving to a "free zone" (typically within 15 miles of the border, but including most of Baja California). Just arrange your insurance and go.

However, you need a Temporary Car Importation Permit to drive your car beyond the free zone. To get one, you must present both the original and a copy of your vehicle's title certificate and registration at a border station, about 12 to 16 miles below the border. If you're in a car registered in the name of someone else (another individual, a bank or credit union, a corporation, or a leasing company), you must also have a notarized letter or affidavit from the legal owner authorizing you to drive the car into Mexico.

The permit fee (about $11) is payable only by a credit card issued in your name by a bank outside Mexico; cash or traveler's checks won't do. (That hassle is meant to ensure that you won't sell the car in Mexico.) A hologram is then applied to the inside of the vehicle's windshield and must be removed by Mexican border officials when you return to the U.S.

DRIVING A U.S. RENTAL CAR. Company policies vary. Some rental offices near the border may prohibit any driving in Mexico; others may limit how far below the border you can go or cap the distance you can drive in Mexico before you start paying per-mile charges.

Mexico puts you through the same car-permit rigmarole with a rental car as with your own car. However, the rental company provides the necessary proof of ownership. Be sure to let the rental agent know you intend to drive into Mexico.

RENTING IN MEXICO. Renting a car from a Mexican rental office avoids the border-crossing paperwork. All you need is a

BY CAR OR TRAIN

driver's license, a charge card, and Mexican insurance sold by the rental company. But be aware that Mexican rental costs can be a lot stiffer than they are in the U.S. Despite the red tape, you're much better off with a U.S. rental as long as the geographical restrictions don't interfere with your plans.

If you run into a problem while driving through Mexico, you can get directions, emergency referrals, information, and other assistance through a 24-hour hot line: 91-800-90392 (250-0151 in Mexico City).

C H A P T E R 12

CARS AND TRAINS IN EUROPE

Travelers who want to tour Europe have three main transportation options. Flying is usually expensive, though it may be the only way to cover large distances in a short time. For most tourists, the real choice is between road and rail.

Trains are faster than driving for long-haul touring, and you needn't worry about traffic or parking. However, you're the slave of their schedules and routes. Driving affords high flexibility and, if you enjoy the smaller towns and the countryside, you can escape big-city hotel gouges. On the other hand, not everyone is eager to cope with unfamiliar roads and traffic rules. Many travelers use relative cost as a tie-breaker.

COMPARING THE COSTS

In 1998, *Consumer Reports Travel Letter* compared the per-person costs of touring Europe by train and by car on a one-week trip covering 1,000 miles and a two-week jaunt of 3,000 miles.

Driving costs include rental charges, taxes, and fuel. The table "Car vs. Train" below gives the details, but here are some highlights:

• We priced first for two adults. On a short trip, a rented car beat the train substantially in the primary EuroPass area (France, Germany, Italy, Spain, and Switzerland, where the only available rail passes were in first class) and in Germany and the U.K. (where even second-class rail is relatively expensive). The train beat the car by a wide margin in Italy, where rail fares were low and car-rental rates high. Car and train were a virtual tie in France. The same general relationships were true for a long trip, except that car and train costs were closer in Germany.

• We next compared costs for four adults. On a short trip, a

TRAVEL IN EUROPE CAR VS. TRAIN

COSTS PER PERSON FOR SHORT TRIP (1 WEEK/1,000 MILES)

	By car		By train	
	2 persons	4 persons	Travel 4 days or less	Travel 7 days
EuroPass area	$117	$86	$230	$230
France	152	104	162	170
Germany	117	86	141	228
Italy	191	166	110	110
UK	114	81	219	240

COSTS PER PERSON FOR LONG TRIP (2 WEEKS/3,000 MILES)

	By car		By train	
	2 persons	4 persons	Travel 8 days or less	Travel 14 days
EuroPass area	$302	$223	$362	$563
France	372	258	282	504
Germany	302	223	228	308
Italy	451	382	195	221
UK	279	199	315	395

Driving costs includes rental charges, taxes, and operating expenses. In most cases, rail costs are based on using a flexible rail pass (a pass that allows travel on a limited number of days during its validity period) that meets the trip requirement: First Class EuroPass for EuroPass areas (France, Germany, Italy, Spain, Switzerland); Second Class national pass in individual countries; and companion passes in the EuroPass area and Germany.

shared midsized car beat the train everywhere except in Italy, where the train retained a big advantage, and for itineraries in France and Germany that permitted use of a flexible rail pass (travel x days during the pass's validity period), where car and train costs were about a dead heat.

• Though we didn't include the calculations in our table, a solo traveler would have been better off traveling by train than renting a subcompact car in all cases except on the short trips in the EuroPass area and the U.K., where car and train costs were about even.

Note, however, that both driving and train travel carry some hidden extras:

• Overnight parking is seldom included in European city hotel rates; it can add $10 to $20 a day to your costs. Highway tolls can add $5 to $15 a day to the cost of driving in Austria, France, Greece, Italy, Portugal, and Spain.

• Rail passes usually don't cover seat-reservation charges on express trains—a necessity on many top trains. If you buy individual tickets, the express supplements and other fees can add a good bit to your cost. Since rail passes seldom include local transit, you have to pay extra for station-to-hotel transport—as much as $20 per each arrival or departure if you take a taxi.

You don't have to choose between an all-rail or all-driving trip. Many rail passes offer options that include several days' use of a rental car in addition to the train travel.

WHICH COMPANIES RENT OVERSEAS?

There's no shortage of companies that rent cars abroad. You'll see many of the familiar logos of multinational rental companies or their European affiliates at Europe's gateway airports—Alamo, Avis, Budget, Hertz, National, Payless, and Thrifty are all represented. In fact, National (U.S.) has severed its Europcar affiliation, acquired Eurodollar, and put the National Car Rental sign up on all its European agencies. Meanwhile, Dollar (U.S.) picked up Europcar, National's former European affiliate; it retains the Europcar name. Three European-based renters—Kenning, Town & Country, and Woods—have U.S. representatives.

You can also rent a car from several U.S.-based wholesale tour operators—Auto Europe, AutoNet, DER Car, Europe by Car, European Car Reservations (ECR), International Travel Services (ITS), and Kemwel Holiday Autos. Those companies arrange rentals through various Europe-based renters, multinational as well as local.

Typically, tour operators require full payment up front and multinationals have you pay when you return the car. But some multinationals offer you a choice between prepayment at a rate guaranteed in U.S. dollars and payment in local currency when the car is returned. (Unless the prepaid price is significantly lower, we recommend the pay-at-return option. There's less hassle if your plans change.) Payment in soft-currency countries may be specified in U.S. dollars or German marks.

Minus a price advantage, those differences aren't important to most travelers. However, you might lean toward a multinational if you have a discount or upgrade deal with one of them or if you want to earn extra frequent-flier miles.

RIGHT-SIZING A RENTAL. It's false economy to rent a car that's too small to be comfortable for extended driving. It's also a mistake to try to save by selecting a stick-shift model if you're used to an automatic.

Rental companies charge according to a car's letter code, but with no great consistency. In a given country, one company's B-class car may be another's C. In fact, a single company may class the same model as A in one country and B in another. For that reason, the rental-rate tables in this report group cars by car model. You should shop the same way: Ask for cars by model, not letter code.

Cars and trains in Europe **131**

The table "Car-rental rates abroad," on pages 141–149, gives prices for specific groups of comparable models, no matter how rental companies classify them:

Standard subcompacts are the smallest cars we recommend for two touring adults. Typically, those cars are two- or three-door models, okay for two adults and their baggage but with rear-seat room for only one or two infants or very small children. Specific models include Alfa Romeo 145/146, Citroën Saxo/Xsara, Fiat Brava/ Bravo/Punto/Uno, Ford Fiesta, Hyundai Accent/Elantra, Lancia Delta, Mazda 323/Lantis, Mitsubishi L Sedan/Lancer, Nissan Micra/ Sunny, Opel (Vauxhall in the U.K.) Astra/Corsa, Peugeot 306, Renault 5/Clio/Megane, Seat Cordoba/ Ibiza/Marbella, Skoda Favorit/Felicia, Subaru Justy, Suzuki Swift, Toyota Corolla/Starlet, and VW Golf/Polo.

Standard midsized cars are the smallest we recommend for parties of three or four adults or grownups with large children. They're usually four-door sedans, two classifications up from standard subcompacts, with adequate rear seat room for two adults. Specific models include Alfa 155/156, Alfa Romeo 164, Audi A4, Citroën Xantia, Fiat Croma/Marea/Regatta/Tempra, Ford Mondeo/ Sierra/Tempo, Hyundai Sonata, Lancia Dedra/ Thema, Mazda 626/636, Mitsubishi Galant, Nissan Bluebird/ Primera, Opel (or Vauxhall) Cavalier/Omega/Vectra, Peugeot 405/406/505/ 506, Renault Laguna/Safrane, Rover 414/620, Seat Toledo, Toyota Camry/Carina, VW Jetta/Passat/Vento, and Volvo 440/S40.

Rental companies (and tour packagers that also offer rental cars) often push four-door models of some of the roomier subcompacts (Citroën Xsara, Renault Megane) or cars that bridge the gap between subcompact and midsized (Ford Escort) as adequate for four travelers. But we think those cars are too tight for rear-seat passengers.

CHEAPEST RENTAL. As a come-on, some rental companies feature cramped, severely underpowered subsubcompacts at lowball prices. While those models may do for tooling around town, we think they aren't suitable for the open highway. Models here include Fiat Cinquecento/Panda, Ford Ka, and Renault Twingo. If the table notes a cost for the cheapest rental that's less than the entry for a standard subcompact, the cheapest rental is an undersized subsubcompact.

CHEAPEST AUTOMATIC. Now fairly common in many European countries, automatics are no longer the extravagance they once were. The table lists the cheapest automatic available, no matter what size the car is. Often, it's just one category up from the standard subcompact group—fine for two, but skimpy for four. But in some countries, you find automatics only on large, luxury cars. That's why the table's entries for automatic-shift models vary so broadly.

OTHER MODELS. Air conditioning has become more popular— and less expensive—in the last few years, expecially in the warmer countries. If it's important to you, check when you reserve your car. Minivans and van campers have also become popular in Europe, but rental rates are also high—especially in the summer.

FINDING THE BEST DEAL

No single company was consistently either the cheapest or the most expensive from country to country—or even for all models within the same country. Our table will help you comparison-shop.

WEEKLY TOURING RATES. Our table gives weekly touring rates —usually the best deals you can find—for cars booked in the U.S. for summer driving in Europe. (Rates for longer rentals are usually prorated at one-seventh the weekly rate per day.) Typically, you must keep your car five days to qualify for the weekly rate. If you return the car early, the company may recalculate your bill at the local daily rate—often resulting in a much higher total. The rate quotes are for summer 1998; '99 quotes,

Cars and trains in Europe **133**

not available at this writing, should be comparable.

Basic rates are usually uniform throughout each country. However, you can expect to pay a surcharge at many large airports (see "Airport bites" and "Highway charges," page 135). And rates in Greece and Spain may vary at island locations. We list the rate for rentals that began at each country's major gateway city, excluding airport surcharges.

All listed rates provided unlimited mileage. In a few countries (see table), rates are higher in July and August than in other summer months. In any event, rates are always subject to change. And some companies' rates are more volatile than others—check before you rent.

Can't set your itinerary in advance? If you don't decide to rent until after you're in Europe, a local office will probably quote you a much higher rate than the one we tabulate—maybe with a mileage cap, too. Unless you're renting for just a day or two, don't pay a high local rate. You can probably get the weekly touring rate by calling a multinational rental company's North American reservation office or your travel agent at home.

Alternatively, Kemwel will sell you a *CarPass* good for three consecutive rental days in any of seven countries. You must return the car in the same country, but not necessarily in the same city, in which you rent it. Rates are higher per day than weekly rates, but lower than you'd pay on the spot.

ONE-WAY RENTALS. Most companies don't charge extra for a rent-it-here, leave-it-there rental within a single country. If you want to rent in one country and return in another, check first with the multinationals—some provide one-way rentals between a few adjoining countries at no extra cost. (You pay the originating country's rate and tax.)

CHANGE GATEWAY? Most tourists pick up their rental car in their country of arrival. In a few cases, you might want to choose your gateway country for its low car-rental rates:

134 BY CAR OR TRAIN

• If you're planning a multicountry trip, note that Belgium and Germany were offering the lowest rental rates. Also, airfares to these destinations from the U.S. and Canada were generally at least as good as to neighboring countries. Other low-rate countries were The Netherlands, Portugal, Spain, and Switzerland.

• For a long-term rental, the availability of French leases makes Paris an inviting gateway.

• A reader touring Finland recently recommended renting in Sweden and taking a low-cost ferry to Finland as a way to avoid Finland's sky-high rates.

EXTRAS AND LIMITATIONS

European rentals entail some add-ons and restrictions. Some you can't avoid—but a few you can.

VAT. European auto rentals are subject to a value-added tax (VAT) that can boost your rental cost by as much as 25 percent. To put the different companies and countries on the same footing, we added VAT to any rates that didn't include it. Brochure rates usually exclude tax. (The table also shows VAT rates for each country.)

Services such as car rentals are "consumed" locally, so in most European countries vacation travelers can't claim the VAT refunds that are available on goods bought locally but "exported" outside Europe. While most rental companies list identical VAT rates, a few tour operators apparently get a partial VAT refund —which they pass along to customers—because they're "exporting" car rentals to travelers who live in North America. Listed rates reflect the refund.

INSURANCE. European rental companies try just as hard as their U.S. counterparts to push collision- or loss-damage waiver (CDW/LDW). Costs are even higher—CDW/LDW can run up to $54 a day for some cars.

Cars and trains in Europe   135

Savvy tourists generally rely on their charge cards to cover collision damage to or theft of a car rented in Europe (see Chapter 11). However, you can't always avoid the insurance gouge:

• Theft insurance is mandatory on all car rentals in Italy and Slovenia, adding as much as $20 a day to the cost. Some companies include that charge in their published rates. Since it's mandatory, we added the theft-insurance cost to any rate that didn't include it.

• The American Express card no longer provides collision coverage in Ireland, Italy, or Israel.

A few companies include CDW/LDW in their published rates in some locations. Since many travelers don't buy it, we didn't add the cost to the rates of companies that don't build it in. However, if your charge card doesn't cover collision damage, you'll have to buy the insurance.

Other insurance sold by car-rental companies—accident, personal effects, and such—is just as overpriced in Europe as it is here.

AIRPORT BITES. Quite a few European airports impose fees that the rental companies pass along to renters. Most are trivial—in total, they add up to less than the cost of a taxi from the airport to a downtown rental office. But in Austria, Belgium, Italy, Luxembourg, Switzerland, and the U.K., renting from an airport location can add as much as 10 to 14 percent to the total cost of your rental—enough to make you consider dealing with an off-airport office. (The fees don't apply to cars that you simply return at an airport.)

GO FIRST CLASS?

First-class rail travel makes sense for some leisure travelers. Its extra room and comfort are particularly welcome on long trips. So is its freedom from the bustle of summertime second class, jam-packed with vacationing Europeans. The 34 to 54 percent premium you pay for first-class rail is far less than the premium for first-class airfare, often more than 10 times the price of an economy ticket.

CAR OR TRAIN

HIGHWAY CHARGES. Any car driven in Austria or Switzerland must have a sticker indicating payment of that country's highway fee. Local rental cars normally have that sticker. But if you rent in an adjacent country, you (not the rental company) must buy the sticker or pay a stiff fine. Rental cars in such border-area cities as Milan and Munich often have a sticker already—ask for one if you plan to drive in Austria or Switzerland.

GEOGRAPHIC LIMITS. At some locations, car-rental companies limit your driving destinations. The most common ban is on driving cars rented in the West into Eastern Europe, with some exceptions (cars rented in Austria and Germany can often be driven into the Czech Republic, Hungary, and Slovakia). There are far too many specific cases to list here. Whenever you reserve a rental car, ask the reservationist if your entire itinerary is acceptable. If not, check other rental companies.

AGE RESTRICTIONS. Minimum and (occasionally) maximum age limits vary by company and country. If your party includes an under-25 or over-70 driver, be sure to check minimum or maximum age limits on rentals when you reserve.

GETTING ON THE ROAD

The companies we list in the back of the book rent directly or through any travel agency; you'll pay the same either way. The multinational rental companies maintain rental counters at most European gateway airports; follow the signs in the arrivals area. Check a local phone book for addresses of city offices. If you rent from a tour operator, you get a voucher that lists the name and location of the company that actually provides the car.

At the rental counter, you'll need a reservation confirmation or voucher, a valid U.S. driver's license, a charge card, and your passport. We've found that European car-rental agents speak

Cars and trains in Europe **137**

enough English to handle the transaction. An International Driving Permit (obtained through local American Automobile Association offices) isn't legally required, but we recommend one for Austria, Germany, Italy, Spain, Eastern Europe, and the Middle East.

WHEN TRAINS MAKE SENSE

Though a rented car is a good choice for touring, trains are better if you travel alone, stay mainly in big-city centers, or plan to rack up a lot of intercity mileage. A travel-all-you-want rail pass is usually your best bet. However, separate tickets may be cheaper —especially if you qualify for a senior discount—if most of your trips will be short.

Rail travel's good points go beyond economics. New tracks permit very-high-speed (186 mph) service from Paris through to Brussels. And new tilt trains allow somewhat lower (but still high) speeds on conventional roadbeds. Today's trains can take you just about anywhere on the continent. On the main routes, they run often, and they're convenient and comfortable. They also spare you the need to cope with parking, traffic, and foreign road signs.

WHAT'S OUT THERE?

Rail passes come in several versions:

Full-time passes let you travel as much as you want on every day in their validity period—on each of 15 or 21 days, say, or even daily for a month or two. They're your least restrictive option, and are especially good for extensive city-hopping with only short stopovers. However, full-time passes are expensive.

Flexible passes provide unlimited train travel, but only on some days during their validity period—say, on any 10 days dur-

138 BY CAR OR TRAIN

ing two months. (The travel days needn't be consecutive.) For any given validity period, flexible passes are cheaper than full-time ones; they're a better bet if you plan to stay in each destination for several days.

Rail/car and (in Greece) rail/air passes combine rail and rental-car or air-travel days, a fixed number of each. These let you combine the speed and comfort of a train for long hauls with the flexibility of a rented car (or air travel to outlying islands) for local touring. Rail/car passes are a lot cheaper than renting a car, one day at a time, in several locations. If you plan extensive driving, however, you're better off with a weekly rental.

Companion passes give a price break to parties of two; group passes, to parties of two to five. Holders of those passes must travel together at all times.

Senior and youth passes give discounts to special age groups.

Most passes cover at least some supplemental fees, such as surcharges for express trains and some very-high-speed ones. But you almost always have to pay extra for seat reservations and berths on sleepers and overnight ferries.

THE AREAS THEY COVER

MULTINATIONAL PASSES. These permit travel in several countries:

• Eurailpass covers the most territory: all of Western Europe except the U.K., plus Hungary, for a total of 17 countries. It also entitles you to free or discounted travel on suburban trains (but not city-transit systems) that are operated by national railways, on some private railways, on most long-distance buses, and on some ferries and excursion boats. The newer Europass covers less territory, but at lower prices: It's good in France, Germany, Italy, Spain, and Switzerland. (Austria, Belgium, Greece, Hungary, Luxembourg, The Netherlands, and Portugal are extra-cost options.)

Cars and trains in Europe **139**

Adults can buy Eurailpass and Europass only in first-class versions; second class is limited to young travelers.

• The Benelux (Belgium, The Netherlands, Luxembourg) and Scanrail (Denmark, Finland, Norway, Sweden) passes are considerably cheaper than Eurailpass for travel within their limited areas. Moreover, adults can buy them in second-class as well as first-class versions, for a saving of 20 to 40 percent. But see the sidebar "Go First Class?" on page 139 before you make up your mind.

• You have two options in Eastern Europe. European East Pass covers Austria, the Czech Republic, Hungary, Poland, and Slovakia, and Balkan Flexipass covers Bulgaria, Greece, Macedonia, Romania, Serbia, Montenegro, and Turkey.

NATIONAL PASSES. Most European national rail systems sell passes for their own country. If your travels are confined largely to a single country, its national pass will probably be a lot cheaper than a multinational pass of the same validity. Unlike Eurailpass, many national passes are available in second class, too. National passes are especially good deals in Germany, France, Italy, and The Netherlands.

A national pass may not provide all the extras you get with a multinational pass. Then again, some offer extras or features of their own. The Swiss pass, for example, provides free or discounted travel on important private railroads that Eurailpass excludes. If you're unsure if Eurailpass covers any given trip, check with Rail Europe, the official Eurailpass representative in the U.S.: 800 438-7245 or *www.raileurope.com*. BritRail Pass last year introduced reduced-price deals for three or four traveling together, a major improvement for families.

REGIONAL PASSES. Rail systems in some large countries sell area passes, which cost less than the national pass and cover less territory. For the most part, they're designed for local residents, but most can be used by tourists, too.

FOR SENIORS AND JUNIORS

Most European railroads provide reductions for senior travelers and youngsters. While the discounts target mainly residents, visitors may find that they're often better off buying individual discounted rail tickets, with reductions as high as 50 percent, than buying travel-all-you-want rail passes.

• Seniors who show ID (typically a passport) can get discounts on tickets in Denmark, Finland, Norway, and Portugal. Travel may be blacked out on peak days or at peak times.

• Seniors who buy an official ID from the railroad, good for a year, get discounts in Austria, France, Greece, and Sweden. You can have a card issued on the spot at a main rail station booking office. In most cases, you'll need a passport-sized photo—but many stations have photo machines. Austrian cards are also available in advance by mail.

• Youth/student ticket discounts are available in many countries. Check a student travel agency or a youth-travel guidebook for specifics.

CITY PASSES

Many European cities sell local or regional transit passes covering metro, light rail, and bus services. These are popular with tourists and are good deals for getting around town.

Many cities sell transit passes that target visitors. They're usually priced so that you break even at three or four trips a day—just enough to make the passes unattractive to local commuters. Travelers age 60 or over should also check out local senior options.

Cars and trains in Europe **141**

CAR-RENTAL RATES ABROAD

COUNTRY-BY-COUNTRY COMPARISON OF WEEKLY RATES
Source: *Consumer Reports Travel Letter,* August 1998

Company	Cheapest rental	Standard subcompact	Standard midsized	Cheapest automatic
AUSTRIA *21.2% tax included*				
Auto Europe	$152	$154	$166	$302
AutoNet	144	168	241	326
Budget	161	161	262	350
DER Car	176	246	314	382
ECR	163	163	272	362
Europcar	185	217	325	366
Europe by Car	181	193	314	375
Hertz	245	245	445	478
ITS	168	168	285	381
Kemwel Holiday	144	156	273	321
National	188	188	280	356
BELGIUM *21% tax included*				
Alamo	113	113	184	312
Auto Europe	92	93	120	289
AutoNet	108	108	168	277
Avis	146	146	224	359
Budget	106	106	167	273
DER Car	137	137	221	241
ECR	79	79	155	205
Europcar	132	132	208	253
Europe by Car	108	132	180	253
Hertz	116	116	189	316
Kemwel Holiday	103	103	188	241
National	127	127	199	300
BULGARIA *22% tax included*				
Auto Europe	387	411	484	—
Avis	409	409	842	683
Budget	282	282	411	411
DER Car	376	376	638	—
National	268	306	464	551
CZECH REPUBLIC *5-22% tax included*				
Alamo	228	228	399	270
Auto Europe	196	196	238	312
AutoNet	240	240	366	335
Avis	314	314	470	470
Budget	229	229	325	325
DER Car	441	441	747	877
ECR *high*	231	231	412	—

CAR OR TRAIN

CAR-RENTAL RATES *continued*

Company	Cheapest rental	Standard subcompact	Standard midsized	Cheapest automatic
CZECH REPUBLIC *cont'd*				
ECR *low*	$198	$198	$357	—
Hertz	471	471	708	$723
ITS	262	262	376	350
Kemwel Holiday	267	267	401	—
National	254	254	385	326
Thrifty	279	279	544	—
DENMARK *25% tax included*				
Auto Europe	221	234	261	471
AutoNet	261	261	399	524
Avis	366	366	656	1094
Budget	261	269	431	529
DER Car	300	300	360	603
ECR	220	222	358	447
Europcar	326	326	466	559
Europe by Car	286	286	424	674
Hertz	350	350	475	579
ITS	233	238	366	534
Kemwel Holiday	256	261	374	636
National	242	268	358	537
EGYPT *5-17% tax included*				
Auto Europe	313	313	—	374
Budget	300	300	650	650
Hertz	242	242	557	594
FINLAND *22% tax included*				
Auto Europe	389	399	545	655
AutoNet	450	450	487	645
Avis	498	498	527	883
Budget	401	401	551	—
DER Car	549	549	—	645
ECR	368	378	502	494
Europcar	487	487	572	630
FRANCE *20.6% tax included*				
Auto Europe	141	153	189	262
AutoNet	168	168	228	373
Avis	252	276	380	693
Budget	200	200	459	870
DER Car	144	166	216	187
ECR	173	219	302	509

Cars and trains in Europe

Company		Cheapest rental	Standard subcompact	Standard midsized	Cheapest automatic
FRANCE *cont'd*					
Europcar		$233	$287	$351	$361
Europe by Car		180	180	240	312
Hertz		222	286	291	308
ITS		236	282	338	—
Kemwel Holiday		168	180	228	240
National		193	193	296	296
GERMANY *16% tax included*					
Alamo		114	114	184	232
Auto Europe		89	92	101	194
AutoNet		92	99	150	219
Avis		171	171	253	432
Budget		116	116	232	186
DER Car		97	97	130	210
ECR		108	108	145	201
Europcar		96	96	129	179
Europe by Car		99	103	184	242
Hertz		85	121	175	143
ITS		108	108	155	215
Kemwel Holiday		89	99	161	231
National		118	118	154	259
GREECE *18% tax included*					
Alamo		171	171	289	271
Auto Europe		126	150	162	232
AutoNet	high	191	223	406	354
	low	140	164	388	282
Avis		256	295	531	584
Budget	high	245	295	—	475
	low	213	237	—	397
ECR	high	224	267	576	473
	low	146	191	455	334
Europcar	high	211	249	404	397
	low	160	174	292	272
Europe by Car		211	235	447	506
Hertz	high	190	290	409	447
	low	148	148	290	286
Kemwel Holiday	high	164	188	—	376
	low	136	159	—	317
National		155	172	—	303

CAR-RENTAL RATES *continued*

Company		Cheapest rental	Standard subcompact	Standard midsized	Cheapest automatic
HUNGARY *no taxes*					
Auto Europe		$177	$187	$237	$307
AutoNet		209	209	329	349
Avis		396	396	610	610
Budget	high	268	268	1027	345
	low	233	233	893	317
DER Car		280	280	420	420
ECR	high	228	228	350	368
	low	184	184	306	324
Hertz		360	360	560	550
ITS		216	216	375	360
Kemwel Holiday		219	225	469	299
National		210	210	343	350
ICELAND *24.5% tax included*					
Auto Europe		372	372	—	—
Avis		705	705	—	1241
IRELAND *12.5% tax included*					
Alamo		181	181	267	288
Auto Europe		168	177	255	323
AutoNet	high	376	376	488	552
	low	179	179	258	348
Avis		224	224	286	280
Budget	high	367	367	459	520
	low	199	199	283	321
DER Car		189	189	—	347
ECR	high	200	200	384	346
	low	113	145	246	232
Europcar	high	283	364	574	658
	low	190	203	245	326
Europe by Car		145	145	235	258
Hertz	high	383	383	504	566
	low	214	214	275	343
ITS		124	124	329	312
Kemwel Holiday	high	332	348	460	505
	low	145	156	246	269
Kenning	high	296	296	417	505
	shoulder	197	197	285	363
	low	158	158	230	278
National	high	289	289	439	535

Cars and trains in Europe

Company		Cheapest rental	Standard subcompact	Standard midsized	Cheapest automatic
IRELAND *cont'd*					
National	shoulder	$168	$168	$236	$364
	low	136	136	214	246
Payless		146	156	196	320
Thrifty		459	459	688	765
ISRAEL *no taxes*					
Auto Europe		149	149	219	239
Avis		133	133	—	237
Budget	high	243	243	700	350
	low	138	138	595	245
ECR	high	312	312	831	476
	low	207	207	726	371
Hertz		154	154	—	280
Kemwel Holiday	high	206	206	592	326
	low	129	129	515	249
National	high	287	287	—	434
	low	203	203	—	336
Thrifty		133	133	378	238
ITALY *20% tax included*					
Auto Europe		179	224	320	356
AutoNet		269	269	499	459
Avis		398	398	796	874
Budget		315	315	567	441
DER Car		245	245	474	569
ECR		263	263	501	394
Europcar		293	293	596	—
Europe by Car		309	309	673	539
Hertz		371	371	634	649
ITS		283	283	510	424
Kemwel Holiday		282	282	539	426
Thrifty		241	271	463	—
LUXEMBOURG *15% tax included*					
Auto Europe		114	123	146	215
AutoNet		114	114	160	194
Avis		146	146	200	266
Budget		130	130	174	190
DER Car		129	151	210	245
ECR		123	144	190	219
Europcar		216	216	313	231

CAR OR TRAIN

CAR-RENTAL RATES *continued*

Company	Cheapest rental	Standard subcompact	Standard midsized	Cheapest automatic
LUXEMBOURG *cont'd*				
Europe by Car	$183	$183	$263	$194
Hertz	114	137	182	242
Kemwel Holiday	120	194	286	252
NETHERLANDS *17.5% tax included*				
Alamo	106	106	—	256
Auto Europe	102	114	137	220
AutoNet	112	128	234	234
Avis	189	189	254	323
Budget	175	175	286	279
DER Car	115	115	230	311
ECR	111	111	208	236
Europcar	105	136	214	245
Europe by Car	116	128	187	234
Hertz	118	224	—	266
ITS	113	118	204	253
Kemwel Holiday	116	128	182	276
National	123	130	245	304
Thrifty	103	149	314	282
NORWAY *23% tax included*				
Auto Europe	269	279	304	476
AutoNet	257	306	466	503
Avis	556	556	818	798
Budget	419	484	615	615
DER Car	333	333	504	609
Europcar	328	328	474	538
Hertz	376	376	517	635
Kemwel Holiday	355	368	523	577
Thrifty	267	267	420	—
POLAND *22% tax included*				
Auto Europe	228	240	314	—
Avis	589	589	765	—
Budget	340	340	441	401
DER Car	376	376	551	676
Europcar	253	253	341	—
ITS	262	287	464	—
Kemwel Holiday	279	279	401	—
National	239	265	325	265

Cars and trains in Europe

Company		Cheapest rental	Standard subcompact	Standard midsized	Cheapest automatic
PORTUGAL *17% tax included*					
Alamo		$140	$140	—	—
Auto Europe		113	113	$184	$406
AutoNet		135	135	350	362
Avis		161	161	417	660
Budget	high	220	220	456	360
	low	169	169	351	266
DER Car		160	160	428	374
ECR	high	180	206	655	963
	shoulder	145	166	572	521
	low	99	112	357	650
Europcar	high	252	252	774	615
	shoulder	172	172	427	461
	low	157	157	387	341
Europe by Car		139	146	221	280
Hertz		150	150	391	—
Kemwel Holiday	high	209	221	684	—
	low	146	181	619	—
Kenning	high	238	238	—	446
	low	191	191	—	352
ROMANIA *18% tax included*					
Auto Europe		341	341	—	—
Avis		455	455	762	1155
Budget		342	342	544	555
ITS		520	520	520	—
SLOVAKIA *6% tax included*					
Hertz		264	264	329	435
SLOVENIA *5% tax included*					
Auto Europe		228	249	354	784
Avis		441	441	956	772
Budget		383	383	569	—
ECR		315	315	717	—
Hertz		187	187	585	543
Kemwel Holiday		251	293	671	587
National		257	257	579	—
SPAIN *16% tax included*					
Auto Europe		103	124	147	194
AutoNet		126	126	196	196
Avis		153	153	246	239

CAR-RENTAL RATES *continued*

Company		Cheapest rental	Standard subcompact	Standard midsized	Cheapest automatic
SPAIN *cont'd*					
Budget	high	$144	$144	$232	—
	low	132	132	215	—
DER Car		136	136	235	$240
ECR	high	174	174	282	279
	low	161	161	261	279
Europcar		155	155	232	296
Europe by Car		138	145	300	—
Hertz		140	140	231	237
ITS		155	180	—	295
Kemwel Holiday		145	145	266	261
National		179	179	308	366
SWEDEN *25% tax included*					
Auto Europe		209	221	246	484
AutoNet		261	261	374	524
Avis		276	276	419	639
Budget		223	223	310	—
DER Car		234	234	350	436
ECR		281	281	384	562
Europcar		329	329	384	—
Hertz		395	395	499	583
ITS		280	280	403	598
Kemwel Holiday		319	349	411	599
National		279	279	427	632
Thrifty		241	241	344	608
SWITZERLAND *6.5% tax included*					
Alamo		160	160	200	232
Auto Europe		114	125	178	252
AutoNet		137	148	212	223
Avis		208	208	249	445
Budget		190	190	226	233
DER Car		127	127	224	226
ECR		120	120	240	223
Europe by Car		133	137	223	212
Hertz		174	181	217	252
ITS		209	209	273	261
Kemwel Holiday		122	137	265	240
National		167	167	222	236

Cars and trains in Europe

Company		Cheapest rental	Standard subcompact	Standard midsized	Cheapest automatic
TURKEY					
Auto Europe		$215	$215	$284	—
Avis		283	283	389	—
Budget	high	266	266	692	—
	low	217	217	588	—
ECR	high	304	304	—	—
	low	255	255	—	—
Europcar		291	291	—	—
Hertz		421	421	607	—
Kemwel Holiday		293	293	—	—
National	high	221	221	—	—
	low	189	189	—	—
UNITED KINGDOM 17.5% tax included					
Alamo		201	201	240	$277
Auto Europe		116	161	173	267
AutoNet		128	140	222	246
Avis		222	236	301	444
Budget		243	243	389	681
DER Car		148	148	214	320
ECR		144	144	267	248
Europcar		179	185	243	309
Europe by Car		128	135	227	222
Hertz		182	187	244	310
ITS		117	124	244	205
Kemwel Holiday		140	152	241	234
Kenning		143	156	351	282
National		185	193	251	346
Payless		127	135	170	293
Thrifty		195	214	215	289
Town & Country		117	124	244	205
Woods		197	220	336	284

most cases, figures are for 1-week rental with unlimited mileage, including VAT but not collision-damage waiver (CDW). es established in local currency were converted at mid-March 1998 exchange rates. Where a company offers both ance-payment and after-rental payment, the lower of the two options is shown. Where applicable, seasonal rates are indi- ed by *high, shoulder,* and *low.* High season is generally July and August, but exact dates vary by company and country. See t for definition of car classes and rental limitations and conditions. All rates subject to change.

exceptions: Foreign visitors are exempt from VAT on car rentals in Hungary (25%) and Israel (17%); renters may be ed to show passport at rental counter. In the Czech Republic some rental companies quote 5% VAT, others 22%. In Egypt, quotes range from 5 to 17%. Entries are based on tax quoted by each company.

W and other exceptions: Rates for Italy include mandatory theft insurance; so do Budget rates in Egypt, ITS rates in nania, and ECR and Kemwel Holiday rates in Slovenia. CDW included in Budget and Hertz rates in Egypt, most Italian rates, rates in Romania, and ECR rates in Slovenia. Thrifty rates in U.K. include liability insurance, required when CDW is declined.

C H A P T E R

MAPS FROM YOUR COMPUTER

Computer-based mapping programs and mapmaking web sites allow you to plan a trip before you hit the road—and stay on course come driving time. These digital tools can plot the best route, print a map, suggest places of interest along the way, calculate distances and travel time, and budget gas expenses. Video tours and audio clips allow even armchair travelers to explore destinations and collect information.

When you hit the road, several programs can even track your car's path. Whizbang gadgetry that you plug into a laptop computer can link up with global positioning satellites (GPSs) that tell you where you are and in which direction you're headed—provided you can navigate a laptop PC while you steer a car (see "A Bird's-Eye View," page 162).

We looked at nine web sites that allow you to create maps that you can print before a trip or forward by e-mail to other web users. The Internet services are free (one, Mapquest, lets you navigate worldwide), but they dispense limited information.

152 BY CAR OR TRAIN

This report also looks at three CD-ROM computer programs that focus on city-to-city routing, five programs dedicated to finding local addresses, and one that combines both intercity and local mapping. They retail for less than $100, though you may need to buy separate packages for intercity and local routings.

How good are those trip planners? Some allow you to find virtually any street address in the country and comb databases that list thousands of tourist attractions and millions of businesses. The best can calculate routes in seconds and produce customized maps and driving directions.

But a computer-generated itinerary can be thrown off course by detours, turn restrictions, and other road regulations, as well as by traffic. (Several programs offer updates on road conditions via their web sites.) Some routings are quirky. And a computer-generated map is no match for a detailed foldup one if you want to venture from a preplanned route. (One map vendor, Rand McNally, provides cross-references to its road atlas.)

CITY-TO-CITY TRAVEL

Of four programs that specialize in city-to-city travel, three are limited to intercity routing. You need companion programs, sold separately, to plot a course between the highway and your final destination address (see "Local Maps," page 158). The fourth program handles both intercity and local chores. All provide directions optimized for the fastest and shortest trip or for scenery, along with sightseeing or lodging suggestions based on your interests or budget.

Most of the intercity programs start by displaying a national or area map or interactive screens on which you enter starting and destination cities. You can then zoom in and out on your chosen route, add markers for hotels, restaurants, or sightseeing attractions, and print an itinerary and map.

Maps from your computer **153**

Two programs (listed alphabetically) stand out:

• AAA Map'n'Go 3.0 is a cooperative effort from DeLorme, one of the first to market digital maps, and the American Automobile Association, which has dropped its own clunky AAA Trip Planner program. Information from the AAA's TourBook database of 64,000 accommodations, restaurants, and points of interest is keyed to DeLorme's first-rate maps and routings. The program works seamlessly with the company's Street Atlas U.S.A. for local mapping and with DeLorme's Tripmate GPS device for navigation on the go (see "A Bird's-Eye View," page 162).

Map'n'Go starts with a map of the U.S. or your last-viewed map. You aim your mouse at any North American city and click on a starting point, then click elsewhere on the map to choose a destination (and any intermediate stops). Another click and you can summon the command that tells the program to calculate the quickest, shortest, or preferred routing between the two. One more mouse click and you can have the program display an itinerary.

You can use pull-down menus to access dialog boxes that let you type in the trip's target locations. Or you can point to icons that will search for locations by city name, area code, or zip code. Clicking on map symbols produces a listing of attractions, lodgings, restaurants, and landmarks tied to the auto club's TourBooks, which you can choose by price or quality criteria based on AAA's one- to five-diamond rating system. You can also connect online to DeLorme's web site to download current information on road construction and weather, and to overlay the data on the maps.

DeLorme's maps (U.S., Canada, Mexico, and the Caribbean) allow you to zoom in and out at 16 levels of magnification. Colored markers indicate the presence of additional information about hotels, campgrounds, restaurants, and points of interest.

154 BY CAR OR TRAIN

Want to find a radio station somewhere? Click on the map to see a list of stations (and formats) for that area of the U.S. or Canada. The program includes descriptions of and videos about key attractions.

Map'n'Go's biggest asset is its ability to print strip maps in the style of AAA's Triptiks, with a typical panel covering about 75 miles. The printouts, the clearest of any program's, contain directions and cumulative mileage figures.

• Rand McNally TripMaker 1998 Edition and Deluxe 1998 Edition has the most polished interface with users. It uses a talking "Trip Guide," a cartoon character dressed as an explorer, who asks questions about the journey you want to take. The guide prompts you to type answers in a series of dialog boxes that steer you through the steps needed to plan a trip in the U.S., Canada, or Mexico, starting with your origin and destination and including any stopovers. As you type a few characters, an alphabetical list of city names pops up.

The fill-in-the-blanks approach continues as Trip Guide asks about your choice of route (quickest, shortest, or scenic) and travel dates (just click on calendars to indicate starting and ending dates). Answer a few more questions about stopovers and attractions (you can display information about side trips, including photos and videos, before choosing any), and TripMaker cranks out an itinerary. You can also feed it details about driving speeds (what pace you keep on interstates, U.S. highways, state, and rural roads) and road habits (how many hours you like to drive in a day and when you take breaks).

For those who prefer less hand-holding, the program also has buttons and pull-down menus for inputting trip data quickly. The results are the same: a chart with detailed driving instructions on one side of the screen (including highway exit information) and a route map on the other.

The itinerary contains page and map references to the 128-

Maps from your computer **155**

page "Rand McNally Road Atlas." In addition, the program has ties to Rand McNally's web site, which posts information on current road conditions and has links to other travel sites where you can make travel bookings. The program also integrates with Rand McNally's StreetFinder for local mapping.

At any point, you can revise your route (TripMaker lets you avoid certain roads by right-clicking on any trip segments on the electronic map), adjust your schedule, compare two travel options side by side on the computer, or ask for suggestions for additional nearby attractions. The scenic tours include narratives and driving instructions.

The maps and information can be printed in whole or part. The program can print a TripPack that contains an overview map, a list of attractions, phone numbers for each of the attractions you've selected, and segmented maps with corresponding itineraries. If there's a downside to TripMaker, it's that the printouts lack the sparkle of its onscreen maps, and the strip maps are less detailed than the ones AAA Map'n'Go generates.

In addition to Rand McNally's own inventory of eateries and lodgings, featured in the standard version, TripMaker Deluxe presents the complete Mobil Travel Guide database of restaurants, hotels, resorts, and inns, which can be searched based on rates or Mobil's one- to five-star rating system. The Deluxe version can also pinpoint the nearest highway turnoffs for your preferred hotel, gas, or fast-food chains. It also allows you to use a laptop with a GPS receiver to chart your locations while you're on the road.

Compared with TripMaker and Map'n'Go, the following two programs (also alphabetically listed) fell down a bit:

• Microsoft Expedia Trip Planner 98 for Windows and Microsoft Automap Road Atlas 2.0 for Macintosh are from the software giant, which entered the mapmaking field by acquiring Automap Road Atlas, a program with some rough edges. It

156 BY CAR OR TRAIN

retained the core functions and added a number of embellishments to the Windows version (the Macintosh version has not been upgraded in several years). The Windows program, described next, was rechristened Microsoft Automap Trip Planner, with the latest version renamed Microsoft Expedia Trip Planner 98.

Trip Planner 98 employs dialog boxes to find out where you'd like to visit (and any sights along the way), how you want to get there (quickest, shortest, preferred routes), how fast you'd like to travel (on interstates, limited-access highways, or arterial roads; lead-footed drivers can increase the default speeds), and whether to measure distances in miles or kilometers. You can also input information about gas prices and your car's average mileage (in miles or kilometers per gallon, city and highway), which it uses to estimate the cost of each journey. The program lets you type in your starting, stopover, and destination points anywhere in the U.S., Canada, or Mexico and choose from a checklist of sights and activities that interest you.

The routings and calculations produce detailed charts with driving instructions, distances, and travel times. Like the DeLorme and Rand McNally products, Trip Planner 98 is tightly integrated with a companion program, Microsoft Expedia Streets 98 and Streets 98 Deluxe Edition (see "Surfing for Maps," page 161), to handle localized routings and to connect with GPS-software, allowing drivers to track their movements on a map.

Expedia Trip Planner 98 begins each mapping session with a menu of options that allows you to find a city or an attraction, plan a route, revisit a trip you've already begun planning, or go online to Microsoft's web site, where you can book hotels through the Microsoft Expedia travel service and connect to other sites for weather and tourist suggestions. The CD-ROM alone contains information on 19,000 hotel accommodations and 14,000 landmarks, plus scenic photos (some with 360-degree panoramic views), samples of regional music, and articles from Moon

Maps from your computer **157**

Publications, a publisher of travel books. It also contains 17,000 listings from the popular Zagat restaurant guides.

Microsoft touts the program's ability to adorn maps with "pushpins" that can be linked to text, pictures, video files, sound, and web sites. Indeed, the program is rich in multimedia features, but some of the silicon turns to sawdust when you print maps, which have shadings that can make route tracings difficult to follow. And it's the maps that you'll carry on a trip.

• Road Trips Door-to-Door 1997 Edition (TravRoute Software), which bills itself as the "single answer" to block-to-block and city-to-city navigation, is a hybrid of local (any address in the U.S.) and intercity (U.S., Canada, and Mexico) map programs. It packs a complete street atlas in one program, making it a particularly good buy.

It does so by depositing a large chunk of its data on your hard drive from its installation program, and then cramming the rest of its database onto a second, active CD-ROM. The upshot: a program with almost 7 million miles of highway and street maps, 200,000 cities, towns, and ZIP codes, 95 million home and business street addresses, and one million "points of interest." Door-to-Door lacks video and audio walk-throughs and other multimedia features, but its maker maintains a web site where you can retrieve lodging, dining, and attraction information, as well as weather updates.

You set up a trip by opening a window and working through a series of screens for Trip Start/Trip End (using city names or exact addresses), Intermediate Stops (up to 15 waypoints), and Options (quickest, shortest, or custom routes). For custom routes, the program lets you set speed limits and preferences on a scale of 1 to 10 for travel on each of eight route types, from local roads to divided highways to multilane no-toll highways—and even ferry crossings.

Though it has 12 zoom levels, Door-to-Door's screen maps

158 BY CAR OR TRAIN

lack some of the adornments of competing programs. Still, route markings are clear and the driving directions are well organized, showing road names, directions, segment distances, driving times, and cumulative travel times for each stage of the journey. Printouts, fast because of the lack of map detail, are not a work of art, but they suffice. The itinerary must be printed separately from the maps, and the program has no option for generating strip maps.

LOCAL MAPS

Picking up where the intercity planners (except Road Trips Door-to-Door) leave off, local mapping programs start at street level and can pinpoint your own address or find your old neighborhood anywhere in the U.S.

• Rand McNally StreetFinder 1998 Edition and Deluxe 1998 Edition has the crispest maps and the most features of the five programs we reviewed; it's our top choice. The cousin of Rand McNally TripMaker, this street locator combines ease of use with a vast collection of planning tools and detailed travel information. A business traveler, for instance, can launch an address search by street address, ZIP code, area code plus prefix, intersection, or attraction. When a category such as "business-out-of-towner" (one of a dozen prepackaged map styles) is then selected, up comes information about hotels, transit, car rentals, and other items of interest. The listings can be added to a trip itinerary, and the traveler can employ an address-to-address directions feature to display routings, say, from a hotel to a business appointment automatically.

Using a Concierge button on the Deluxe version's screen, you can summon an overview of an unfamiliar city, get recommendations for restaurants near a hotel, or get information on top attractions, local business services, or medical services. If you haven't

Maps from your computer **159**

booked a hotel, you can search the Mobil Travel Guide according to price, Mobil rating, or amenities.

Both versions include a database of 1 million businesses searchable by name, address, or location. For air travelers, the program features maps showing the location of terminals at 47 of the nation's busiest airports, plus highway access, parking, and car-rental lots. When you have trouble finding an airport, the program's GPS capability might be your last, best hope.

All the other programs have features to recommend them; we list them alphabetically:

• DeLorme Street Atlas U.S.A. 4.0 gives you a complete street map of the U.S.—down to remote dirt roads—with the purchase of a single CD-ROM. You can zoom in on any city or rural area, including more than 1 million lakes, rivers, parks, railroads, airports, colleges, malls, and other landmarks.

To go exploring, enter the city name, the ZIP code, or the area code and local exchange. (For larger cities, you also can search by street numbers.) You can then zoom in on your target. At mid-magnification, you'll begin seeing highway numbers; at higher levels, towns, lakes, and rivers appear, then railroads and streets. Crank it up a notch or two and you'll see street names.

Street Atlas U.S.A. can fetch information from Phone Search U.S.A. (sold separately by DeLorme), a digital phone directory that contains more than 80 million residential and business listings. The program also connects to an online database, where you can get updated information on road and weather conditions and event information that can be displayed on your map.

• Microsoft Expedia Streets 98 and Deluxe Edition is functionally similar to its highway cousin. It transports you to any street address, city, town, or ZIP code in the U.S., and is smart enough to recognize abbreviations such as 1st for First, NE or N.E. for northeast, or St. for Saint or Street. (Capitalization isn't necessary, either.)

The program can track restaurants and lodgings within a specified radius (one-half mile to 50 miles) of the spot you click, consulting a database of more than 350,000 restaurants (including Zagat listings) and 13,500 hotels (you can connect to Expedia's online travel service to make reservations). The Deluxe Edition allows you to search an additional 14 million business listings on an accompanying American Yellow Pages CD-ROM, locate the addresses, and create custom maps showing the business names, addresses, and phone numbers.

• Precision Mapping Streets 3.0 (Chicago Map Corp.) displays street-level views of virtually every U.S. street segment, park, waterway, railway line, airport, landmark, and political boundary, and it includes a "layer" control to hide any of the markings when creating custom maps. You can search by city, county, state, crossroads, street name, ZIP code, landmarks, area code and prefix, address, and latitude/longitude coordinates. A "street hints" feature automatically displays street name and block number next to any map segment you point to with the mouse.

In addition, Precision includes a symbol library for customizing maps, and it has drawing and editing tools that allow you to scale, move, rotate, color, or shade map objects. An image underlay feature lets you import images such as photos or scanned drawings to use as a backdrop. The emphasis on customization extends to the printing phase, where a mural option lets you create large-scale maps that span multiple sheets of paper.

• Select Street Atlas and Atlas Deluxe is a business-oriented mapping program from ProCD, a publisher of electronic

---

POCKET MAPPING

Microsoft also offers Pocket Expedia Streets 98, a scaled-down version of its digital street atlas that's specially designed for pocket computers. A free demo copy is available on Expedia's web site, *www. microsoft.com/ expedia* (a full-featured version is included with its CD-ROM Expedia Streets 98 program).

Maps from your computer **161**

business directories. Besides offering street-level maps of the entire U.S., the program comes with a database that lists about a million businesses, including hotels, restaurants, stores, and banks, which you can plot on the maps. The Deluxe package includes separate sets of atlas and phone CD-ROMs for East and West, which can be searched by name, address, city, county, state, ZIP code, telephone number, SIC (Standard Industry Classification) business code, and general geographic location.

A toolbar keeps all the mapping functions close at hand. Select has 10 levels of zoom magnification and the ability to annotate the maps with labels and drawings, mark locations with any of 200 icons, and measure distances. The program also allows you to import up to 5,000 addresses and phone numbers from personal databases.

SURFING FOR MAPS

You can't beat the price of the free mapping services on the Internet (advertisements pay the freight on most of the sites). Mapmaking online is a bit slower than with the CD-ROM programs, and there's a chance a site may be down. But you'll be able to track addresses and generate maps that you can view, print, e-mail to friends, or embed in web pages. The better sites allow you to plot trips and create itineraries.

A good place to start is MapBlast! *(www.mapblast.com)*, home page for interactive map designer Vicinity Corp., or Yahoo! Maps *(www.proximus.com/yahoo)*, which uses Vicinity's maps as part of its Internet search tools. Both allow you to locate places by typing in addresses, intersections, cities, and states, then to create overview and thumbnail maps and turn-by-turn driving directions. (With Yahoo!, you can also search for nearby businesses.)

Mapquest *(www.mapquest.com)*, using digital maps and databases from several sources, allows you to browse and zoom your way to cities and towns worldwide and perform city-to-city or door-to-door routing in major U.S. cities. Maps on U.S. *(www.mapsonus.com)* uses technology from Bell Labs to route travel (you can click on a button to hear voice directions), create customizable maps of U.S. addresses, and search Yellow Page listings.

Two primarily Yellow Page sites, Zip2Yellow Pages *(www. zip2.com)* and BigBook *(www.bigbook.com),* house business databases that offer some mapping capabilities. Additionally, there's Tiger Mapping Service *(tiger.census.gov),* a large but pokey database run by the U.S. Bureau of the Census, DeLorme Cyber-maps *(www.delorme.com/cybermaps),* a watered-down version of the mapmaker's atlas and routing software, and Etak Guide *(www.etakguide.com),* a scaled-down version of the maps it provides for Rand McNally and others.

A BIRD'S-EYE VIEW

Several mapping programs use the GPS system to give directions and track your position as you drive. DeLorme's Tripmate carries the lowest entry price: For $149, you get a package that combines its standout Street Atlas U.S.A. software with a GPS receiver. Just add a laptop and go. Other mapping-system suppliers provide more expensive software-receiver packages or software that is compatible with GPS receivers that you buy separately.

However, the map-program adjuncts still aren't as fully realized as the integrated systems available on some rental cars. In rental-car systems (also available as options when you buy some luxury cars), both receiver and computer are built in, and the system issues detailed voice instructions ("exit the next off-ramp . . . turn right . . . get into the left-hand lane . . . turn left at the next stoplight"). In contrast, most map-program adjuncts provide locations and directions only through screen displays on a

Maps from your computer **163**

laptop computer. If it's chancy to drive while talking on a cellular phone, driving while following a laptop-screen display would be foolhardy.

Still, two systems are closing the gap:

• Compass, $200 from Chicago Map, combines its Precision Mapping Streets local-map software with a hand-held Eagle Explorer GPS receiver that displays your current position and gives directions on its own small screen. You must still connect it to a computer for trip planning, but once you've set an itinerary, you upload your route data and use the receiver unit by itself.

• Door-to-Door Co-Pilot, $300 from TravRoute, includes a GPS receiver and provides voice instructions through a laptop's audio system. As with the built-in systems, you can keep your eyes on the road.

Overall, today's add-on systems don't quite equal the convenience of built-in systems. If you don't already have a laptop computer, the buy-in price can be extremely high. But if you have a laptop and like high-tech gadgetry, give one of the programs a try.

PART FOUR

HOTELS

14 How to get the best deals 165

15 Hotels at half price 181

16 Budget hotels 189

17 Extended-stay hotels 195

18 Deals for frequent stayers 203

19 Hotel deals abroad.....................213

20 Villas, condos, other rentals 221

C H A P T E R 14

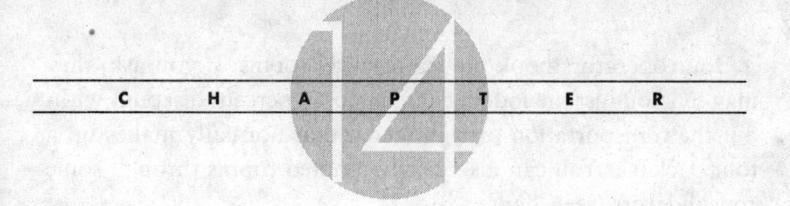

HOW TO GET THE BEST HOTEL DEALS

Smart travelers rarely pay full price for a hotel room. Rates vary widely, even for the same room in the same hotel on the same day. Hotels use complex pricing systems formulated on predictions of room-occupancy rates for each date and location. Rates for empty rooms drop as a given reservation date approaches.

For most travelers, it's too risky to show up at a hotel hoping to get a room at a good price. And it's unnecessary, when there are so many good sources for bargain hunters.

FINDING THE DISCOUNTS

Room deals can be had through either private or public sources.

Private channels. Hotels sell off excess room capacity through half-price hotel programs, which often offer the best deals for travelers (see Chapter 15). Their biggest drawback? You may have to be flexible about locations or dates, especially during a peak-demand period.

Tour operators book blocks of hotel rooms. If you ask, they may sell you just the lodging at a 20 to 40 percent discount without the transportation or sightseeing that normally makes up a tour package. You can also get discounted rooms through some consolidators (see Chapter 5).

In some cities, local reservation services can provide good deals. If you're heading off for a week or so on an island, in the mountains, or in a distant major city, be aware that a hotel or resort isn't your only choice. A vacation rental or home exchange can be cheaper, roomier, or more fun.

Public channels. Every type of hotel—from economy to full-service (business) deluxe, and even resort properties—gives discounts off rack rate (list price). It's generally best to call individual hotels directly to check for the best rate; national reservations operators aren't always informed of local short-term deals.

Direct discounts come in several forms:

Sales and promotions. Rates at hotels catering to business travelers during the work week are dramatically lower on weekends. So are rates at resort hotels during off-season.

Bargain destinations. Overbuilding in a region affects hotel rates dramatically. Ask your travel agent which destinations offer the best deals.

Advance-reservation deals. A number of chains will reward you with lower rates if you do your booking ahead (anywhere from 7 to 29 days in advance). In one such deal, you pay for your first night's stay within a week of reserving; if you cancel without giving at least a 15-day notice, you lose your deposit. However, penalties for cancellation vary, as do prepayment requirements and the amount of the discount; check before you book.

Deals on the web. Many chains allow you to room-shop right from your computer; some offer special, Internet-only bargains. The next section of this chapter will tell you where to look.

Other sources. Membership associations, such as the American

How to get the best hotel deals **167**

Automobile Association (AAA) and the American Association of Retired Persons (AARP), negotiate special rates for their members with selected hotel chains. Many marketing partnerships are formed around discount hotel offers. Some banks offer lodging discounts as benefits with their credit cards (usually rebates of 5 to 10 percent, often with a minimum hotel bill of $100 or so).

Special rates. Most hotels that serve business travelers offer *corporate* rates—often available to any traveler who can produce even vague evidence of corporate or professional employment when checking in (a business card will usually do). Regular corporate rates are available at thousands of hotels. However, they usually run no more than 20 percent off rack rate, and many are even stingier. They may even be a bit higher than the lowest rack rate, to cover some extra amenity: a "superior" room, an "executive" floor, or a few pleasant but minor perks.

Preferred rates are a special kind of corporate rate, specifically negotiated by a big travel agency, an independent booking service, or a travel club. These rates may provide substantially better deals than ordinary corporate rates—average discounts are around 20 percent, and some are as high as 40 percent. Furthermore, they're typically available on a "last room" basis: You'll get the discount as long as a hotel has any rooms at all open for sale, even if the hotel is close to full. Some preferred-rate programs even have their own "blocked space" at some hotels and may be able to confirm you a room—at the discount rate—when the hotel's inventory is booked.

On the other hand, preferred rates are available at far fewer hotels than are regular corporate rates (perhaps a fifth to a quarter as many) and only through the individual travel agencies, travel clubs, booking organizations, and corporate travel offices that have negotiated them. Furthermore, some preferred discounts are 10 percent or less.

To arrange the discount, ask to see your travel agency's current

168 HOTELS

preferred-rate directory and the latest "Hotel and Travel Index" when you plan a trip. Check the listings and prices for the places you want to visit, then have the agent make your reservations. Directories are now available on CD-ROM: If you travel a lot, your agency may be able to give you a copy.

You can also ask to see a display of available preferred rates on your travel agent's computer screen. The big multioffice chains and large independent networks (including ABC Corporate Services and THOR24) have their own preferred rates listed in most of the airline-sponsored computer reservation systems. Computer access to those rates is restricted to participating retail travel agencies.

If you prefer to arrange your own deals, the Travelgraphics preferred-rate program is available directly to consumers ($29; 800 644-8785; AE, Disc, MC, V). Buy a directory, find a hotel that fills your bill, and call that hotel directly, mentioning the Travelgraphics booking code.

HOTEL CHAINS ON THE INTERNET

Dozens of hotel chains maintain web sites, and new ones crop up every week. We found more than 70 such sites when we checked in late February 1998, a few with Internet-only deals you might find interesting. (Web addresses are in the Resources Guide in the back of the book.)

In general, the hotel-chain sites followed the same patterns as airline web sites:

Short-notice deals. A few of the better Internet hotel deals paralleled the airlines' short-notice approach, with special rates as much as half off regular rates but available with little advance notice and for an extremely limited time. In some cases, the deals applied just to the following weekend; in others, they were good for a week or more. Most chains posted deals on their sites;

How to get the best hotel deals **169**

Radisson enrolls you through the site, then notifies you by weekly e-mail messages.

Internet-only discounts. Several chains promoted special deals that they claimed were available only for bookings made over the Internet. Other chains are likely to adopt that strategy.

Other promotions. More than half the chains' sites listed promotions and packages of one sort or another. As far as we could tell, those listings were simply another way of communicating promotions that were also available through travel agencies and to travelers who called the chains' central reservation offices.

Bookings. Most of the chains took bookings online, through either an entry form on the site or an e-mail link.

WHERE TO LOOK ON THE WEB

It's all too easy to spend endless hours chasing travel deals around the web—especially with chains that, however large, may not have any hotels in areas you want to visit. Here are a few sites that seemed especially useful and attractive:

Radisson's site was, we thought, the most fully realized one. It offered a chance to get a weekly e-mail listing with several dozen outstanding short-term deals worldwide, often more than 50 percent off. It also listed associated airfare deals (Continental's COOL program and Northwest's CyberFares deals) that offered significant savings on short-term weekend trips, as well as rental-car specials from National. The listing is at least partially reciprocal—Continental's site regularly includes Radisson listings.

Hyatt and **Inter-Continental** also listed short-term discounts, as much as 45 percent. Their listings, however, weren't as extensive as Radisson's, and they didn't include airfare deals.

Shoney's site listed Fall Back Weekend specials of particular appeal to budget travelers. The rates were seasonal and weren't Internet-only deals.

Outrigger showed Web Surfer Special reductions up to 35 percent at some Hawaiian locations. The promotions were presented as Internet deals, but we found that the same ones were available through the chain's central reservation office. In addition, the site listed the chain's ongoing promotions, including senior deals, AAA offers, an ongoing airfare promotion, first-night-free packages, and such. If you're heading for Hawaii, Outrigger's web site is an obvious first stop.

Best Western offered a chainwide Internet-only 10 percent discount the first time we looked, but a few weeks later it had disappeared from the site. Although 10 percent off isn't much, the possibility of future chainwide deals warrants an occasional visit to the site.

Sofitel's site listed that chain's usual seasonal promotions. Those deals are among the better chainwide European promotions, but they're available to anyone, not just through the Internet.

OTHER WIRED-IN DEALS

Theoretically, you could use the Resource Guide on page 285 to check sites that offer promotions or packages and find exactly what you're looking for. However, that could entail a lot of fruitless surfing and, unless you have a high-speed access hookup, many online hours. Quite a few sites provided little but fluff—descriptions of properties, locations, and such. Unless a site promises promotions, a visit isn't worth the time.

Instead, you might try one of several other wired-in ways to find hotel deals:

• Thousands of individual hotels maintain web sites. The Hotels Worldwide button on Travel Weekly's site (*www.traveler. net/two*) leads you to a geographical menu of individual hotel sites, some of which include extensive reviews from the Official Hotel Guide (OHG). Those sites may or may not include deals. When we

How to get the best hotel deals **171**

went through the menu (U.S., then Hawaii, then listings by city) to the Royal Waikoloan, we found the same Web-Surfer Special that was listed on Outrigger's site.

• Another umbrella site, Hotels and Travel on the Net (*www.hotelstravel.com*), provides links to "more than 100,000 hotels worldwide." You can reach some hotel-chain sites only by going through it or other similar travel-booking sites. Deals, if any, depend on the individual hotel's site.

• Several booking agencies offer discounted rates over the Internet. Among the larger are Hotel Reservations Network (*www.180096hotel.com*), probably the most active broker for U.S. accommodations—it's linked to several other Net sites—and U.K.-based Expotel Interactive (*www.expotel.co.uk/expotel/*), which provides worldwide coverage.

• Full-service booking agencies, such as Expedia (*www.expedia.com*) and Travelocity (*www.travelocity.com*), provide hotel reservations. Discounts, if any, are available through links to a discount hotel broker.

SENIOR HOTEL DISCOUNTS

Two booms—economic and demographic—are gradually choking off senior hotel discounts. The booming economy is fueling steady growth in both business and leisure travel, hiking demand for hotel space just about everywhere. As the baby-boom generation enters its 50s, many hotels seem to have decided they can't be overly generous to such a large part of the population.

The upshot is a trend to smaller discounts and vaguer promises. At several chains, the typical senior discount is now substantially lower than it was in 1996, when we last covered senior hotel deals.

Happily, though, senior hotel deals aren't yet an endangered species. Dozens of hotel chains and thousands of individual hotels still use price incentives to attract over-50 travelers. In

172   HOTELS

fact, with the proliferation of hotel brands, a few more chain-wide programs turned up this year than in 1996. Nonetheless, things will probably continue to tighten up—you're apt to hear "sorry, the senior discount isn't available tonight" more often.

THE PLAYERS. Senior programs are commonly set up in one of two ways:

• Most offer relatively modest (10 to 15 percent) discounts, but usually offer them as long as a hotel has any vacancy at all.

• A few provide reductions up to 50 percent, competitive with the best reductions you can get through a half-price program (see Chapter 15) or a hotel broker. But those big-discount deals are usually subject to availability or limited by some other restrictions.

Chains operate any of three types of senior program: Some give a discount to anyone with proof of age, some restrict deals to members of the AARP or other senior group, and some limit discounts to members of the hotel chain's own senior club. Several chains operate under two different sets of rules, and a few have entries in all three categories.

ANY-SENIOR DEALS. A majority of the chains offer a senior discount to anyone at or over some minimum age. All you need to qualify is a driver's license or other official ID:

• The most generous discounts—25 percent or more, subject to availability—are offered at Aston, Colony, Cross Country, Four Points, Hawaiian Hotels & Resorts, Hyatt, Marc/Hawaii, Outrigger, Radisson, Sheraton/Luxury, Vagabond, and West Coast. You can also do as well at the several Choice brands and at MainStay, if you reserve in advance. With some chains, however, the generous senior discount may not apply to minimum-rate rooms.

Unsurprisingly, Hawaiian-based chains are prominent among those offering generous reductions. Business from Asia has fallen off, making Hawaii one of the few major destinations where the hotel market is soft.

How to get the best hotel deals   **173**

• Many chains give reductions of only 10 to 15 percent. While that's better than nothing, senior travelers at those chains would be wise to check for some other, bigger discount—through a half-price program, a travel agent's preferred-rate program, a hotel broker, or a chain's own any-age promotion. At most of those hotels, a low-percentage senior deal is the fallback position if you can't find anything better. However, budget hotels seldom give more than 10 to 15 percent off to anyone, so a senior deal there is probably as good as any you'll find.

The minimum age for membership in the AARP is 50, and a goodly number of the any-senior programs apply the same minimum. However, more than a quarter use age 55, about another quarter use 60, and a few require that you be 62 or 65.

AARP DEALS. AARP has arranged official discount programs with about two dozen chains, listed in the members' AARP Purchase Privilege Program directory. At least that many more chains unofficially honor AARP membership for senior discounts. Many of the chains in both groups also honor memberships in the Canadian Association of Retired Persons and other senior membership organizations.

• Among the chains that honor AARP, officially or unofficially, only a dozen don't offer an any-senior discount program at all—at those chains, no AARP card, no discount.

• While most chains give discounts to seniors who aren't AARP members as well those who are, AARP membership lowers the minimum qualifying age from 55 to 65 to 50 at 24 of the listed chains.

• At five chains with both types of program, the AARP deal is better than the any-senior deal.

• Generous discounts of 25 percent or over are limited to AARP (and other senior-association) members at Canadian Pacific, Doubletree, and Marriott.

Membership in AARP is open to seniors of 50 and over at $8

a year. In addition to hotel discounts, AARP offers other services for seniors, including arrangements for reduced-price prescription drugs and Medicare-supplement insurance. New this year is a discount-ticket deal with Virgin Atlantic—the first time in many years that AARP has been able to arrange a deal with a big airline.

HOTELS' OWN 'CLUBS.' Five of the chains run their own membership programs for senior travelers but, for the most part, members get only modest discounts. Only at Days Inn and Hilton do the reductions (subject to restrictions) run as high as 50 percent; at Ramada, the standard is 25 percent. In those three cases, the hotel-club deals can be quite a bit better than the same chains' any-senior deals.

The minimum age for a hotel membership program ranges from 50 (the same as with AARP) to 60. If you don't already belong, you can usually sign up on the spot when you arrive at the hotel.

Beyond room discounts, the Days Inn, Hilton, and Disney clubs offer a variety of other benefits, including discounts at hotel restaurants and gift shops, reduced admissions, and even promotional deals with airlines, cruise lines, and car-rental companies. The Hilton and Ramada senior programs are extensions of their frequent-stay programs: Stays at a participating hotel earn credit toward free hotel stays, air tickets, and other awards.

MAKING YOUR DEAL. You usually can't combine a senior discount with any other reduction—half-price, corporate, weekend, group, meeting, or such. And even an advertised chainwide discount may not be available at all times or at all locations.

Senior discounts are usually available through a chain's toll-free national reservation line. Many chains now also provide web sites of varying sophistication; some merely provide information, others accept reservations. Still, it's often a good idea to call each hotel's own reservation office. You may learn of a better choice of discount options and local promotional deals, as well as of local senior offers.

How to get the best hotel deals **175**

Several notable names have no chainwide policy, but you'll often find senior rates at their individual locations. (On the other hand, very upscale small chains and independent hotels may not offer any.) If you're 50 or over, always ask about senior discounts when you reserve.

BROKERS: NO-HASSLE HOTEL DEALS

Brokers are agencies that provide a way for hotels to unload rooms they don't expect to sell at full price. They don't always get you the biggest discounts, but they're among the most reliable sources of decent ones.

Some brokers focus on their hometown; those can provide first-hand advice about new hotels, locations, special events, and the like. Others cover many cities and may provide only a few choices in some areas. Still others are wholesalers who usually package discounted rooms with airline tickets or other travel services but will also sell rooms by themselves.

Brokers provide far and away the easiest route to hotel deals. Usually, one phone call is all it takes: You tell the broker where you're going and when you need a room; the broker lists the current deals, and you choose the one you like. You needn't call around, hotel by hotel, to see which if any is giving sizable deals, as you do with 50-percent-off programs (see Chapter 15). A broker may also be able to get you a discount when half-price rates are blacked out. A few can even provide rooms when a hotel says it has nothing available.

On the down side, most brokers offer a limited selection of hotels. Broker deals are usually confined to fairly upscale properties, midpriced and up. Some brokers handle hotels in only one or two cities—and seldom in small cities. Most handle only downtown locations, with only occasional choices in suburban or airport locations.

176   HOTELS

Many brokers require prepayment in full. If you have to cancel or change your plans, prepayment can be a hassle. You may be on the hook for at least one night's room charge. Even brokers that don't make you prepay may impose a cancellation charge.

While brokers are often sources of good deals, there are no guarantees—they sometimes provide only a modest discount. If you're willing to put in some telephone time, you may do better with a half-price program, a hotel's own promotion, or (if you're 50 or over) a senior deal. Before you accept a broker's rate—or a discount from any source, for that matter—check out the hotel's own asking price for the time you're considering.

BROKERS AND WHOLESALERS

Brokers fall into two broad categories:

Booking agencies act as a limited sort of travel agent, making a reservation for you at a discount rate. You pay the hotel when you check out, by cash, charge card, or check, just as you would for a room you had booked on your own. Usually, booking agencies can handle last-minute arrangements. Most booking agencies don't give commissions to other agencies; you must deal with the broker yourself.

Booking agencies get some of their deals from hotels that need to fill rooms on a short-term basis. Discounts may be more than 50 percent during slow times and disappear when rooms are tight. Other booking-agency deals are "preferred" rates, typically 10 to 40 percent off the hotel's rack rate (its published list price). Those are the same rates that many full-service travel agencies arrange for their corporate clients (see earlier in this chapter). Preferred rate programs sign hotels up for an entire year, so those deals are generally available whenever a hotel has a vacancy.

Wholesale brokers generally contract with hotels by the year to sell rooms at a discounted price. Many of them are tour oper-

How to get the best hotel deals **177**

ators who sell rooms to independent travelers at the same rate they sell them in package tours. (Tour operators who don't promote themselves as brokers may do the same; you can sometimes find additional deals by checking a range of tour brochures.) Some wholesalers even control their own inventory of block-booked rooms, at least at some hotels: They "own" a certain number of rooms.

Wholesalers generally require you to prepay them for your entire stay; the broker then mails you a room voucher. (On bookings less than a week or so in advance, the voucher is held for you at the hotel. Wholesalers often can't accommodate last-minute bookings at all.) Most of these do give commissions, so your regular travel egency can deal with them for you.

Like preferred rates, wholesaler discounts are generally in the range of 10 to 40 percent, although occasionally they're higher. On the other hand, when rooms are tight, a wholesale broker may not give any discount at all; instead, the broker sells the room to travelers who are happy to pay full price just to get a booking. Unlike booking agencies, wholesalers typically quote an all-in-all rate, including tax and service charges. But beware: A few wholesalers quote prices on a per-person rather than a per-room basis; the true price for a couple is double the price quoted, and the true single rate includes a hefty single surcharge.

PICKING A HOTEL

In the U.S. at least, the most widely used hotel grades are probably those published in the OHG. When a tour brochure or newspaper ad promises a certain grade of hotel, the claim is probably based on OHG classifications.

OHG ratings combine two elements: quality of lodgings (room size and standard of furnishings) and extent of facilities (number and size of public and meeting rooms, restaurants, and shops).

178 HOTELS

When you use them, or any other hotel rating, be sensitive to nuance. The travel industry is reluctant to say flatly that any hotel is really bad. So the OHG and other sources often resort to code words and euphemisms. When the description says "may not be well kept" or "should be used only in a pinch," read it as "this hotel is a dog."

COMPETING RATINGS. OHG is published for the travel industry, not consumers. But quite a few other hotel-classification systems are designed mainly for use by the traveling public:

• Government agencies assign hotel ratings in many countries, among them Australia, Austria, Belgium, France, Greece, Indonesia, Italy, Mexico, the Netherlands, New Zealand, Spain, Switzerland, and the UK. Those ratings may be noted in hotel and tour brochures in place of, or in addition to, OHG ratings. However, many important tourist countries (including Denmark, Finland, Germany, Japan, Norway, Sweden, and the U.S.) don't rate hotels. Travelers headed for those countries, as well as tour operators and travel agencies, have to rely on nongovernmental sources for ratings.

• Certain major guidebooks—including the AAA Tour-Books, Michelin's Red Guides, and the Mobil Travel Guides—have hotel ratings of their own. Others (for instance, the Birnbaum, Frommer, Let's Go, and Lonely Planet series for consumers, and the Star Service for travel professionals) provide only descriptive prose.

All the systems are similar to some extent. Government systems tend to rely on such statistical measures as dimensions of guest rooms and public areas, percentage of rooms with bath, and so on. The OHG and the guidebooks lean more on the personal judgments of authors, professional inspectors, or voluntary reports from travelers, travel agents, and travel writers.

BUDGET ROOMS. In many parts of the world, hotels more basic than those OHG rates can be quite adequate. (The guide doesn't even list many low-end hotels.) Budget travelers in Paris, for

How to get the best hotel deals **179**

instance, may be perfectly happy in hotels with a government rating of only one or two stars, if they know what to expect. Similarly, travelers in the U.S. find budget hostelries a great buy even at list price.

DECODING OFFICIAL HOTEL GUIDE RATINGS

The OHG divides hotels into three main categories—Deluxe, First Class, and Tourist—with subcategories under each. Here's what each of the rating terms really means (reprinted with permission of the Official Hotel Guide).

DELUXE. Superior Deluxe describes an exclusive and expensive luxury hotel, often palatial, offering the highest standards of service, accommodations, and facilities; elegant and luxurious public rooms; and a prestigious address. Establishments in this category are among the world's top hotels.

Deluxe refers to an outstanding property offering many of the same features as Superior Deluxe. These hotels may be less grand—and more reasonable—than the Superior Deluxe properties, yet in many instances just as satisfactory.

Moderate Deluxe is basically a Deluxe hotel, but with qualifications. In some cases, accommodations or public areas may possess a less-pronounced degree of luxury than that found in fully Deluxe properties. In other cases, the hotel may be a well-established famous name, depending heavily on past reputation. The more contemporary hotels may be heavily marketed to business clients, with fine accommodations and public rooms offering Deluxe standards in comfort, but with less emphasis on atmosphere and/or personal service.

FIRST CLASS. Superior First Class is an above-average hotel, perhaps an exceptionally well-maintained older hotel, more often a superior modern hotel specifically designed for the First-Class market, with some outstanding features. Expect accommo-

HOTELS

dations and public areas to be tastefully furnished and very comfortable. These establishments can be good values, especially the commercial hotels.

First Class indicates a dependable, comfortable hotel with standardized rooms, amenities, and public areas, and maybe a superior executive level or wing. Don't expect deluxe facilities or special services.

Limited-Service First Class denotes a property offering full first-class quality accommodations but limited public areas, food service, and facilities. Usually moderate in size, these hotels often utilize a residential scale and architecture, and many offer complementary breakfast and evening cocktails in the lobby or in a small, informal restaurant. This bracket is geared to the individual business/pleasure traveler.

Moderate First Class is essentially a First Class establishment with comfortable if somewhat simpler accommodations and public areas. These may lack some features (e.g., restaurant), and, while adequate, some of the rooms or public areas may tend toward basic and functional. However, rates are also reasonable.

TOURIST. **Superior Tourist Class** primarily signifies a budget property, with mostly well-kept, functional accommodations, some up to First Class standards. Public rooms may be limited or nonexistent. Often just a place to sleep, but it may have some charming or intimate features, and may be a good value. The amenity/low rate ratio may balance for individuals or groups on a budget.

Tourist Class means strictly a budget operation with some facilities or features of Superior Tourist Class, but usually no (or very few) First Class accommodations. Use these with caution.

Moderate Tourist Class refers to low-budget operations, often quite old and sometimes not well-kept. Should only be used in a pinch if no other accommodations are available.

CHAPTER 15

HOTELS AT HALF PRICE

With room rates continuing to zoom, hotels again shape up as travel budget-breakers. A half-price hotel directory will be one of the handiest tools in your cost-cutting kit. Your savings from just a night or two's use will more than offset the cost of joining a half-price program ($40 to $99 a year).

The major-program directories promise more opportunities than ever to score a big discount. Each of the top three we report on here listed over 3,500 individual half-price properties in North America, we found when we checked their 1998 offerings. (The '99 programs hadn't been announced as of press time, but they should be much the same.) The directories also included hundreds of locations that honor smaller chainwide deals. (They offer deals in overseas hotels as well; we cover those in Chapter 19.)

All the major half-price programs offered the same basic deal. The big differences were in geographic scope—the more hotels and locations in a program's directory, the bigger your chances

182   HOTELS

of finding discounted lodgings when and where you want them. Accordingly, this chapter ignores smaller programs, focusing instead on seven programs with a relatively large number of North American listings.

Although the programs we've omitted sell directly to consumers, they're distributed mainly through tie-ins with travel clubs, oil companies, banks, retail merchandise chains, charge cards, and such. If you get one of their directories free through such a deal, by all means use it. But in view of their sparse hotel listings, there's little reason to seek one of them out.

THE HALF-PRICE GAME

From a hotel's perspective, joining a half-price program is a good way to try out yield management. That's a gambit, pioneered and perfected by airlines, for selling essentially the same service at a variety of prices.

Here's how it works. The hotel establishes an artificially high rack rate (list price), which it knows it can get only rarely—during a big convention, say, or a major sports event. But that price serves as a baseline for a variety of "discounts," some offered openly, others limited to certain guests. Typically, a half-price program will get you a discount that's the biggest you're apt to get from any given hotel.

The big programs offer a broad mix: independent and chain hotels at a range of prices in downtown, suburban, airport, and highway locations. However, the offerings are thin at the price extremes. Some budget-hotel rates are already so low that there isn't room for big discounts. Deluxe properties often opt out because they don't need to discount, or they prefer to do it in other ways.

From a traveler's angle, playing the game requires you to enroll in a club (or buy a discount directory). The program operator

Hotels at half price **183**

then gives you a list of participating hotels and an identification card that's good for at least a year.

Before a trip, you check your program's directory for participating hotels along your route. The directories indicate each hotel's price range (usually with a symbol), address, phone number (some also list a fax number), and sometimes a brief list of its services.

You contact hotels of interest directly, name the half-price program you're using, and ask if a discount rate is available when you want it. If so, you make your reservation (guaranteed by charge card, if necessary). If not, the hotel may offer you a lesser discount. Alternatively, you can try for a different date or check with another hotel. You must usually call at least a few hours ahead for a reservation, not just show up at the desk.

On checking in, you show your ID card. You pay when you leave, by cash or charge card. Your half-price ID is supposed to cover only one room each night. Though some clerks may bend the rules if you're in a party requiring two or more rooms, assume that your party should have a separate membership for each room.

WHAT THEY OFFER

Directories generally include a laundry list of additional features, discounts, and other deals. Probably the most useful offers are dollars-off airline coupons, which let you knock as much as $175 off the regular price of a coach excursion ticket—usually with not too many restrictions. Some programs said they offered additional discounts through HRN, a large hotel broker. But you needn't belong to any program to use HRN (800 380-7666).

Most of the hotels offer half-price rates on any day of the year, subject to availability. That means you won't get the discount at times when a hotel expects to be more than about 80

184 HOTELS

percent full (seasonal blackouts often apply, too). Peak-season discounts are often available only on weekdays in resort areas and on weekends in cities. A few hotels impose a minimum or maximum stay. These restrictions are usually noted in the program directories.

All the programs we list accept enrollments (or sell directories and coupon books) by phone, with payment by a charge card. Entertainment directories are sometimes available at bookstores and other outlets. Except as noted, all directories and memberships are valid for one year from date of purchase.

Membership in a listed program may also be included as a benefit in some other program you've joined. Some are occasionally also offered as premiums in promotions and charity drives, or as an employee benefit through corporate personnel offices.

WHICH ONE FOR YOU?

Here's a rundown of the seven major programs. They're listed in order of estimated overall attractiveness, based on the number of locations listed in their '98 directories and the extras that were included.

Entertainment Publications ranks number one in total North American (as well as worldwide) locations, offering a broad range of directories for U.S. and European hotels, as well as local books that feature hotel, dining, and entertainment discounts. Its "Hotels & Travel Ultimate Savings Directory," a blockbuster, covers most prime travel destinations, and also includes discounts on airfares, car rentals, cruises, and admissions to visitor attractions. Entertainment offers a catalog, and buying one book gets you others at reduced prices. 800 445-4137. The $62.95 cost includes ID cards valid for 12 to 18 months. *MC, V. Editor's Choice.*

ITC-50 is used as an enhancement to many oil-company

Hotels at half price **185**

charge cards, road-service programs, memberships in associations and alumni groups, and the like. It contains fewer U.S. listings than Encore (see below) but is significantly ahead in Canada and overseas. It offers minimal hotel discounts, some car-rental discounts. 800 987-6216. $52. *AE, DC, Disc, MC, V. Best Buy.*

Encore ties for second place with ITC-50 in North America for overall offerings. Besides the hotel listings, a separate section features small inns and B & Bs. It has discounts on hotels, airfares, car rental, cruises and admissions to visitor attractions—as well as price breaks on flowers, auto-painting, carpet-cleaning, and the like. 800 444-9800. $59.95. *AE, Disc, MC, V.*

Great American Traveler ranks well below the top three in total North American listings and has meager hotel, airfare, car rental, and cruise discounts. However, the parent company, Access, offers breaks on condo rentals; percent-off greens fees at hundreds of golf courses; and admission discounts for hundreds of amusements and theaters. 800 548-2812. Total Portfolio Package costs $99.95 for the first year, $49.95 to renew. The hotel program is $49.95 for the first year, $29.95 to renew. *AE, Disc, MC, V. Best Buy* for golfers and amusement-park enthusiasts.

Quest has considerably fewer offerings than in the past but remains relatively pricey (though it's discounted through associations, charge cards, and the like). It offers small hotel and airfare discounts, breaks on car and condo rentals, and on cruises. 800 742-3543; $99; quarterly hotel-directory updates, $8 a year. *AE, Disc, MC, V.*

GetAway Travel Club offers almost entirely first-class or better hotels, lists some not available from other programs. 800 218-5862. $49.95. *MC, V.*

Impulse also concentrates on a small number of upscale hotels through its web site. Connect to *www.impulsepreferred.com* for

186 HOTELS

deals on city-hotel rooms in North America, condo-rental offers in the U.S. and Mexico, airline reservations, and auto rentals. You must contact hotels directly to ask for a deal. Enroll through the site: $15 for a 90-day trial; $44 for a year; $5 for a printed directory. *MC, V.*

WATCH YOUR BACK

Despite their virtues, half-price programs aren't the answer to a traveler's every prayer:

• Hotels really mean their "subject to availability" limitations. You won't get a discount when a hotel expects to be busy. Don't join a program expecting to pay half-price for all your stays.

• The real deal may be less than a full 50 percent off the price other travelers pay. In a number of cases, our readers have found that their "half-price" rate was only a few dollars less than they'd have paid had they just walked up to the desk and asked for a room.

• Don't be surprised if the reservationist at a listed hotel tells you that it no longer honors a program's card. There's extensive turnover in participant lists.

• You won't get a half-price deal just by mentioning the name of a big program. Hotel clerks generally ask you to produce a valid card.

• Don't expect to combine a half-price discount with any other reduction—a corporate, senior, or weekend rate, say—for which you might otherwise be eligible.

• Half-price rates aren't commissionable, so your travel agency won't arrange them for you.

On balance, we still recommend a half-price program. In screening the directories, we found some fine hotels, where just one night at a true 50 percent off would justify a program's annual cost. Even if you don't get a true 50 percent discount, you

Hotels at half price **187**

usually get the best deal a hotel offers, without haggling.

Nonetheless, you should also be aware of alternatives, for times when a half-price deal won't work:

• If you're heading for a major U.S. city, a hotel broker may offer better rates and a wider selection (see Chapter 14).

• A competent full-service travel agency can arrange preferred rates (up to 40 percent off) at thousands of hotels throughout the world (see Chapter 14).

• If you're traveling along highways, a budget motel can usually provide a comfortable room, with all the features you really need, at a list price (sometimes with a modest senior or auto-club discount) that won't put a big dent in your budget.

C H A P T E R 16

BUDGET HOTELS

Looking for decent lodgings at a sane price? Budget hotels throughout the U.S. can fill the bill nicely. You'll get a good-sized room, a well-equipped bathroom, and only the facilities and extras you absolutely need.

Budget hotels/motels are called "economy/limited-service lodgings" in hotel lingo; for convenience, we call them just hotels in this book. Most belong to chains—the biggest now offer more than 100,000 rooms in more than 1,500 locations. Some chains are independent; others are subgroups of giant chains. But whatever the genealogy, $50 or less a night (once you're outside the big cities) usually gets you all you need in overnight lodgings.

To be sure, a few individual budget hotels are dogs, once-pricey establishments fallen on hard times. Fortunately, those don't last very long: Intense competition demands that even the cheapest chains renovate, redecorate, and update facilities and services on a regular basis.

THE PROS AND CONS

Budget hotels are generally located outside city centers—along major highways, in suburban areas, and near airports. Typically, they provide modern bathrooms and clean, comfortable rooms equipped with two doubles, two queens, or one king bed; a writing table or dresser; a color TV with local cable; and a phone or two. You'll usually find ice machines (free) and vending machines for soft drinks and snacks nearby.

Most budget hotels provide 24-hour front-desk service, choice of a nonsmoking or smoking room, and individually controlled heat and air conditioning. Some chains offer "free" breakfast, newspapers, local phone calls, and other extras. Except in central-city locations, you get free parking, too. But it's rare to find new, comfortable budget hotels in the central business districts of major cities—and when you do, they're often in marginal areas.

You usually give up a few features that midpriced chains offer: fancy lobbies, large meeting rooms, health clubs, business centers, and such. But many travelers don't need or use these features. Nobody will help with your bags either—but nobody will extend a palm for a tip.

You also ordinarily sacrifice food service. Instead of finding an on-site restaurant, you'll have to go afield a bit—but a fast-food outlet or family restaurant usually won't be far away. The hotel probably won't provide room service, but it will permit (even encourage) delivery from local restaurants.

BY THE NUMBERS

Average room size in budget hotels varies from well over 400 sq. ft., at some suite chains, down to 210 sq. ft. or so. But most chains offer a room size between 250 and 300 sq. ft., an area typical of a midpriced hotel room. Rooms at the low end of the range

Budget hotels **191**

are all right for a couple, at least for a short stay. However, if you're in a larger family group or plan to hang out for a few days, you're probably better off with chains that offer biggish rooms.

Most of the chains characterize themselves as budget operations (or use fancier code words that mean the same thing), but there's no precise definition of the "budget" price range. As a practical matter, rate classes depend on location: What passes for budget in a city center would be mid- or high-priced along the highway. Similarly, a highway budget rate would barely buy a flophouse bed in central Chicago or New York.

Average room rates are generally near $50. Rates start at under $30 (a bit below the then-current average for Motel 6, which promotes its rates as the lowest of any national chain).

Most chains offer at least a modest reduction to seniors (typically 10 percent; you may have to be a member of AARP), as well as discounts to members of American Automobile Association affiliates (or other auto clubs). A few individual units also participate in other discount programs—half-price or preferred-rate—that offer discounts of 20 to 50 percent. Check your half-price directory for particulars.

All but a handful of chains allow one or two kids, usually with an age limit in the teens, to stay "free." Generally, however, that doesn't mean that the hotel provides an extra bed or bedding. As an alternative to stuffing an entire family into one room, families may want to head for one of the all-suite chains listed on pages 198-199. Those often provide two separate rooms, or at least separate areas, at budget rates.

BY THE FEATURES

Many chains are generous with features:

• Quite a few budget chains let you make local and toll-free calls without charge.

192   HOTELS

• Except in some city-center or cold-weather locations, pools have become virtually universal at hotels in all price ranges. But not every budget chain offers a pool at every location. If a pool is important to you, check when you reserve.

• Many chains provide a free breakfast, though it may be confined to rolls and coffee or tea. But even a basic breakfast can save you up to $5 a day per person in restaurant costs.

• Chains are responding to economy-minded business travelers with more and more business-oriented features, such as incoming fax services and modems. Hotels near airports may provide free airport shuttles, too.

• Many of the least expensive hotels have outside-corridor room entrances. However, many travelers prefer the security of inside corridors.

• Cable TV is an attractive extra in cities, and it's almost a necessity in rural areas. Basic cable service has become so common these days that it's not really a feature. However, a few hotels include free access to such premium channels as HBO and Showtime. Some offer in-room VCRs—some free, some at a daily charge—with an on-site library of rental tapes.

ANY ALTERNATIVES?

A half-price program can bring the cost of staying at a midpriced hotel down to the budget range (see Chapter 15). A hotel broker or preferred-rate program can also do about the same (see Chapter 14). A discounted midpriced room is likely to be bigger and to have more facilities and features than a budget room at the same price.

However, your chances of finding a budget room are usually a lot better. Budget-chain rack rates aren't subject to limited availability or blackouts. And you needn't join a club or buy a discount directory.

Budget hotels

Of course, many locations don't offer a real choice. In rural areas, budget properties may be the only option—you can drive several hours along an interstate without seeing a hotel in a mid-priced chain. On the other hand, if you're looking for a comfortable room in the center of a big city, budget chains may have nothing to suit you.

CHAPTER 17

EXTENDED-STAY HOTELS

Staying out of town for two or three weeks for a family crisis and prefer a substitute home to a cramped hotel room? Need a place to crash while your house is being renovated? On temporary assignment for a few weeks and need a home away from home? If so, several hotel chains target you as a customer for their "extended-stay" subchains.

Two factors mark an extended-stay chain: long-term rates and features (such as full kitchen facilities) that appeal to visitors staying more than a few days. However, most extended-stay hotels also accept transient guests, provided space is available; many offer one-night rates. Ultimately, the differences are in perception and promotion: A hotel chain is "extended stay" when it says it is.

The extended-stay segment of the hotel business somewhat overlaps the all-suite group. Many all-suite features—notably food-preparation facilities—appeal to touring families as well as to extended-stay visitors. However, not all extended-stay chains are all-suite, and not every all-suite chain offers long-term rates.

196 HOTELS

MAJOR AND MINOR PLAYERS

By industry standards, extended-stay chains are small. Residence Inn by Marriott, by far the largest, has more than 250 locations nationwide. Only two others—Extended Stay America and Villager Lodge—have 100 or more locations, and several have only a handful. The "Rates and Features" table on pages 198–199 even lists a prototype chain with no units open at the time this chapter was written (mid-1998).

Most chains are national. The sites are generally in the suburbs, with many others in or near office and industrial parks or close to shopping malls or airports. But you find quite a few downtown, as well.

Several of the major chains, including Cendant, Choice, Doubletree, Holiday Inn, and Promus, have developed their own extended-stay brands or subchains. Marriott has even set up a second extended-stay brand (TownePlace) to compete in a price niche below Residence Inn. Other big players (among them Hilton, Sheraton, and Radisson) remain on the sidelines.

Two other brands, BridgeStreet Accommodations and Oakwood Corporate Housing, offer downtown and suburban apartments in major urban areas. In some cases, they run an entire apartment complex; in others, a portion of a larger building or complex.

RATES AND DISCOUNTS

The table's Rates entries show what you'd pay: typical nightly, weekly, and monthly rates, plus weekend and senior discounts if available. As with other types of accommodation, the rates vary widely, from $150 or so a week at two budget-oriented operations to nearly $2,000 a week for a two-bedroom suite at one of the upscale chains. And as with most chains, rates vary by location and often by season.

Extended-stay hotels   **197**

Extended-stay hotels usually offer a discount when you contract, in advance, to stay more than one week. Some chains don't quote weekly and monthly rates; they negotiate extended stays individually. If you're traveling on your own, call a hotel directly. Tell the reservationist or sales manager how long you plan to stay, and ask what sort of deal you can arrange for that period. Corporate travel offices may negotiate long-term rates for their business travelers—especially in the case of ongoing training programs or offsite assignments.

Only about half the chains offer weekend reductions and only about half offer senior discounts of any kind. Beyond those, there are few deals.

AmeriSuites has a unique getaway gimmick: If you rent a room at one location for a full week or more, you can enjoy a change of scene by moving to a different AmeriSuites location for two weekend nights at no extra cost. Since you're still checked into your original room, you can keep some of your stuff there while you're away. Ask for the AmeriStay program.

LAYOUTS AND FEATURES

Unit configurations range from studio to two-bedroom. Most of the chains provide some studio rooms and about one-quarter offer nothing but a studio—one room for both sleeping and daytime living with, at best, some sort of furniture as a divider. Studios might satisfy a single relocating employee, but they're apt to be inadequate for either a business traveler who needs work space or a family on vacation.

Most of the chains offer at least some one-bedroom suites, with bedroom and living areas in two rooms separated by walls and doors. Separation of sleeping and work/relaxation areas is ideal, but it's confined mainly to the upper-end chains.

About half the chains feature two-bedroom suites. They're

HOTELS

HOTELS: RATES AND FEATURES

RATES AND FEATURES OF EXTENDED-STAY HOTELS

Source: *Consumer Reports Travel Letter*, June 1998

Hotel chain	Locations	RATES		
		Nightly	Weekly	Monthly
AmeriSuites	75 national	$79–109	$483–693	$1920–2820
Bradford Homesuites	3 SW	$79	$349–359	$1475–1495
BridgeStreet Accommodations	1000 + national, international	$63–275	$441–1925	$1350–6000
Candlewood Suites (Doubletree)	38 national	$50–85	$413	$1470
Extended Stay America	138 national	—	$199–299	—
Crossland Economy Studios	7 MW, SE, SW, NW	—	$159–199	—
Hawthorn Suites	30 MW, NW, SE, SW	$89–248	Call	Call
HomeGate Studios & Suites	21 national	$59–69	$350–500	$1375–1600
Homestead Village	92 national	—	$209–399	—
Homewood Suites (Promus)	65 national	$95	Call	Call
InnSuites	10 SW, West	$49–99	$299–699	$999–2199
MainStay Suites (Choice)	11 national	$55–65	$350	$1350–1400
Oakwood Corporate Housing	1000+ national	$50–200	$350–1400	$1500–6000
Residence Inn by Marriott	268 national	$75–105	Call	Call
Sierra Suites	12 NE, SE, SW, West	$69–109	$343–623	$1170–2370
StayBridge Suites by Holiday Inn	[1]	$75–110	$450–675	$1500–2700
StudioPlus Deluxe Studios	73 MW, NE, SE	—	$299–399	—
Suburban Lodges of America	75 national	$49	$169	$676
Summerfield Suites	32 national	$89–270	Call	Call
TownePlace Suites by Marriott	6 national	$55–65	$385–455	$1650–1950
Villager Lodge (Cendant)	100 national	$36–42	$150–225	—
Woodfin Suites	7 MW, NE, West	$99–189	Call	Call

[1] New brand; expects to open 25-40 units in U.S. and abroad through 1999.

[2] AmeriSuites Club members only.

[3] By special arrangement.

[4] All locations except Charleston, S.C.

Room discounts	Layout	EXTRAS					
		Free local phone calls	Free breakfast	VCR	Office equipment	Exercise equipment	Pool
✔	1-bdrm	[2]	✔	✔	✔	✔	✔
	Studio and 1-bdrm	✔	—	—	✔	✔	✔
	Studio, 1-, 2-, and 3-bdrm	✔	—	Some	[3]	Some	Some
✔	Studio and 1-bdrm	✔	—	✔	Some	✔	Some
	Studio	✔	—	—	—	—	—
	Studio	✔	—	—	—	—	—
✔	Studio, 1-, and 2-bdrm	Most	✔	Most	✔	Most	[4]
✔	Studio, 1- and 2-bdrm	—	—	Some	Some	Some	Some
	Studio	✔	—	—	✔	—	—
	1- and 2-bdrm	✔	✔	Most	✔	✔	✔
✔	Studio and 1-bdrm	✔	✔	—	✔	✔	✔
✔	Studio and 1-bdrm	✔	✔	—	✔	Some	Some
	Studio, 1- and 2-bdrm	—	—	Most	Most	Most	Most
✔	Studio, 1- and 2-bdrm	—	✔	Some	✔	✔	✔
✔	Studio	✔	✔	✔	—	✔	✔
✔	Studio, 1- and 2-bdrm	✔	✔	Some	✔		Most
	Studio	✔	—	—	—	✔	Some
	Studio	✔	—	—	—	—	—
✔	1- and 2-bdrm	Some	✔	✔	✔	✔	✔
✔	Studio, 1- and 2-bdrm, 1-bdrm w/office	—	—	—	—	✔	✔
✔	Studio and 1-bdrm	Most	—	Some	Some	Some	Most
✔	1- and 2-bdrm	—	✔	✔	✔	Most	✔

For **reservation numbers** and web addresses, see Resource Guide in back of book. **Locations**: MW=Midwest; NE=Northeast; NW=Northwest; SE=Southeast; SW=Southwest. Rates listed are as of June 1998; call where indicated. Chains that allow **discounts** usually do so for weekends and for seniors; discounts range from 10 to 30 percent. Most chains provide full kitchen in at least some rooms (AmeriSuites provides minikitchen only).

fine for larger families on vacation or two-person business teams who want separate bedrooms but a common living area. Others convert the second bedroom into an office.

Room/suite size varies with layout and price. Rooms at the budget Crossland chain are a skimpy 227 sq. ft. But in most chains, the minimum total room size (for a studio) is at least 300 sq. ft. Rates at the low end generally buy you no more than a studio, either in an all-studio budget unit or as the low-cost choice in a unit with different layout options. Larger, multiroom units go as high as 1,000 sq. ft., with prices to match.

The kitchen marks the primary difference between extended-stay hotels and typical all-suite properties. A large majority of the extended-stay chains include a full kitchen with full-size appliances, while many all-suites provide only minikitchens (possibly just counter areas with a microwave and a minirefrigerator). A decent kitchen, with stove, refrigerator, tableware, and utensils, is desirable even if you eat mainly takeout or delivered food.

EXTRAS

The special features and facilities of each chain reflect the two basic markets that the extended-stay hotels target: families on vacation and long-term business travelers. Some features, including free local calls and free breakfast, appeal to both markets.

The business orientation of many chains is clear. Beyond what we show in the table, some feature two phone lines per room or a single line with extra data ports, and some provide a central business center with fax, copier, and such.

Several chains provide CD players and VCRs. The hotel may provide a small tape or disc library; if it doesn't, you'll probably find a rental outlet nearby. Of course, you won't find all the traditional services and facilities of a full-service hotel. Extended-stay hotels tend to have a relatively small staff; at a few, even check-in is automated. You may find towels and bedding changed only once or twice a week (or when a new guest arrives), not every day.

You're not likely to find an on-premises restaurant or coffee shop, either, though there's probably one nearby. Although you won't have 24-hour room service, chances are that the hotel will permit (or even encourage) delivery from neighboring restaurants and fast-food outlets. At most locations, parking is free.

You'll find no spacious lounges and lobbies or meeting and convention facilities, nor will there be attendees filling the public spaces and elevators. You'll also have to give up proximity to major tourist attractions. As with hotels generally, those at the budget end of the price scale may have outside rather than inside-corridor entrances—undesirable from a security standpoint, especially in hotels with limited full-time personnel.

ALTERNATIVES

Of course, if you're planning to stay somewhere for a few weeks, the extended-stay hotel chains aren't your only options. In big U.S. cities, you'll find independent apartment buildings that have been converted to weekly or monthly rentals. Check the classifieds and the phone book under "apartment rentals" in a city you plan to visit for individual units or brokers. Also, if you're heading for a popular tourist destination, a vacation rental may be a better bet (see Chapter 20).

But the extended-stay chains bring to the table the same advantages you find in chains in general: an assurance of standards that you can't get with independent units. And "no surprises" remains important for many travelers.

CHAPTER 18

DEALS FOR FREQUENT STAYERS

Hotel frequent-stay programs have never had the marketplace clout of airline frequent-flier programs. Maybe that's because the airline plans pay off better. Even so, a frequent-stay program can provide a decent return in free stays and other payoffs if you spend as few as 8 to 10 nights a year in hotels.

The basic principle of frequent stay is the same as with frequent flier: You get a reward in proportion to your use of the sponsor's service. But most big-airline programs are virtual clones, while the hotel programs vary widely.

This chapter gives an overview of 29 frequent-stay programs. All let you earn credit at any participating hotel in a chain, pool the credit you earn at different locations into a single account, and use that credit for a free stay at any participating hotel (or for some nonhotel award). Some are based on building up points, the way airlines run their frequent-flier programs. Others are based on how many nights you stay.

We didn't look at the pseudo-frequent stay programs that

many hotel chains run. Some offer free rooms or other rewards for repeated stays at a single hotel, but you can't use the credit anywhere else. Some offer discounts or other perks to good customers, but not free stays.

POINT-BASED PROGRAMS

Eleven programs resemble those of the big airlines, with a long list of earning options, awards, and partners. Most of the 11 give you points or some other credit based on what you spend at the hotel—in many cases for food, room service, merchandise, and other on-site purchases as well as for the room. Some give credit for rooms occupied at a preferred, senior, half-price, or other discounted or promotional rate (though they may not give credit for the deepest discounts). The others typically limit credit to travelers who pay rack (list-price) rate or the hotel's published corporate rate. Program literature often limits earnings to "qualifying" rates —check whether a rate you're quoted qualifies when you reserve.

• Some of the programs give additional points for patronizing car-rental or airline partners, usually in conjunction with a hotel stay. With most, you can choose between getting hotel or airline credit during each stay. Hilton and Westin allow you to "double dip"—to earn both hotel and airline credit for the same stay.

• Several programs offer one or more levels of very-frequent-stay (VFS) status, similar to very-frequent-flier status in airline programs. As with the airlines, VFS status provides some combination of faster earning or more generous benefits. Our comparisons, however, are based on the lowest level of membership.

• Some chains give you an unlimited time to accumulate enough credit for a free stay or other award; others give you only a year.

• Hilton, Holiday, Marriott, and Westin cosponsor credit cards (MC or V) that earn frequent-stay credit for all purchases billed to the card, not just hotel stays.

Deals for frequent stayers **205**

• Membership in most hotel programs is free. Holiday and Sheraton charge a fee, noted in the Frequent-Stayers Program table.

HOW GENEROUS?

All the point-based programs provide free hotel stays as awards. Most also let you redeem hotel points for a wide range of other travel services as well as merchandise. The table includes our assessment of the minimum worthwhile award. It's the lowest-credit award that we consider to be broadly desirable (and to which we can reliably assign a dollar value). It includes free nights, room discounts, and such—but not such less tangible awards as a room upgrade or free use of a health club or a business center.

The minimum worthwhile award is also a fairly good yardstick of a program's generosity. The typical minimum award is simply one free night—at any time in some programs, during a weekend (or on an off-peak night at a resort location) in others. Since half-price weekend deals are common, we've valued a weekend night at half the dollar value of a weekday (or any-day) night.

In many programs, higher-credit awards are simply multiples of a basic award: If 10 paid nights earn a specified award, 20 paid nights earn double the specified award.

The table also shows a payoff figure for both benchmark awards. Payoff is the value of the award, expressed as a percentage of what you'd have to spend to earn it. Where a program offers either hotel or airline credit, we calculated payoff on the value of the hotel award. Where credit is awarded per stay (rather than per dollar or per night), we based the cost of a minimum award on a two-night stay and assumed that the 10-night award was earned during three stays.

We didn't adjust our payoff calculations to reflect credit earned for nonroom expenditures or use of a partner airline or car-rental firm, since any assumptions we might make about those would be

HOTELS

FREQUENT-STAYER PROGRAMS

PROGRAMS THAT ACCUMULATE CREDIT BASED ON POINTS

Source: *Consumer Reports Travel Letter,* April 1998

Hotel chain	Program	How you earn points	Partners
Best Western	Gold Crown Club	1 point per dollar on qualifying rates	Avis, Dollar
Hilton	HHonors	10 points per dollar on qualifying rates and purchases; 500 points per stay at HHonors Resorts; HHonors charge card	Alamo, Avis, National, Thrifty; many airlines
Holiday Hospitality [1]	Priority Club ($10 or 250 points per year)	10 points or 2.5 airline miles per dollar at regular rates; some MCI calling plans; Priority charge card	Hertz; many airlines
Howard Johnson	SuperMiles	1 point per dollar on qualifying room rates and all room charges	—
Hyatt	Gold Passport	5 points per dollar on most room rates	Alamo, Avis; some airlines; Royal Caribbean cruises
Independent B&Bs, Inns	InnPoints	4 points per dollar on room rate	—
Marriott [2]	Marriott Rewards	5/10 points per dollar for room rate/all charges, depending on property; Marriott charge card	Hertz; some airlines
Ramada	Ramada Business Card	10 points per dollar for room at most rates and other hotel charges; 50% bonus for seniors	Avis
ITT Sheraton [3]	Sheraton Club (Gold Level $50 per year or 10 stays)	2 points per dollar on room rate and other hotel charges; some AT&T calling plans	National
Travelodge [4]	Travelodge Miles	1 point per dollar on room rate	
Westin	Premier	2,000 points plus 500 airline miles on most rates; Westin charge card	Many airlines

For **reservation number and web addresses**, see Resource Guide in back of book. You can earn additional points by patronizing partners' products.

[1] Includes Crowne Plaza, Inter-Continenal, and StayBridge suites.

[2] Includes Courtyard by Marriott, Fairfield Inn, Marriott Vacation Club, Renaissance, Residence Inn, TownePlace, and some Ritz-Carltons.

Deals for frequent stayers **207**

MINIMUM WORTHWHILE AWARD			Other awards	Membership benefits
Points	**Award**	**Payoff**		
1,300	$25 at some locations	1.9%	Car rental, meals, merchandise, tours, airline tickets, or miles	Breakfast, free calls
20,000–30,000	1 weekend night	2.5	Car rental, merchandise, tours, airline tickets, or miles	Late checkout, priority reservation, free stay for companion
7,500–45,000	1 night	3.5	Car rental, meals, merchandise, tours, airline tickets, or miles	Priority reservations, discounts in hotel restaurant, shops
2,000	1 night	3	Car rental, airline tickets, or miles	—
8,000	1 weekend night	3.8	Car rental, tours, airline tickets, or miles	Late checkout, priority reservations, discounts in hotel restaurant, shops
5,000	$30 or 1,500 miles	2.4	Tours, airline tickets, or miles	—
7,000–10,000	1 night at Fairfield Inn	5	Tours, airline tickets, or miles	Priority reservations, free stay for companion at some locations
20,000	1 night	3	Car rental, merchandise, tours, airline tickets, or miles	Breakfast and free calls at some location, car-rental discounts, late checkout, room upgrades, free stay for companion
3,000	1 night at some hotels	5	Car rental, tours, airline tickets, or miles	Late checkout, room upgrade
750	1 night	6.7	Car rental, meals, merchandise, airline tickets, or miles	Discount rooms, free calls
20,000	1 weekend night	1.5	Tours, airline tickets, or miles	Breakfast at some locations, priority reservations

3 Includes The Luxury Collection, Sheraton, and Four Points.

4 Includes ThriftLodge.

208　HOTELS

FREQUENT-STAYER PROGRAMS

PROGRAMS THAT ACCUMULATE CREDIT BASED ON NIGHTS STAYED

Source: *Consumer Reports Travel Letter,* April 1998

Hotel chain	Program	How you earn points	Credit life
Adam's Mark	Gold Mark Club including discount rates	1 credit per stay, unlimited time to use	1 year to earn, unlimited time to use
AmericInn	Inn-Pressive Club	1 credit per night, 1 year to use	Unlimited time to earn, 1 year to use
AmeriSuites	AmeriSuites Club	1 credit per night	Unlimited time to earn, 1 year to use
Baymont (formerly Budgetel)	Roadrunner Club Card	1 credit per night, including discount rates	1 year to earn, 1 year to use
Best Inns & Suits	BIP Club	1 credit per night, including discount rates; 2 credits for reservations 10 days in advance	Unlimited time to earn and use
Clubhouse Inn	Best Guest	1 credit per night	1 year to earn, 1 year to use
Cross Country Inn	Traveler's Dozen	1 credit per night	Unlimited time to earn, 1 year to use
Drury Inn	Preferred Customer	1 credit per night	Unlimited time to earn and use
Exel Inn	Insider's Card	1 credit per night	Unlimited time to earn and use
Hawaiian	Coconut Club	1 credit per night, including discount rates	1 year to earn, unlimited
LaQuinta	Returns Club	1 credit per night, including discount rates	Unlimited time to earn, 18 months to use
Masters Economy Inns	Preferred Guest	1 credit per night, including discount rates	By 12/99
Meridien	L'Invitation	1 credit per night	2 years to earn, 1 year to use
Omni	Select Guest	1 credit per night	1 year to earn and use
Sofitel	Exclusive Card ($70 per year) and use	1 credit per night	Unlimited time to earn nights
Susse Chalet	Susse VIP Club ($10 per year)	1 credit per night	Unlimited time to earn, 1 year to use
Vagabond Inns	10th night free	1 credit per night	By 12/98
Wingate	Frequent Travelers Club	1 credit per night	Earn by 10/99, use by 12/99

For **reservation number and web addresses**, see Resource Guide in back of book.

Deals for frequent stayers

MINIMUM WORTHWHILE AWARD			Airline partners	Membership benefits
Credit	Award	Payoff		
10	1 night	10%	—	Late checkout
10	$35 credit	7	—	Car rental discounts, free calls, room upgrade
12	1 night	8.3	—	Car rental discounts, discount rooms, late check out, free calls, free stay for companion
12	1 night	8.3	—	—
12	1 night	8.3	—	Discount rooms, priority reservations, free stay for companion
12	1 night	8.3	—	—
12	1 night	8.3	—	—
10	1 night	10	—	Discount rooms, priority reservations
12	1 night	8.3	—	—
10 time to use	1 night	10	—	Car rental, discount rooms, room upgrade, food/beverage discount
11	1 night	9.1	—	Discount rooms, priority reservations, free stay for companions
9	1 night	11.1	—	Discount rooms, late checkout, free calls, priority reservations, room upgrade
10	1 night	10	—	—
10 night	1 weekend	5	—	Late checkout, priority reservations
12	2 weekend	8.3	—	Discount rooms, late checkout, priority reservations
8	1 night/ 500 miles	12.5	American, Delta, USAir	Late checkout, priority reservations
9	1	11.1	—	Free calls
9	1	11.1	American, Continental	—

too arbitrary. Because discount coupons are so widely available for a variety of travel services, we assigned no value to discount awards.

For most dollar-based programs, the payoff percentages are in the 2 to 5 percent range. That's far below the airline programs, at least for travelers who earn credit by buying cheap coach/economy excursion tickets.

We didn't tabulate the payoffs for nonhotel awards—discount certificates for air tickets, tours, merchandise, and such. But note that they're generally lower than what you'd get in free nights. Where offered, payoff in frequent-flier credit is stingy, too. Since a mile of credit is worth 1 to 2 cents, the 500 miles per stay you get in several programs amounts to $5 to $10. Nonetheless, you may prefer adding mileage to an airline account to accumulating separate hotel credit that you might not be able to use.

Our payoff calculations apply to average travelers and may be quite different for other people. If, say, you normally pay discounted or promotional rates, the payoff of a program that doesn't honor promotional rates is zero. If your average stays are just a day or two, you'll pile up per-stay credit faster than you would by staying at one hotel for extended periods.

The payoff on the hotel-sponsored credit cards is about 1 percent. Since the payoff on airline cards is 1 to 2 percent, most travelers are probably better off with an airline-sponsored card than with a hotel card.

NIGHT-BASED PROGRAMS

The Night-Based Programs table on pages 208 to 209 gives an overview of 18 programs that resemble Southwest's frequent-flier program. The hotel versions operate on a simple "stay x nights, get a free night" formula, or a minor variant of it. They're used mainly by midpriced and budget chains.

Of the night-based programs, only two have airline partners.

Deals for frequent stayers　**211**

Wingate gives you a choice of room or airline credit, and Susse Chalet gives you both hotel and airline credit.

Figuring the payoff for these simple programs is straightforward. It ranges from 7 to 12 percent. Given their emphasis on leisure travel, we valued a free weekend night at a midpriced or budget chain at the same value as an any-day night. In general, the payoff range for the night-based programs is substantially higher than for the more complex, point-based programs.

JUST FOR BELONGING

About half the programs offer at least some worthwhile benefits even if you never earn enough credit for a free stay. The Membership Benefits portions of both Awards and Payoffs tables show the enrollment perks we consider to be of greatest value, either in dollars or convenience: room discounts, free breakfast, late check-out, free local calls, priority reservations (or a special reservation phone line), and such.

Some programs tout all sorts of other features that we consider mere fluff. They range from free coffee or a free newspaper to a "space available" free upgrade that nobody ever seems to get.

Rather than operating a frequent-stay program, some big chains feature "customer-recognition" programs. These don't provide free stays and other cash-value awards but do offer a variety of membership benefits comparable with those we tabulate.

CHOOSING A PROGRAM

Don't forgo a really good hotel discount just to get a little frequent-stay credit. But if you can get the discount and the credit, too—or if a big discount isn't available—the credit can provide at least a modest payoff.

Most travelers will probably find it a bit tougher to decide which frequent-stay program is best for them than to make a similar choice among the airlines:

• For many travelers, the number of participating hotels is critical—if your travels take you to a wide range of destinations, you'll be far better off with a program in which you can earn credit in hundreds of cities worldwide. On the other hand, if your travels are concentrated in just a few destinations, a small chain with convenient locations may well fill your needs.

• Other measures being equal, payoff is probably the most important choice factor. The most generous hotel programs are generally run by the midpriced and budget chains. They give you a free night for every 8 to 12 paid nights—about as big a payoff as you get with a major airline's frequent-flier program. Our tables identify the openhanded and the miserly chains.

• Earning opportunities can also be important—the more chances you get, the better. Among the upscale chains, Hilton and Westin let you earn both hotel and airline credit for the same stay. However, the payoff, even including the airline miles, is lower than that of many other programs.

If you're a relatively infrequent traveler, here are further tips:

• As long as it's free, join the program of any chain where you plan to stay more than two or three times a year. You'll get worthwhile benefits—free local calls, late checkout, and the like—even if you never earn a free night.

• Look for a program that provides an attractive list of benefits you can use without racking up a minimum number of stays (see the tables' Membership Benefits entries) or one that awards frequent-flier mileage that you can add to your airline account.

CHAPTER 19

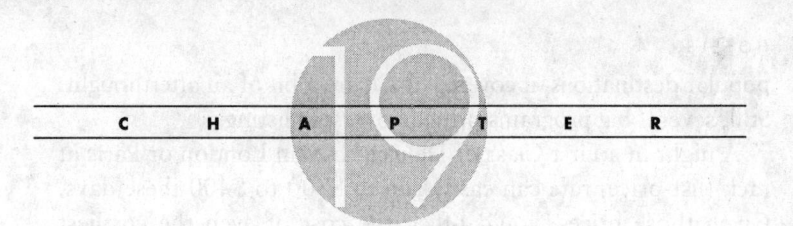

HOTEL DEALS ABROAD

With today's high hotel prices overseas, it's more important than ever to get a good rate. U.S. half-price programs also offer some discounts on rooms in Canada, Mexico, the Caribbean, Europe, and elsewhere; check those programs first. But if you're going to Asia, you'll find the offerings meager. In that case, ask your travel agent to find a wholesale or preferred rate for you.

When you can't get a large discount, smaller ones are often available. But failing even one of those, you can still save by comparing costs from different sources. Check directly with a hotel's reservation desk, through a travel agent's computer-reservation system, or through a U.S.-based hotel representative. Or consider a budget hotel.

FOREIGN HOTELS AT 50 PERCENT OFF

The major half-price programs (see Chapter 15) concentrate on North American and Caribbean hotels. Europe, Asia, and other popular destinations, if covered at all, are a bit of an afterthought. Still, several big programs provide overseas listings.

A night in a First Class or Deluxe hotel in London or Paris at rack (list-price) rate can easily run to $300 to $400 these days. Given those prices, you'd offset the cost of even the costliest half-price programs in just one night. And, of course, your membership fee entitles you to discounts at participating U.S. hotels, too.

Half-price programs operate the same overseas as at home. When you sign up, you get a directory of participating hotels and an ID card. About a month or two before you plan a trip, you call or fax hotels of interest directly, mention the program you belong to, and ask for a room at the half-price rate. The

ALTERNATIVES IN FRANCE

If a French budget motel sounds a bit dreary to you, consider these:

RURAL FRANCE. The French countryside is full of small inns where you can often find accommodations in the same price range as the subbudget chains. Very few of them are listed in guidebooks published in the U.S. The easiest way to find them, almost anywhere in France, is to study the current edition of the Red Michelin Guide. Look for two types of entry:

Hotels listed under the Guide's "quite comfortable" or "modest comfort" symbols often show rates as low as the subbudgets.

Countryside restaurants that are noted as *restaurants avec chambres* can sometimes offer better room deals, although the main business of these establishments is food service.

Many city tourist offices maintain lists of *gîtes* (cottages) available for rent in the nearby countryside. Although rentals are usually by the week, you can sometimes negotiate a deal for a shorter stay.

CITIES. Hotel booking offices, run by the local community or its tourist office, are located in most French cities (as well as in cities throughout the rest of Europe), usually in or near the main rail station. Stop there to check room availability and make a reservation for one of the many inexpensive hotels that use the system.

Hotel deals abroad **215**

hotel will (supposedly) provide one if it doesn't expect to be more than 80 percent full.

When you arrive, you show the program ID and check in. Each membership covers just one room per night. If you need two rooms for a stay, you'll need two memberships.

If the hotel expects to be too full to justify offering a half-price rate, it may counter with a lesser discount, which you're free to accept or reject. Alternatively, you might want to try one of the discount hotel brokers that some programs also list or to check the program's central reservation center. But such less-than-half-off discounts are often available to anyone, program member or not (see Chapter 14).

HALF OF WHAT?

"Half price" seems to be a less precise term for hotels than for airlines and other travel suppliers. Theoretically, you get 50 percent off the rate the hotel regularly offers to other travelers. But in our experience, it doesn't always work that way.

Many hotels offer a range of discounts to seniors, to anybody who can produce a business card, and often even to anyone who walks up to the desk. Rack rates are often inflated to cover those discounts. Only a few travelers who book at peak times pay full price.

A 50 percent discount from a fake rack rate that hardly anybody pays, then, may be less than it seems. But at that, the half-price rate, whether it be 50 percent or only 25 percent less than most travelers pay, is still likely to be the best deal anyone other than a regular corporate customer gets.

Readers occasionally complain that their so-called half-price rate was actually higher than a rate some other guest got without using a program. Always ask about the going rate—and any other discount you might qualify for—before you go for a "half-price" rate.

HOTELS

WHOLESALE DEALS AT ASIAN HOTELS

While the Asian offerings of half-price programs have improved a lot in recent years, they remain pretty thin for some areas. Depending on your destination, you might instead want to try a wholesale agency, basically a tour operator that guarantees suppliers a certain volume of bookings in exchange for price cuts. Travel Interlink and VacationLand are two that are probably fairly typical of the group. (See also Chapter 14.) Several years ago, we compared rack rates with what the wholesalers were offering for hotels in six Asian cities: Bali, Bangkok, Hong Kong, Kuala Lumpur, Singapore, and Tokyo. (Both agencies had deals in other major Asian cities as well.) The discount agents' rates on standard rooms averaged about 35 percent less than rack rate, but discounts at some hotels ran up to 50 percent, occasionally a bit more. (A later follow-up for Bangkok and Hong Kong included those two agencies plus a third, Absolute Asia. The results were similar.)

There was a broad choice of hotels—from Superior Tourist, just below the middle of the ratings of the Official Hotel Guide, through Superior Deluxe. Individual agencies may use a different classification in their brochures, so it's useful to have some knowledge of the hotels in each city you're visiting, from the OHG or a guidebook, before you call a discount agency.

When arranging your room, tell the agency where you're going, when, and any preferences for location or specific facilities. If you already have one or two favorite hotels, ask what deals the agency might have there. Otherwise, ask what's available in your price range.

You reserve in advance and prepay by check; neither Travel Interlink nor VacationLand accepts charge cards. The wholesale agency sends you a voucher that you present on arrival at each hotel. (In some cases, the vouchers are sent directly to the hotel.) Cancel well before your departure and you get a full refund, less a modest

Hotel deals abroad **217**

fee; cancel closer to departure and you forfeit the cost of one night's lodging. If you'd rather have your own travel agent make arrangements for you, note that VacationLand's listings are commissionable.

One warning: As with any prepaid lodging, once you get past the cancellation deadline, you're locked into the deal. Book through a wholesale agency only if your travel plans are firm and you know the hotel where you'll be staying. For other situations, a preferred rate—even though not quite such a good price—may turn out to be a better overall deal.

ANY OTHER DISCOUNTS TO BE HAD?

If you can't get a 50 percent discount or the 35 percent-and-more reductions we've described above, do you have any other recourse? Try aiming for at least a 20 to 25 percent discount off rack rates. Here are some other options:

- Try to get preferred rates—deeply discounted corporate rates (see Chapter 14).
- Discount through a tour operator's package (see Chapter 2).
- Weekend, holiday, and off-season sales promotions run by hotels and resorts.
- Use senior discounts. As in the U.S., hotels abroad may offer discounts for travelers of even not-so-mature years; ask before you book.

LIST-PRICE BARGAINS

Even dedicated discount shoppers are sometimes forced to reserve a room at rack rate. In those cases, you can still save yourself some money by comparing rates among different hotels in the same location. There are generally three ways to find out if a room is available—and what it will cost—in overseas hotels that don't have U.S. reservation numbers:

218 HOTELS

Reserve by computer. Many hotels abroad are listed in the computer-reservation systems that travel agents use. Rooms at those hotels can be booked in the same way you'd book a domestic hotel. For most agencies, the commission on a hotel booking for a few nights would never cover the costs of extensive comparison shopping. But once you've identified your preferred hotels, a travel agent will probably at least be willing to check the prices in a reservation computer—especially if you then book the accommodations through the agent.

Contact the hotel directly. International phone calls can be expensive and cumbersome, especially with time-zone and language barriers—but they may be your best bet. Although fax messages are convenient, they may be ignored by hotel personnel when received from an unknown individual traveler.

Check hotel reps. Many overseas hotels are represented in the U.S. by one or more hotel representatives, independent booking services that will sell you a room at whichever facilities they represent in the location and time period you desire.

Overseas reps are the least attractive option: You often pay more than rack rate. However, if you feel that the convenience is worth the extra cost, you may want to book your overseas lodgings that way. Many reps list their rates in the computer-reservation systems used by travel agents and then book overseas hotels through those systems. (A hotel is often listed more than once in a reservation system at different rates—in the hotel's own listing and through one or more representatives.)

Reps can usually issue immediate space and rate confirmations by phone. Most require a deposit (the cost of one to three nights), or a charge-card number, to confirm reservations. Some require full prepayment. Some reps may charge extra for last-minute reservations (booking one day ahead, say). Most impose some limits on cancellation. You're usually charged one night for a no-show, but some reps charge for three nights. If you've

Hotel deals abroad **219**

booked resort accommodations during high season, the cancellation policy may be more stringent than for low season.

Payment procedures also vary. Some reps accept payment directly. You either remit payment for one to three nights as a deposit or prepay the entire stay. In most cases, you can pay by cash or charge card; a few reps accept personal checks. The advantage of going through a rep who takes payment is that your deposit is refundable from a U.S. organization in case you cancel. Also, a few reps who work that way accept the U.S. dollar payment converted at the exchange rate in effect at the time of booking and honor that rate regardless of any subsequent currency exchange fluctuations.

Other hotel reps obtain charge-card guarantee information and forward it to the hotel. Your rate is computed and paid in foreign currency at the time you check out; any refunds due you have to come through the hotel.

YOUR PERSONAL BEST BUY

Your travel agent or your company's travel department can help you narrow your list of hotels or find the names and phone numbers of reps to call for information about hotel prices and room availability. You could also consult a copy of the Hotel and Travel Index, Official Hotel Guide, or Star Service, available in large libraries as well as at travel agencies.

Regardless of how you make the reservation, be sure to get the information: confirmation number, deposit requirements, guarantees, credit or charge cards accepted, and cancellation provisions.

BUDGET MOTELS

If you're looking for efficiency rather than charm, European budget motels are a great bargain. In the U.K., there's the

Granada Inns chain, located next to Granada gas stations and restaurants along the motorways. Even cheaper are the Little Chef Lodges, affiliated with a U.K. fast-food chain.

You'll find more budget-motel chains in France, however, than in any other European country. They come in several flavors: subbudget and something a notch or two above.

There's no real U.S. counterpart to the French subbudget hotel. At somewhere near 100 square feet, the rooms are less than half as big as those you find at even the bottom-end U.S. chains, and they're not air-conditioned. You get one standard double bed (with, perhaps, an overhead bunk or a foldout mini-single as well). Bathrooms are tiny, with a shower down the hall. Check-in counters may be open for only a few hours in the morning and again in the evening. (At other times, guests can check themselves in automatically with a charge card.) The rooms are spartan, but they're clean and efficient.

You must go upmarket two levels to find something close to the U.S. budget motel. Chains such as Climat de France and Campanile approximate what you find at Motel 6 or Hampton Inn. Even then, the rooms are smaller than those found in U.S. chains—but cost more. The bath is a bit more like what you're used to, but air conditioning is still relatively rare.

CHAPTER 20

VILLAS, CONDOS, AND OTHER RENTALS

Planning to vacation in one spot for a week or more? Consider a rental. You can get more space than in a hotel, save money, or both. A rental can also make for a more interesting vacation.

Vacation rentals range from rustic one-room cottages to deluxe houses with private swimming pools to estates that can accommodate a dozen or more vacationers. Some units are designed specifically as vacation rentals; others are owner-occupied and rented or exchanged only occasionally.

You can book your accommodation through an agency or a web site. While some sites merely augment the standard rental-agency catalogs, other sites let you arrange rentals or house-swaps directly with owners.

RENTAL PLUSES

Rentals provide an ideal way to "hang out" in a destination area —they're fine for vacations on which you don't have a long must-do checklist or plan to see three countries in 10 days:

Room cost. You can often save a bundle if you're willing to occupy a rental as you would a hotel room. Many one-bedroom rentals, for example, include two double beds in a bedroom and a convertible sofa in the living area. That one rental could accommodate six people—a party that would require two or three hotel rooms.

Space. Alternatively, a rental allows you to enjoy a lot of extra space at about the same cost per person as a hotel. Many travelers especially like having completely separate living and sleeping quarters.

Living costs. A rental with a kitchen lets you cut food costs. Preparing some of your own meals is a good bit cheaper than eating in restaurants, especially for families with kids. You'll often have a washer and dryer, too.

Convenience. Rentals frequently include access to private yards, pools, and other recreational facilities. In resort areas, rentals may be handier to beaches or ski slopes than hotels, and they usually have free on-site parking. You can live and dress as informally as you like, too.

Local color. Resort hotels often cocoon you from interaction with the local community. In a rental, you can live like a local. In an overseas rental, you can—often must—hone your language skills as you cope with village or city life.

RENTAL MINUSES

Vacation rentals have a downside, too:

Minimum service. For some travelers, a resort hotel's cushy amenities—daily maid service, fresh towels, evening turndown, cable TV with HBO or pay-per-view, on-site restaurants and entertainment, recreational facilities, room service—are what make a vacation enjoyable. Even if your rental provides access to

Villas, condos, and other rentals **223**

some of those services, you usually have to pay extra. Many rentals don't have TV or, if they do, they don't have cable. Many rentals aren't air-conditioned, even in areas where hotels are.

Extra work. Cooking meals, making beds, doing laundry, and cleaning aren't everyone's idea of a vacation.

Uncertainty. In the absence of quality standards, you often can't be sure of what you're buying. Your only protection is whatever screening the rental agency may have done.

Inflexibility. Rentals typically lock you in. You have to reserve and prepay the full price far in advance. If you find your rental unsatisfactory, you can't just pay for the first night, check out, and move elsewhere.

Still, there are ways around most of these problems. Want housekeeping services, on-site restaurants, or some other amenity? Look for a rental that provides them as part of the package or as an option. Worried about what you'll find when you arrive? Check a rental with someone who has rented there before. Or rather than take a chance on someone's remote cabin, look for a large complex that caters to short-term renters, with an on-site manager.

RENTAL MECCAS

Most vacation-rental action centers around a few popular areas:

Resorts. U.S. vacation rentals seem to be concentrated in central Florida, around the Walt Disney World complex; in California, Colorado, New England, and Utah ski centers; and in Hawaii.

Beaches. Outside the U.S., you find big rental concentrations in most highly developed warm-water beach areas, especially in the Caribbean, Mexico, and the coasts of Spain.

Big cities. Rental apartments are becoming increasingly popular as hotel alternatives in the world's primary tourist cities—London, New York, Paris, San Francisco, and such.

224   HOTELS

Rural Europe. Rentals are also attractive in the European countryside. The biggest concentrations are in France (especially the Dordogne and Provence), northern Italy, and Britain.

A RENTERS' WHO'S WHO

Chances are you'll arrange a rental through an agency that specializes in them.

WHOLESALE BOOKING AGENCIES. These agencies focus primarily on developing extensive rental listings. Some large wholesalers publish elaborate, full-color brochures. Typically, wholesalers provide commissions to retail travel agencies that book their rentals. Some wholesalers also act as retailers (see the following paragraph).

RETAIL BOOKING AGENCIES. Along with rentals, these agencies sometimes arrange airline tickets and rental cars as well. Some retailers develop a portion of their own listings; others simply sell from a wholesale catalog. For European rentals, quite a few U.S. retail booking agencies use wholesalers based in Europe.

Like a full-service travel agency, a good broker should be able to provide professional advice about destination areas and individual rental properties. Quite a few retail agencies now maintain web sites, where you can view rentals and check prices.

TRAVEL CLUBS AND HALF-PRICE HOTEL PROGRAMS. Both may offer vacation rentals exclusively or include vacation rentals in their larger mix of accommodations (see Chapter 15). Half-price programs may claim to offer "discounts" on vacation rentals. But since many rental properties have no official published rate, you can't tell if a quoted rate is really discounted. Clubs and half-price programs charge annual membership dues or charge for directories.

OTHER RENTAL CHANNELS. Some tour operators sell package tours that include vacation-rental accommodations. House-exchange agencies list houses and apartments for exchange. You

Villas, condos, and other rentals **225**

generally pay to be listed in their periodic lists or to receive them. Realtors in popular vacation areas often handle local vacation rentals as a sideline; we don't list those in our directory. You can also make your own arrangements (see "Arranging Your Rental" on page 226).

CRACKING THE CODE

No matter how you rent, your main source of information about individual properties is likely to be a brochure. Whether it's a simple photocopied tear sheet or an elaborate, full-color catalog, the brochure normally at least lists an accommodation's location, number of rooms, number and type of beds, and kitchen facilities. Many include photographs, drawings, or floor plans.

But many brochures overaccentuate the positive. Here's how to decipher them:

• Concentrate on the hard facts and examine photos closely. Clever wording can transform a shack into a quaint cabin, and a wide-angle lens can make a broom closet look like a ballroom.

• The specified number of people a rental "sleeps" is often more appropriate to an army barracks than a comfortable vaca-

HOUSE EXCHANGE

Switching houses with another family opens you to some risks, mainly of damage to your property. The organizations that list houses for exchange take no responsibility for the behavior of temporary tenants; you do your own screening and take your own precautions. Be sure your homeowner's insurance covers you for any damage a house-exchange visitor might do, as well as for liability if a visitor is injured in your house. Securely store anything you don't want a visitor to use. At a minimum, that means a locked closet or storeroom, but it's safer to cart your things to a storage locker. When renting, make sure the contract calls for tenants paying the replacement value of anything damaged. Ask for an upfront security deposit, too.

HOTELS

226 HOTELS

tion property. Unless you're willing to stack your travel party like cordwood, judge your space needs by the number of rooms and the numbers and types of beds, not the number of people the brochure says you can sleep.

• Assume that you won't find anything that isn't promised specifically. That's especially important in Europe. If a brochure doesn't specify a shower, say, you're apt to have nothing more than a tub.

ARRANGING YOUR RENTAL

As with resort hotels, vacation-rental rates go up and down seasonally. Peak summer season in the European countryside is extremely short—often just August and the latter part of July.

Some accommodations offer reduced rates for long-term rentals (a month or more) or for large groups. Feel free to haggle—list prices often aren't firm. Rentals may involve a few other idiosyncrasies, too:

WEB RENTALS

To find a homelike setting for your holiday, call up *www. vacationspot.com.* The site lists more than 30,000 vacation rental properties worldwide, with photos, price ranges, and accommodation details. You can search for your spot by region or by interests, including "family fun," "skiing getaways," and "secluded and romantic."

• Though rental agencies are paid by property owners, many vacation-rental brokers demand an up-front payment—as much as $50—as a "registration" fee or as a charge for brochures. You can usually apply that fee to the rental cost.

• Beyond normally having to prepay the full rent months in advance, even on fairly long rentals, you may also have to prepay for bedding or maid service. The rental agent may ask for an additional cleaning or security deposit, too. Cancellation fees may be stiff, especially if you cancel close to the occupancy date. *Consumer Reports Travel Letter* strongly

Villas, condos, and other rentals **227**

recommends trip-cancellation insurance for any vacation rental (see Chapter 22).

• Many brokers don't accept charge cards; you have to write a check.

• A vacation rental usually requires a long lead time—as much as six months ahead for popular destinations at peak season. Of course, most agencies will work with shorter notice—if space is still available—but you may have to pay extra for phone calls or express delivery of paperwork.

• Many vacation rentals require a minimum stay of a week. You may also have to rent on a fixed weekly schedule—Saturday to Saturday is the most common—that may not suit your itinerary. On the other hand, during the low season rental properties may be glad to get your business on your terms.

• Moving into a vacation rental is often a bit of a hassle. You might have to make an appointment with a property manager, local agent, or neighbor to obtain the keys, turn on the utilities, and arrange phone service. Not all rentals come equipped with linens.

• If you're swapping homes with someone, you have to coordinate schedules more or less exactly with some other family. You're also entrusting much of your personal property to that other family's care. Some travelers therefore prefer to exchange only with families they already know or with those who belong to a group that promises a close match in interests.

DO-IT-YOURSELF RENTALS

Rentals typically involve several markups—the owner, wholesaler, and retailer all get their cuts. You can avoid some of that markup by arranging your own rental:

• Classified ads in magazines and newspapers offer apartments, cottages, and houses as vacation rentals. Budget guidebooks may list rental accommodations as well as hotels. And English weekend newspapers, which you can find at foreign paper stands, typically contain classified ads for a wide variety of vacation rentals—extensive listings for the U.K. and France, spotty listings for many other countries.

• Tourist offices in some localities maintain lists of nearby vacation rentals. You can write ahead for those lists or get them when you arrive. In Europe, we've found on-the-spot country-side vacation rentals available at very low prices (except during July and August).

• Some property owners list individual rentals on their own web sites. You can track them down by searching for a specific destination area plus the word "rental."

• In an unfamiliar destination, you may want to wait until after you arrive to arrange a vacation rental. Stay in a hotel for the first day or two, giving yourself enough time to scout out the rental options; then make a deal through a local realtor or the manager of a large rental complex. For a last-minute or short-term rental, an apartment-style or all-suite hotel can provide many of the same advantages as a rental.

BEWARE THE TIMESHARE TRAP

Many of those "free-trip" come-ons you get in the mail—or by phone, fax, and even e-mail—are from timeshare promoters who will foot the bill for your weekend just for the chance to give you a hard sell. Here's the pitch: For a modest price, you can "own" a luxury condo in some fabulous beach or ski area for a week every year (or even every other year). You may even be able to trade your timeshare for a week in some other equally fabulous area, even overseas. But watch out: Timeshare ownership may become a trap.

Timeshares are a refinement of the condo idea. In a condo, a

Villas, condos, and other rentals **229**

building is carved up into individually owned units; in a time-share, the ownership of those units is subdivided into weekly time slots. As with a condo, you pay the purchase price. Then you add a prorated share of the maintenance costs of the individual apartment and the building's grounds.

However, timeshares are not all alike. With some, you buy a specified week each year; with others, you have a floating time slot. You may get an actual deed to a specific occupancy right. Or you may simply join a "vacation club" that promises you space every year.

PAYMENTS AND HEADACHES. With your timeshare, you usually get a chance to join (and pay a fee to) one of two big international timeshare-exchange networks: RCI or Interval International. Through either, you can trade time with other exchange members throughout the world—your week in a ski area, say, for a week in the Caribbean or Europe. The deal may sound okay, but here are the drawbacks:

Owning a week in your own vacation condo may not be any cheaper than simply renting. With maintenance and cleaning fees, membership in RCI or Interval International, and other miscellaneous fees and charges, your week can easily cost $500 to $600.

Worse, it's almost impossible to sell. When you try, you're apt to be competing with the developer, who is often still selling units in your program. Owners who try to walk away lose their investment—while the timeshare's maintenance fees continue to mount. And a foreclosure may put a blot on the owner's credit record.

Once you've bought in, you're again in competition with the developer. When you try to claim a floating time slot, you may find that the developer aims to rent the most desirable weeks to nonowners instead. Some developers actually *oversell* a timeshare, figuring that a certain percentage of owners won't find a suitable time to visit.

If you try to rent out your time slot on your own, the developer

230 HOTELS

REAL-LIFE RENTALS

Consumer Reports Travel Letter staffers have sampled vacation rentals in such diverse locations as Hawaii's Kona coast, the Northern California coast, Upper Michigan, the Yosemite area, Cape Cod, London, Brittany, Florence, Oxford, Paris, Scotland, and Waikiki. Here are a few lessons we learned:

• Assembly-line condos such as you find in Hawaii present few surprises or challenges. You get more space than you'd get in a hotel but fewer services. Housekeeping is available if you want it.

• One-of-a-kind cottages or private apartments, on the other hand, can be quirky. At their best, they're superior to any but the most elaborate hotel suites—for privacy, peace, and living space. At their worst, they're weird—a Paris apartment, for example, where most of the beds were on "mezzanines" reached by climbing steep, spindly ladders. Or a Cape Cod "cottage" that turned out to be a minimally converted garage, with cement floor and screened-over garage door.

• Be prepared to cope like a home-owner if something goes wrong—the person responsible for the rental may not always be available. At least one person in your group should be handy with basic tools and able to improvise fixes out of coathanger wire or the like. Never head for a vacation rental without at least a screwdriver and pliers. Also, be prepared for the challenge of figuring out how to run appliances for which the manuals have long since disappeared.

• If you plan any serious cooking, take some of your own utensils or figure on buying some. In all our vacation rentals, we've yet to find a sharp kitchen knife or a frying pan with a flat bottom.

• Vacation rentals other than city-center apartments usually require a car. That often means a rental car—which can be very expensive in France or Italy.

• Rural rentals often have no phones. If you can't afford to be out of touch, take (or rent) a cellular phone for the duration of your trip.

may try to block you—with obstacles as broad as a flat ban on rentals by individual owners or as small as refusing to have someone on hand to give the keys to a renter. You also have very little control over the property you supposedly own.

BUYING OR SELLING. If despite those problems you still like the timeshare idea, buy a resale unit from an individual owner. There

Villas, condos, and other rentals **231**

are many more sellers than buyers, so you should be able to drive a hard bargain. In some cases, you might even be able to take ownership merely by assuming the current owner's long-term maintenance obligation.

To find a motivated private seller, check the ads in newsletters and local papers in resort areas. You might also nose around some of the more attractive timeshare complexes talking to current owners, checking bulletin boards, and looking for notices. A few real estate brokers also specialize in timeshares. An outfit called Triwest runs periodic timeshare auctions; call 800 423-6377 to find out when the next one will be held.

PART SIX

TRAVEL SAVVY

21 Overseas travel strategist 233

22 Travel insurance.........................245

23 Phoning home............................255

24 Staying healthy 261

CHAPTER 21

OVERSEAS TRAVEL STRATEGIST

Interested in a smooth trip abroad? Take a few preparatory steps: Check State Department advisories for any cautionary information on the region you're visiting. Make arrangements for access to cash overseas. For ready cash, always carry some traveler's checks, perhaps in the currencies of the places you plan to visit. Consider whether it's worthwhile to pursue tax refunds of your foreign purchases. Check out customs allowances if you plan on heavy shopping.

AVOIDING HAZARDS ABROAD

The Centers for Disease Control and Prevention of the U.S. Public Health Service issues lists of countries suffering outbreaks of such diseases as cholera, plague, and yellow fever. Sanitation scores for cruise ships are available from the U.S.P.H.S. Vessel Sanitation Program of the National Center for Environmental Health. The Federal Aviation Administration lists foreign governments that don't comply with established standards for safety oversight of civil aviation. (See Chapter 24.)

Similarly, the U.S. State Department alerts traveling Americans to possible risks abroad with information in two categories:

Travel warnings. These are issued when the State Department decides to recommend that Americans avoid travel to a certain country. The basis for such a recommendation includes unusual security and/or travel conditions—for instance, the potential for unexpected detention, unstable political conditions, or serious health problems.

Consular information sheets. Available for every country of the world, these include such information as the location of the U.S. embassy or consulate, unusual immigration practices, health conditions, minor political disturbances, unusual currency, entry regulations, crime and security information, and drug penalties.

Any instabilities in a country that aren't severe enough to warrant a warning may be included in an optional section of the consular information sheets called "Areas of Instability." Once in a while, that section will also restate any embassy advice given to official employees. Otherwise, the information sheets generally don't include advice.

State Department policy requires that any information that's routinely made available to embassy employees must be made available to the traveling public. But in response to criticism from the travel industry and the General Accounting Office in 1991, Consular Affairs took steps to specify whether an advisory concerns a threat to the general traveling public or just to diplomatic personnel. It has also made consular information and warnings more accessible: You can now get the information by fax or on a free electronic bulletin board instead of by phoning or writing.

Travel agents can get the full text (and for some services, an index) of the consular information sheets and travel warnings through all the major computer-reservation systems.

Overseas travel strategist **235**

Check the announcements for any location you're considering visiting, or ask a travel agent to do so. (Each month, *Consumer Reports Travel Letter* publishes a list of countries for which some sort of warning is in effect.)

If your trip is already booked and you cancel because of a travel advisory that you feel is serious, you risk losing any deposits and being liable for any cancellation fees. Your ability to recoup losses often depends on the policies of the carriers with which you've booked your trip. Trip cancellation insurance may not reimburse you if you cancel because of a travel advisory. (See Chapter 22.)

MONEY MATTERS

Developing a foreign-currency strategy is an important part of trip planning. Here's how to minimize exchange costs:

• Put big expenditures—tickets, hotels, car rentals, and the like—on your charge card. You thus save the percentage point or two of the price that you'd otherwise lose in currency conversion. You also get the protection of the card's chargeback provisions and (with some cards) an extra guarantee on your purchases.

• Use an automatic teller machine (ATM) card for incidental cash whenever you can (see below).

• Carry a small amount of money in traveler's checks just as a backup.

ATM CARDS. If your ATM card works in the Cirrus or Plus network at home, you may be able to withdraw cash from foreign-bank ATMs that belong to the same network. Your withdrawal will be converted at the interbank exchange rate—the "wholesale" rate that banks use for large-scale financial transactions.

That's quite an advantage. If you exchange currency or traveler's checks at a bank exchange counter, you get a retail rate that's often 3 to 5 percent less favorable. At many banks, an additional

TRAVEL SAVVY

fee—per transaction, per check, or a percentage of the transaction—can add another 2 to 5 percent to your cost.

The expense can be even worse if you exchange at hotels and nonbank exchange counters when banks are closed. Foreign cash advances on credit cards or charge cards typically incur interest (charged from the date of cash advance until you pay your bill, regardless of any grace period on purchases), a per-transaction fee, or a percentage of the advance (up to 3 percent).

Overseas, Cirrus and Plus work exactly as ATMs work at home: You punch in your personal identification number (PIN) and the amount of withdrawal (in local currency). The machine issues the currency, and your home account is debited automatically. As in the U.S., the foreign bank may or may not impose a fee. The other possible extra is a per-use fee your bank may impose for using an ATM elsewhere on the network (usually $2 to $3 per transaction, $5 at a few banks). Those fees can add up, though, so plan ahead to minimize the number of transactions you make.

Here are some tips to minimize ATM hassles:

• ATMs outside North America often do not accept PINs longer than four digits. If your PIN is longer, ask your bank for a different number.

• Keypads on many foreign ATMs have numbers only. If your PIN contains letters, use the standard letter-number correspondences from U.S. phones to convert.

• Don't worry about a language problem—most foreign ATMs affiliated with Cirrus or Plus provide instructions in English.

• Overseas ATMs may not give you a choice of accounts to tap. If you want to withdraw abroad, make sure funds are available in your primary checking account.

• However, finding a participating ATM may be difficult, and your card may not work in all locations. Banks in a few important tourist countries still aren't set up to handle ATM debit

Overseas travel strategist **237**

withdrawals—travelers from the U.S. can get cash only by using a credit card (and paying interest on the withdrawal as a cash advance). But the situation is getting better, as both Cirrus (MasterCard) and Plus (Visa) extend their ATM networks. Both systems now publish directories of overseas locations, which should be available from the issuing bank.

Caution is usually still the watchword with foreign ATM technology. Don't rely solely on ATMs to replenish your cash supply while you're traveling, unless you're sure (from a prior trip) that your card will work.

TRAVELER'S CHECKS. Widely accepted in hard-currency countries, traveler's checks offer protection against loss or theft. Most provide worldwide refunds and emergency services if your checks are lost or stolen.

You can purchase traveler's checks at a bank or thrift, a credit union, an American Automobile Association office (checks are free to members), an American Express Travel Service Office, or a currency-exchange service such as Thomas Cook or Ruesch International. Fees vary, but the average is 1 to 2 percent of your check purchase. (Two-thirds of American Express offices don't charge for traveler's checks.)

American Express and Visa also offer two-signature traveler's checks. When a couple buys, both sign. Then, the check can be cashed by either person. Two-signature checks are handy: A couple doesn't need to decide ahead of time how many checks each person is likely to need.

AmEx charges more for its two-signature checks than for regular checks. Visa says it charges member banks the same price for its two-signature checks as for regular ones, but that it can't control what the banks charge their customers.

PLASTIC CHECKS. Visa's TravelMoney card, available at U.S. banks, is meant to compete with traveler's checks. You prepay the selling bank as much as you want plus a 1.5 percent fee, then use the card as you would an ordinary debit card at Visa/Plus ATMs throughout the world. As with ATM withdrawals, you get a good exchange rate.

The 1.5 percent fee is more than you typically pay for traveler's checks, but with TravelMoney you get a much better exchange rate than you do with paper checks. Overall, you probably come out a bit ahead. You can also cut your chance of losses by buying two or more cards, so that if one is lost or stolen, the others are still valid.

What the advantage might be over ordinary ATM cards or charge cards is a tougher question. Visa apparently thinks that some travelers will like the idea of limiting what they can spend to the money tied up in the card, rather than dipping into their bank accounts with an ATM or building up charge-card debt through cash advances.

TRAVELER'S CHECKS (FOREIGN CURRENCY). If you have to cash a U.S. dollar traveler's check overseas at a hotel, restaurant, store, or nonbank exchange office, you can lose 10 to 20 percent on the exchange rate and fees. That's why many savvy travelers buy some of their traveler's checks in foreign currency.

It pays to shop around. Three channels handle foreign-currency transactions: banks with foreign-exchange offices, foreign-currency exchange services, and travel agents. Foreign-currency checks are a good idea if:

• You know you'll arrive in a foreign country at a time when exchange offices are closed.

• You don't want to carry a lot of foreign cash, don't want the bother of exchanging U.S. dollar traveler's checks at a bank every day or so, and don't want to charge purchases.

• You want to lock in the exchange rate at the time you buy checks. But don't overbuy—you're apt to lose a bit of money when you change leftover checks back into U.S. dollars.

Be aware that foreign-currency checks don't let you avoid exchange losses. You still take a hit; the only change is in where

Overseas travel strategist **239**

you take it. When you buy foreign-currency checks from a U.S. source, you lose about as much as when you exchange dollar checks overseas. There's another problem, too. Overseas hotels, restaurants, and even local banks occasionally refuse to accept local-currency traveler's checks.

HOTEL MONEY EXCHANGE. Holders of Diners Club cards can exchange up to $1,000 per week for local currency at participating Inter-Continental hotels around the world. You get the bank rate, less a service charge of 4 percent. That's only a bit worse than you get at a bank, and it's a much better deal than you usually get at a hotel desk. The service is handy and relatively inexpensive if you're in a country where you can't use an ATM or if you need to pick up some foreign currency when banks are closed.

OTHER CURRENCY SERVICES. Foreign-payment services are also available through large banks, exchange services, and travel agents. Upon receipt of your U.S. payment in check or money order, a bank draft or wire transfer is issued in local currency to the foreign hotel, air, rail, or other travel company you specify. (By making your deposit or even prepaying the full amount in the local currency, you may be able to save yourself some money if the dollar's exchange rate weakens by the time the bills are rendered.) Ruesch International and Thomas Cook both offer check and wire-transfer services at modest fees.

It's also a good idea to carry a small amount of the local currency with you for transportation, phone calls, and incidentals on arrival. Most airports abroad have exchange booths, but you may not get the best exchange rate. U.S. exchange offices can also sell you foreign currency before your trip.

VAT REFUNDS—MAYBE

Travelers who shop abroad are supposed to be able to get a refund of the value-added tax (VAT) that's added to the retail price of merchandise in most European countries. You can save a good deal—VAT accounts for as much as one-fourth of an item's retail selling price. But there are stiff minimum-purchase requirements.

Global Refund (formerly Europe Tax-free Shopping—ETS), run by Europe's largest tax-refund specialist, helps American tourists reclaim the value-added tax (VAT) added to the price of most overseas purchases. (The new name reflects an expansion to Canada and Singapore, with several other Asian countries targeted for future expansion.)

Participating merchants will display a blue and silver "Tax Free for Tourists" sign or sticker (in English) in the window or on the door. (The new Global Refund logo is similar to the old ETS logo.) When you finish shopping in each store, you ask for a Tax-Free Shopping Cheque for the amount of the tax refund.

You have your refund check stamped by a customs officer when you leave the country—and since you must show your purchases to a customs official, keep them handy in your carry-on baggage.

Then you redeem the check at a Global Refund desk, located at most major gateway airports. In most cases, you can request the refund in the form of local currency, U.S. dollars, or a credit to your charge card. There are three possibilities:

• For countries within the European Economic Community, you get your refund at a Global Refund desk after you've passed through departure customs in the last country you visit before returning to the U.S.

• In non-EEC countries, you receive your refund when you leave each country; ask about local procedures.

• You may also request that you get your refund after you return home, by mail or as a charge-card credit.

In almost all countries, you must make a minimum purchase in each transaction to be eligible for a refund. For the most part, the minimum is under $100. However, minimums are high enough in Switzerland ($340), France ($210), Italy ($180),

Overseas travel strategist **241**

Singapore ($172), The Netherlands ($160), Canada and Greece ($150), and Belgium and Hungary ($145) to mean that many tourists may not qualify for a refund. For more information, call Global Refund, 800 566-9828, or visit their web site, *www. globalrefund.com*.

Take note of three pitfalls:

• The minimum purchase you must make to qualify for a refund typically applies to all the goods you buy during one shopping session (one visit to one store). In Italy and Luxembourg, however, it applies per individual item. If you go to more than one store or revisit a store, the minimum applies separately to each shopping session.

• Global Refund deducts as much as 20 percent of the refund as a handling fee (the percentage may go down on large refunds).

• Many of the goods you might be tempted to buy in Europe are cheaper in the U.S.

Any visitors to Europe can take advantage of VAT refunds on merchandise they buy. But tourists aren't eligible for VAT refunds on the travel *services* they use while vacationing. People who travel on business, on the other hand, can get refunds of the VAT charged on hotel, restaurant, and rental-car bills in some countries.

The paperwork for refunds is complex and exacting. Even big companies generally rely on a few VAT-refund specialists, which typically handle all the details in exchange for a 12 to 50 percent cut of the refunds. If you spend just a few hundred dollars a year abroad, the rebate probably isn't worth the hassle, either to you or to a VAT-refund specialist. But if you spend several thousand dollars a year, a refund should repay the effort.

BAGGAGE LIABILITY

If an airline loses or damages your checked or carry-on baggage on a domestic trip, its liability to you is limited to $1,250 per person. The limit applies to flights on a plane seating more than 60 and to flights on a smaller plane included on the same ticket with a flight on a larger plane. On international trips, maximum baggage compensation is set by treaty at $20 a kilogram of checked baggage weight (about $9 a pound). The airline is liable only for depreciated value, not replacement value or original purchase price.

The U.S. limit of $1,250 in depreciated value will probably cover most ordinary baggage containing clothing and personal-care items. The international limit, however, is grossly inadequate. With a typical 20-pound suitcase, for example, the claim allowance of $180 would hardly begin to cover the possessions in most travelers' baggage. But the U.S. Department of Transportation (DOT) says that claims are seldom based on actual weight. Most carriers serving the U.S. have filed tariffs stating that rather than weighing every bag at check-in, they will assume that every lost or damaged bag weighed the maximum that they will accept, usually 32 kilos (around 70 pounds). Thus, the international liability limit for most airlines serving the U.S. (both U.S. and foreign carriers) is a flat $640 per bag (32 kilos times $20), regardless of what a bag weighed.

To protect yourself, cover the difference between the value of your personal effects and the maximum airline payment with insurance. Possibilities include a year-round personal-property policy, insurance purchased as a policy or offered by your charge card, or excess-valuation coverage bought from the airline.

Note, by the way, that DOT has no authority to force airlines to reimburse you for lost baggage. The law only states the liability limit; it doesn't provide for enforcement. Most airlines voluntarily accept valid claims up to the maximum amount. When an airline refuses, the best recourse is probably small-claims court.

Baggage is delayed far more often than lost. Though the airlines aren't required to give you anything if that happens, some offer free kits of supplies to tide you over. (As insurance, pack

Overseas travel strategist **243**

what you need for 48 hours, including small valuables, keys, travel documents, and medicines, in your carry-on luggage.)

An airline may also offer to reimburse you for the cost of personal-care products plus a few basic clothing items (shirts, underwear). But if you expect reimbursement, don't buy anything without prior authorization from the airline and save all your receipts. If the delay drags on a day or more, ask the airline to authorize additional purchases.

Always negotiate your baggage problems with the airline on which you arrived. If another airline is involved—either in tracing the baggage or paying for it—the airline on which you arrived will initiate the necessary procedures.

GETTING THROUGH CUSTOMS

Here are a few customs guidelines for overseas travelers:

• If you've been abroad for at least 48 hours and are returning to the U.S., you may bring $400 worth of personal or household articles with you duty-free ($800 if you're coming from American Samoa, Guam, or the U.S. Virgin Islands; there is no time limitation if returning from Mexico or the Virgin Islands). Beyond that, you must pay a flat 10 percent duty on the next $1,000 worth (5 percent from U.S. possessions) and various duty rates for any additional items.

• The duty-free goods can't include more than 100 cigars (non-Cuban), 200 cigarettes (one carton), and one liter of wine, beer, or liquor (none if you are under age 21; some states have other restrictions). Items that may require a permit or license, or that may be restricted, include food, drugs, and certain items not approved by the U.S. Food and Drug Administration; fruits, plants, vegetables and their byproducts; meat and poultry; pets and wildlife; trademarked items (certain cameras, watches, perfumes); lottery tickets; firearms; ammunition; and hazardous materials.

TRAVEL SAVVY

244 TRAVEL SAVVY

• Keep receipts for anything you purchase. If you've spent more than $1,400, you must list in writing all articles acquired on your trip and what you paid for them. It's also wise to carry receipts for any foreign-made articles you take on your trip, to prove that you didn't buy them abroad on the present trip.

• Gifts under $200, except perfume and tobacco, may be mailed duty-free to friends or relatives (the limit is also $200 from U.S. possessions). Postal laws, however, don't allow you to ship alcoholic beverages.

• If you take out of or bring into the U.S. more than $10,000 in currency, you must file a form with U.S. Customs.

• Items designed for personal use, including souvenirs purchased in other countries, can be brought duty-free into most foreign countries (a verbal declaration may be required). Other items may be restricted or prohibited; check with the appropriate consulate before you go if you have questions.

For more information, write the Department of Documents, P.O. Box 371954, Pittsburgh, PA 15250-7954, and ask for the booklet Know Before You Go. Regulations for Canada are similar; for details, write to Canada Customs, Inquiries Unit, First Floor, 333 Dunsmuir Street, Vancouver, B.C. Canada V6B 5R4, or call 604 666-0545 and ask for the booklet I Declare.

CHAPTER 22

TRAVEL INSURANCE: CUT YOUR RISKS

If illness, accident, or emergency strikes before or during a tour or cruise, you could face two major financial risks: the loss of nonrefundable prepayments and the heavy expense of emergency transportation home. Your exposure to either of those risks can total thousands of dollars. Fortunately, travel insurance can protect you against both. But keep in mind that insurance is the most overpriced of all travel services.

Trip-cancellation/trip interruption (TCI) policies cover the losses incurred if you must cancel a trip before you leave home or cut the trip short, reimbursing you for whatever portion of your payment you cannot recover from the travel supplier. Emergency medical-evacuation (EME) policies pay the added cost of having to be rushed to a medical facility far from the site of the accident or illness.

Although some travel insurance covers other risks as well, most travelers can do without that extra coverage. Typically, you pay inflated prices for some combination of coverage you

246   TRAVEL SAVVY

already have (under your regular medical or household policies), coverage for minor risks (such as delayed baggage), and coverage you really may never need (accidental death and dismemberment).

YOUR EXPOSURE

Why pay an extra 3 to 14 percent of your total bill to insure a trip? There are two main reasons:

• Cruises, package tours, and airline tickets typically require 100 percent payment in advance, sometimes months before departure. If you're forced to cancel 60 days ahead, the penalty may amount to pocket change. Closer to departure time, however, cruise and tour suppliers impose stiff penalties for cancellations. In the worst case, you could lose your entire prepayment. Even after you start your trip, your own illness or a problem at home could force you to break off your journey.

• If you suffer a severe accident or illness in a remote area, you might have to be evacuated to a distant medical facility. Just rescheduling your ticket or buying a conventional flight could be expensive; evacuation by helicopter or private jet—unlikely as that might be—could cost a small fortune.

RISK COVERAGE

Coverage for big financial risk falls into three broad categories.

ILLNESS/INJURY/DEATH. TCI policies reimburse you (or your heirs) for extra costs you might incur should either you or a traveling companion fall sick, suffer an injury, or die, either before departure or during your trip. (They don't reimburse you for the companion's expenses unless the companion is also insured.) The policies also provide reimbursement if illness, injury, or death of a close family member at home forces you to cancel or interrupt your trip.

Travel insurance: Cut your risks **247**

Most TCI policies now waive any exemptions for preexisting medical conditions, provided you insure the full value of your trip within seven days of making your initial deposit or prepayment. That's a recent development in TCI, and a major improvement for consumers. As with health insurance generally, preexisting conditions used to be the most contentious element of TCI.

However, some TCI policies won't cover any preexisting condition, controlled or not, for which the insured person received medical treatment or advice within 90 to 180 days before buying the policy. In theory, that means the company could deny a claim if you so much as took an aspirin on a doctor's advice within the exclusionary period—so read the fine print.

Typically, rules on preexisting conditions apply to any person—you (the traveler), a traveling companion (insured or not), or a family member at home—whose medical condition causes a trip to be canceled or interrupted.

EME insurance (or the EME component of a bundled policy) provides for emergency transportation in the event of serious illness or injury. However, both TCI and EME policies exclude a long list of medical conditions—typically, those resulting from unusual risk and those that could be self-inflicted. Those policies won't cover you if your trip is spoiled by a self-inflicted injury, an injury resulting from such hazardous activities as mountain climbing, a medical problem that results from the use of illegal drugs, or a war injury.

OPERATOR FAILURE. All too often, a tour operator fails, leaving its customers stuck with worthless prepaid air tickets and hotel vouchers. Some failures strand travelers abroad without return transportation. TCI can cover those losses, too.

Most policies reimburse you if your operator or cruise line "fails," "defaults," or "ceases operations." But the application can be tricky—know what you're buying. Several policies pay off only if the operator ceases *all* operations for 10 days or more—

248 TRAVEL SAVVY

and a much briefer failure could seriously disrupt your trip. Even worse, some policies (but none of the listed ones) pay off only in case of "bankruptcy"—which could render the coverage useless. Tour operators that fail seldom actually file for bankruptcy; many simply close their doors and disappear.

To guard against losses caused by tour-operator failure, it's wise to buy a cruise or package tour from an operator that belongs to the U.S. Tour Operators Association (USTOA) or one that participates in the escrow program recommended by the American Society of Travel Agents (ASTA). Buy your TCI directly from an insurance company. If you buy from a tour operator who subsequently fails, the coverage would be worthless.

However, if protection against supplier failure is your only

EXCESS INSURANCE

TCI and EME policies often include other benefits. Most aren't worth buying separately, especially since coverage through travel insurance is usually secondary—the insurance company picks up only what you can't recover from your own insurance or from a supplier.

• **Medical/hospital.** Chances are your own medical insurance or HMO covers you even when you're traveling, as do some Medicare-supplement policies. But check your program. If you aren't otherwise covered, go for travel-insurance coverage.

• **Baggage loss.** Your homeowner's or renter's policy probably covers personal effects, even when you travel. Some travelers—especially those on cruises—bring along valuables that may not be covered. But even those folks are probably better off with a year-round floater policy than with by-the-trip baggage insurance.

• **Trip and baggage delays.** Quite a few policies pay up to $1,000 to reimburse you in case of minor hassles. If the coverage is bundled at no extra cost, you might as well take advantage of it, but we don't recommend buying it separately.

• **Accidents.** Some policies include accident insurance, either for the entire trip or just as airline flight insurance. That coverage cynically plays on an irrational fear of flying—you're more likely to die of a bee sting than in an airplane crash.

Travel insurance: Cut your risks **249**

concern, you don't need to buy TCI. Instead, use a charge card to buy your tour or cruise. If the supplier fails, you can get a chargeback that removes the charge from your account. But you can't get a chargeback for any of the other cancellation risks.

UNFORESEEN EMERGENCIES. TCI covers you against a wide range of accidents and surprises that might force you to cancel or interrupt a trip: a fire or flood at your house, a call to jury duty, an accident that makes you miss a flight or a sailing, an airplane hijacking, a natural disaster (fire, flood, earthquake, or epidemic), terrorism, or a strike.

Over the last few years, TCI policies have become generally more liberal in covered risks. In fact, many now include the catchall term "unforeseen emergencies" rather than providing a long list of specifics.

Still, TCI doesn't give you a blank check to cancel a trip for any reason. Even the liberal Travel Guard policy excludes personal financial circumstances, business or contractual obligations, or "change of plans."

INSURANCE PAYOFFS

Should you be hit with a travel problem, TCI or EME bails you out financially.

CANCELLATION FEES/PENALTIES. In the event of a predeparture cancellation or postponement, TCI reimburses you for whatever fraction of your prepayments or deposits you can't recover from the supplier. You must first apply for any refund that may be available from your tour operator, cruise line, or airline, under the terms of the ticket. TCI pays the difference between what you paid and what you can recover.

DOUBLE/SINGLE ADJUSTMENTS. Typically, you buy a tour or cruise at a per-person, double-occupancy rate. Should your traveling companion suddenly be unable to leave on a trip, for a cov-

TRAVEL SAVVY

ered reason, TCI pays the single supplement so that you can complete the trip alone. Similarly, TCI covers adjustments that might be required if your companion has to return home early.

TRANSPORTATION ADJUSTMENTS. If a covered reason forces you to postpone your trip, TCI pays the cost of switching your airline ticket to a later flight, or the extra costs of alternative transportation to join a trip in progress—for example, airfare to your cruise's first port of call.

If a problem arises during your trip that forces you to return home early, TCI covers the extra costs. You must first find the best deal your airline will give you, then apply for TCI to pay for any additional fare or reissuing fee or a replacement ticket home.

If you suffer an illness or accident during a trip and need on-site help, most TCI policies will pay for a family member to travel from home to the site of your accident or hospital confinement.

Should your sickness or accident be severe enough, EME insurance (or the EME component of a bundled policy) typically will cover the cost of getting you from the accident or sickness site to the nearest adequate medical facility— even a special evacuation—as well as your eventual transportation home. Generally, EME services are provided at the discretion of the insurance company's medical adviser.

Most TCI/EME policies include some form of worldwide assistance— a number to call for referral to a doctor, lawyer, or other person or service

---

ASSISTANCE NETWORK

Most TCI/EME policies include some form of worldwide assistance—a number to call for referral to a doctor, lawyer, or other person or service you might need in a pinch. But if you need help for anything other than a covered medical emergency, all you get is a referral: The insurance program will tell you where to go, but it's up to you to pay. Similar services are widely available as free benefits on premium charge cards.

Travel insurance: Cut your risks **251**

you might need in a pinch. But if you need help for anything other than a covered medical emergency, all you get is a referral: The insurance program will tell you where to go, but it's up to you to pay. Similar services are widely available as free benefits on premium charge cards.

POLICY TYPES

TCI/EME insurance comes in several versions:

• Most major travel-insurance companies now feature their bundled (or cruise/tour) policy options as their primary product. The better examples include as much TCI as you want to buy (typically subject to a $10,000 maximum), a moderate amount of EME, plus a handful of other coverages. The price is based on the amount of TCI you buy—but travel insurance is grossly overpriced. The wholesale price of flight insurance is approximately 17 cents per $100 of coverage. Insurance companies, however, take a huge markup; they charge an average $6 per $100 of coverage.

You can buy bundled or custom (see page 33) insurance from a travel agency, through a cruise line or tour operator, directly from the insurance issuer, or from any of several Internet sites. Before you buy, compare coverage and prices.

• Several major insurance carriers also sell custom policies that let you assemble your own travel-insurance package from a selection of options, each priced separately. Once popular, custom policies are losing ground to bundled options that often provide as much or more coverage. A custom TCI option typically sells for about $6 per $100 of coverage. The EME components and other options are usually priced according to the duration of your trip.

• Many big cruise lines and tour operators sell wholesale policies under their own names (although the insurance is actually issued by an insurance company noted in the brochure's fine print). Wholesale policies are typically a bit cheaper than retail bundled policies, but not always—the cruise line or tour operator, not the insurance company, sets the selling price.

Unfortunately, wholesale policies don't cover some important risks—notably operator or cruise-line failure. The risk of tour-operator failure has been a long-standing problem, and these days some cruise lines are wobbly as well.

Still, some wholesale policies have an offsetting advantage: If the insurance company that underwrites the policy rejects a claim for an aborted trip, the line usually offers partial compensation in the form of a substantial discount on a future cruise.

• A cancellation waiver, usually the cheapest form of trip-cancellation coverage, is also the weakest. It really isn't insurance at all. Instead, for a price, the issuing cruise line or tour operator agrees to waive its own cancellation penalties if you have to cancel your trip for a covered reason.

Those waivers typically cover only limited predeparture contingencies, they may not cover cancellations within 24 hours of departure, and they don't cover midtrip interruption at all. Furthermore, you won't recover anything if the tour operator or cruise line fails.

WHICH POLICY?

In a recent study of traveler's insurance policies, we found that four policies stand out.

• Look first at CSA, with rates that are substantially below competitors' rates for most travelers. Among the companies we examined, CSA is the *Best Buy*. It bases its rates on a traveler's age. Travelers over age 70 generate a disproportionate percentage of TCI claims, says the company, so it offers greatly reduced rates for younger travelers. Coverages are comparable with those

Travel insurance: Cut your risks **253**

of other companies, and the policy also includes primary rental-car collision-damage waiver (CDW) at no extra cost. CSA is obviously a smart choice for travelers 55 or under—in some states, CSA offers a full-featured policy at about half the price of its nearest competitor—and a winner even in the 56 to 70 age bracket.

• Travelers looking for the broadest coverage should check out Travel Guard or Travelex Cruise & Tour. Although both are expensive, they include the broadest range of covered causes we've seen, even including the chance that you or your traveling companion might be unexpectedly laid off or terminated (subject to being with the same employer for five or more years). Travel Guard also offers a money-saving extra: a no-questions-asked $250 cancellation benefit if you pay your full premium within seven days of enrollment—paltry, but more than you get anywhere else.

• Although the Travelers custom policy is relatively expensive for our sample trip, its preexisting-condition exemption is not

ANNUAL POLICIES

The TCI/EME policies we studied are designed for—and are adequate for—ordinary travelers who visit popular destinations for a few weeks of the year. They're priced by the trip. But if you travel overseas extensively, especially into high-risk areas, consider buying into one of the programs that feature extended-coverage annual EME, complete with a network of on-site representatives in many parts of the world.

Two of the larger companies providing such services are International SOS

Assistance and Worldwide Assistance; also, Access America offers an annual option with similar provisions.

Heavy-duty EME is a tough call. Your odds of needing evacuation by helicopter or medical jet are minute. But if you should need it, the cost can be astronomical.

Our view is that, for most travelers, the EME you get with a bundled TCI policy is probably adequate. But if you're a real worrier, consider one of the annual packages.

TRAVEL
SAVVY

contingent on your buying enough to cover the entire cost of your trip. If you know you can recover most of the airfare, for example, you can buy just enough TCI to cover the trip components that aren't refundable. If you're concerned about extras, Travelers' medical and baggage insurance is primary—the company doesn't deduct what you can recover from a supplier or other insurance.

We listed the Health Care Abroad policy to illustrate the differences between policies focused on TCI and those that aim mainly at medical benefits. Its medical coverage is far greater than that of any other company, but its TCI, which applies only to sickness, injury, or accident, is by far the weakest of the group. We recommend it only for travelers who need extremely broad medical coverage.

Regardless of which supplier you choose, don't overbuy TCI. You can't recover more than your actual loss, so insuring for an amount beyond your total financial exposure is a waste. Buy any travel insurance only to cover risks you can't afford to absorb.

The safest way to buy TCI is directly from the insurance company. That way, you're protected even if your airline, tour operator, cruise line, or retail travel agency should fail.

CHAPTER 23

PHONING HOME

Telephone companies compete for long-distance business far too hotly to risk gouging you—one outrageous bill and you'd be off to a competitor. Long-distance calls that you place from hotel phones or public phone booths may be something else again: By the time you realize you've been had, it's too late.

Overseas hotel switchboards are by far the worst offenders. Plenty of travelers have been grossly overcharged for calls billed to their hotel rooms—a single call sometimes costs more than the room does. But overseas hotels aren't the only culprits: Some public phones here at home are connected to long-distance operators that charge exorbitant rates—and kick back money to the owner of the premises.

Savvy travelers can avoid those gouges. Overseas, they can usually pay unpadded rates by using a local public phone. And in the U.S., most public phones allow callers to access their preferred long-distance carrier, regardless of the phone's regular carrier.

Though such defensive tactics may spare you a real rooking, you may not realize that your regular long-distance carrier's call-home-from-abroad service may not be the least expensive option. AT&T, MCI, and Sprint were charging close to $5 for a three-minute U.K.-U.S. call, we found when we checked for an early-1998 report. But VoiceNet, for instance, charged less than 85¢ for the same call.

Even within the U.S., it's easy to overpay: The big-company calling cards are among the most expensive. But fortunately, a number of other companies operate calling-card programs with rates much lower than those of the three big carriers. This chapter gives you the rates and features of calling cards from more than a dozen long-distance providers. Specific prices may have changed since we surveyed, but the relative standings should be about the same.

COMPARING CARD FEATURES

Many cards—from AT&T, MCI, Sprint, VoiceNet, and others—can be used regardless of what you use for your home or business long-distance service. Others, such as those from LCI Difference, are available only if you signed up for a complete service package for your home or business. A few companies charge a monthly fee or have a monthly minimum.

CALLING AREA. Cards typically charge the same amount per call, regardless of distance. However, intrastate long-distance calls and calls to or from Alaska, Hawaii, and Puerto Rico may be charged at different rates. There's typically at least one option to let travelers call overseas from the U.S., and most provide for calls from overseas locations back to the U.S. Charges for calls from abroad to the U.S. may well be more important to you than calls from the U.S. to overseas phones, in view of the rapacity of some foreign hotels when guests call home (or phone any other country).

RATE PLAN. With flat-rate cards, you pay the same amount no matter what time of day or day of week you call. Peak/off-peak cards assess different charges for peak and off-peak times. Typically,

Phoning home **257**

peak times are during normal business hours in the area from which you place a call; off-peak times are evenings, weekends, and holidays. Some cards use peak/off-peak pricing in some areas, flat-rate pricing in others. For domestic calls, peak/ off-peak pricing seems to be losing ground.

RATE PER MINUTE. Given the competitive nature of phone rates, we're surprised at the variation in domestic rates among the listed companies. Perhaps customer inertia let AT&T, MCI, and Sprint —giant companies that dominate home-based long-distance service—get away with relatively high rates in all categories.

LONG-DISTANCE SURCHARGE. Many cards impose a surcharge on each call, at least in some calling areas. That's an initial charge that's added to the per-minute charge, something like the flag drop in a metered taxicab. But several cards have low rates and no surcharge. Surcharges are especially high—some over $2.50 a call—on international calls.

PAY-PHONE SURCHARGE. Early last year, a new pay-phone rule allowed owners of public pay phones to collect a charge for toll-free calls that originate from their phones. Those 800 and 888 calls remain nominally free to callers, but not to the phone companies that use pay phones for access. Most calling-card operators pass some or all of that charge along to users. (These surcharges, of course, don't apply to card calls you might make from, say, a friend's phone.) So far, the new regulation hasn't affected the cost of calls to the U.S. from foreign pay phones.

You can't avoid the pay-phone surcharge by buying a prepaid card. Operators of prepaid-card phone services are reportedly deducting a charge equal to the cost of an additional 1 to 3 minutes for each call that originates at a pay phone.

BILLING INCREMENT. Some companies billed in increments of six seconds (usually with a 30-second minimum charge); some billed in one-minute units, and LCI Difference billed some calls in one-second increments. Those quirks can make quite a difference to your bill. On a call that lasts just over a minute—1 minute, 3 seconds, say—some companies would have billed you for a full two minutes, others would have charged you for just 1 minute and 6 seconds (and LCI would have charged for 63 seconds). When rates are comparable, a short increment is clearly preferable.

FOREIGN-TO-FOREIGN CALLS. Several of the cards permit you to call from one foreign country to another. Using a U.S. company's calling card is often less expensive than dialing direct on a local public phone. And you usually save a lot, compared with charging calls to your hotel room.

CALLBACK SYSTEMS

People who make a lot of international phone calls from foreign locations might save with a callback phone system, which capitalizes on low international phone rates from the U.S. Rather than dial directly from a foreign country, you dial a dedicated number in the U.S., let it ring once or twice, and hang up. The "switch" in the U.S. is programmed to dial your overseas number right back and offer you a U.S.-based dial tone. You then dial your calls.

If you hang up quickly, there's no charge for the unanswered call to the U.S. switch: You are billed only for the callback from the U.S. to your foreign location plus the subsequent calls you make using the U.S. dial tone. Even though you pay two tolls, the sum is often less than what you'd pay for a single direct call from a foreign country.

Callback, however, may not work for all travelers:

• With most systems, you must be at a phone that the U.S.-based switch can dial directly—which precludes service to travelers in hotel rooms. A few callback systems provide a computer-generated voice that can be programmed to request a specific extension, but such a system might not work with every hotel switchboard.

• With increasing deregulation, privatization, and competition,

Phoning home **259**

overseas phone utilities are cutting rates closer to U.S. levels. Even the callback suppliers concede they'll have to change their basic product to be competitive.

At this time, we don't recommend callback for individual overseas travelers who travel from place to place, staying in hotels. But if you're renting an overseas accommodation for several months, callback might work for you.

CHOOSING A CARD

Almost everywhere you look these days, it seems that someone is trying to sell you a prepaid phone card. In fact, promotional mailings often include "free" (at least for the first cycle) prepaid cards. We don't include them here because there are so many and because their per-minute rates are higher than the best calling-card deals. We've never seen a prepaid card that charged less than 25 cents a minute, and some charge close to double that figure.

There's no reason not to use any "free" card you might find in your junk mail. Just don't bite when the time comes to "refresh" its prepaid value.

A near-ideal calling card would be stand-alone (so you wouldn't have to switch to a different long-distance service if you didn't want to) and offer a low per-minute charge, a short billing increment, no per-call surcharge, no service fee, and inexpensive overseas calls in both directions.

• In a study conducted for *Consumer Reports Travel Letter,* VoiceNet came closest to meeting all six criteria: Only two cards beat its domestic rate (one by a very thin margin), only three beat its U.S.-to-U.K. rate (again, one by a thin margin), and none came close for U.K.-to-U.S. calls. If you want a low-cost home 800 number, look first at LCI, MCI or, for heavy users, ATN. If you do a lot of away-from-home calling, consider getting two different cards, each optimized for different kinds of calls.

CHAPTER

STAYING HEALTHY

Since illness can wreck a trip, wise travelers prepare for health risks before they pack. This chapter outlines basic trip preparations, as well as the precautions to take once you arrive. The information here isn't a substitute for professional medical advice. We urge readers, particularly those with special health problems or needs (including pregnant or breast-feeding women, older people, those with lowered immunity or with chronic diseases, and anyone traveling with infants and young children), to consult physicians or other professionals for specific advice or treatment.

HEALTH PRECAUTIONS

Most American tourists traveling abroad don't need to be too anxious about their health. In the larger European cities, health conditions are much like those here at home. However, if your itinerary takes you off the beaten path, you may need special health-protection measures.

DOCTOR VISITS. A month or two before your trip, ask your doctor to review your immunization status, to help you plan the full course of vaccinations you'll need, and to see that they are appropriately spaced and on time. Allow at least one or two weeks before departure for possible reactions to subside. You may require even more time because of the need to space certain combinations of vaccines.

If a routine physical exam is in the offing, you may wish to move up the date, or at least get a cursory checkup, before undertaking a long journey. If you suffer from a chronic disease or are on long-term medication, a more complete checkup is essential.

Before an extended trip, see your dentist far enough in advance to allow time for any necessary work. Have your eyes checked. If you wear corrective lenses, take along an extra pair and a copy of your lens prescription, just in case.

IMMUNIZATIONS. You may need certain immunizations before you can enter some countries. For current information about countries you plan to visit, call your county or state health department or contact the U.S. Public Health Service's Centers for Disease Control and Prevention (CDC), in Atlanta at 404 639-3311 or *www.cdc.gov.* The CDC's International Travelers' hot line (404 332-4559) presents programmed responses to questions 24 hours a day for users of touch-tone telephones. Operator assistance is available from 8:00 a.m. to 4:30 p.m. Eastern Standard Time, Monday through Friday. (Information is also available through the CDC web site (*www.cdc.gov*) and in fax-back form.) If you plan to be abroad for more than a month, particularly in a rural area, check with those agencies about any special precautions that may be recommended for that region.

Travelers' health information and international vaccination requirements and recommendations may also be obtained by contacting the U.S. Public Health Service Quarantine Station in your area. (See the Resource Guide, page 285.)

Staying healthy **263**

If any vaccinations are required, it's a good idea to have an International Certificate of Vaccination (Form PHS-731), available from many travel agencies and transportation companies, from your local and state health departments or, at $2 a copy, from the Superintendent of Documents, U.S. Government Printing Office (stock #017-001-004405). Some physicians keep a supply of the forms on hand.

All vaccines except the one for yellow fever can be given, and the vaccination recorded on your certificate, by any licensed physician. Yellow-fever vaccine and certification of yellow-fever vaccination must be obtained at an officially designated Yellow Fever Vaccination Center, where the certificate is validated by the authorized physician or health department. Boosters are needed every 10 years.

Some African countries require a certificate of yellow-fever vaccination from all travelers who enter; other countries in Africa, and some in South America and Asia, require evidence of vaccination from travelers coming from or traveling through areas where yellow fever is present. For the location of the nearest approved center, contact your county or state health department or U.S. Public Health Service office (see the Resource Guide, page 285).

If your physician advises you to omit a required immunization for medical reasons, be sure that he or she records the omission on your certificate and attaches a signed and dated statement on letterhead stationery specifying the reasons.

Infants are often exempt from the vaccination requirements for foreign countries; some countries do not require certificates for very young children. Check with the foreign embassy or consulate for exemption requirements before traveling.

Keep your completed vaccination certificate with your passport and use a separate certificate for each traveler in your party.

When your destination country doesn't require immunizations,

264 TRAVEL SAVVY

your physician can help you decide which vaccinations to have, taking into consideration your destination, the time of year, duration of your trip, your living arrangements and anticipated lifestyle in the host country, and personal risk factors such as your age, your state of health, and your current immunization status.

No vaccine is 100 percent protective. You should still exercise all the appropriate precautions against disease discussed in this chapter.

Routine immunizations are those that everyone should have, whether traveling or not, to protect against common illnesses such as measles and mumps. They're typically administered in early childhood. But adults who don't have an adequate vaccination history should discuss with their doctor the safest immunization strategy for their age, medical condition, and travel plans.

WHICH SHOTS? Traveler's immunizations are typically given to protect against specific diseases. Few if any travelers would need all of them. The following is an overview of ten immunizations and one preventive drug treatment (for malaria). Ask your physician if you fall into a high-risk group (infants, pregnant women, and people with lowered immunity); for such people, the risk from the vaccine may be greater than the health risks of the disease itself.

• Cholera still occurs in parts of Asia, Africa, and Latin America. The disease causes intestinal cramps and diarrhea. In severe cases, dehydration can be fatal unless vigorously treated with intravenous fluid and salt replacement. Antibiotics can also help.

Since the risk of cholera to tourists is now very low, the CDC advises that routine use of the vaccine is questionable. At this writing, no country officially requires you to be vaccinated against it (though local authorities may occasionally require documentation of cholera vaccination). In any event, the cholera vaccine can cause reactions and is effective less than half the time it's administered, so the best precaution is to avoid potentially contaminated

Staying healthy **265**

food and drink (see "Safe water supplies," on page 270, and "Safe food," on 272). For those who must travel into cholera-infested areas, a new oral vaccine (Mutachol, Orachol) is available that seems to be more protective than the injectable vaccine.

• Hepatitis A is also transmitted by contaminated food and drink or by human carriers of hepatitis A virus (HAV). Consider immunization if you're traveling anywhere *besides* Japan, Australia, New Zealand, Northern and Western Europe, Canada, or the U.S.

Hepatitis A vaccine has replaced gamma globulin as the preferred hepatitis A preventative. There are two vaccines available, Merck's VAQTA and Smith Kline Beecham's Havrix, which provide protective antibodies from two weeks after injection; a booster dose is given six to 18 months later. Virtually 100 percent immunity is believed to last for 10 to 20 years.

• Hepatitis B is transmitted by contaminated blood or sexual contact with carriers of hepatitis B virus (HBV). Consider immunization with Recombivax-HB or Energex-B, both genetically engineered in yeast, well in advance (three injections over a six-month period). For those who need more immediate coverage there is a short course (three injections over three weeks) that provides partial (68 percent) protection. The shots should be given in the arm, not the buttocks. Areas where the disease is endemic include sub-Saharan Africa, southeast Asia, South Pacific islands, and parts of the Caribbean—but also other regions of Africa and Asia, as well as Japan, Eastern and Southern Europe, the Commonwealth of Independent States, and most of Central and South America.

The risk of hepatitis B infection is generally low for most travelers. But it rises dramatically for those who have sexual contact with residents of infected areas (or come into contact with their blood). Condoms can lessen the chance of infection (see "Sexually transmitted ills," page 275).

TRAVEL SAVVY

266 TRAVEL SAVVY

• Japanese encephalitis vaccines should be considered by persons who intend to live for extended periods in rural parts of Asia. (The specific areas that pose risk include Bangladesh, Cambodia, China, India, Indonesia, Korea, Laos, Malaysia, Myanmar [Burma], Nepal, Pakistan, the Philippines, Singapore, Sri Lanka, Taiwan, Thailand, Vietnam, and eastern parts of Russia.) But the risk for short-term travelers is low.

• Malaria is transmitted by the female anopheles mosquito. Consider preventive treatment if you're traveling to areas where malaria is known to exist, generally in Central and South America, Haiti, sub-Saharan Africa, South and Southeast Asia, the Middle East, and a few South Pacific island nations. In addition to a drug regimen, travelers to those regions should take precautions against being bitten by mosquitoes (see "Insects," page 274).

Antimalarial drugs help prevent or suppress malaria, but they don't immunize against the disease. If high, spiking fevers develop (that can happen as early as a week after you arrive in a malarial area, or as long as six months after you return home), seek medical help immediately.

Preventive drug treatment should begin as early as two weeks before you enter a malarial area and continue for four to six weeks after you leave. Doses are taken weekly; missing even a single dose will reduce protection.

One 500-mg tablet of chloroquine (Aralen) taken once a week beginning one week before departure, while you're away, and for four weeks after you return home, is a commonly prescribed antimalarial drug regimen. Children's dosages are determined by body weight: The carefully calculated amount can be ground up and put in gelatin capsules, to be mixed with food or drink each week.

Resistant strains of the malaria parasite are now common. Mefloquine (Lariam) is increasingly recommended as the antimalarial suppressant in areas infested with chloroquine-resistant

Staying healthy **267**

malaria (this includes all malarial areas except for parts of Central America and the Middle East, Haiti, and the Dominican Republic). One 250-mg capsule is taken starting one week before departure and continuing weekly until four weeks after return. Mefloquine probably shouldn't be taken by people taking beta-blockers—propranolol (Inderal), atenolol (Tenormin), or calcium-channel blockers such as verapamil (Calan), diltiazem (Cardizem), or nifedipine (Procardia) and so on—by children under 30 pounds, or in areas where chloroquine is still effective.

If you intend to travel in isolated malarial areas, ask your doctor to consider prescribing three Fansidar tablets to take along, strictly as a backup. (Fansidar should be avoided by persons with a history of sensitivity to sulfa drugs and by infants under two months.) That drug contains pyrimethamine and sulfadoxine; it should be taken only if you begin to have malarialike symptoms (high fever, chills, sweating, headache, and muscle ache) and you can't get medical help. Take the pills, but get to a medical facility as soon as possible.

Bring along enough of the prescribed drug(s) to cover four to six weeks *after* your stay in malarial areas. (Warning: Overdoses of antimalarial drugs can be fatal; observe the prescribed dosages carefully and store out of reach of children.)

In all malarial areas, it's also a good idea to protect yourself against mosquito bites. See "Insects," page 274, for the measures to take.

• For plague, vaccination is recommended only for travelers to rural or highland areas of Africa, Asia, and South America who may be unable to avoid contact with infected rodents, rabbits, and fleas. It isn't needed by travelers to urban areas with modern accommodations.

• Poliomyelitis is transmitted by water and food contaminated by the feces of human carriers of the polio virus. Consider having an additional single dose of vaccine (beyond the immunization you probably received in childhood) if you're traveling to tropical or developing countries or to most states of the former Soviet Union. We recommend Ipol (enhanced-potency inactivated polio vaccine), given by injection. It should be taken only once during adult years.

• Spinal meningitis is transmitted by contaminated food and drink and by human carriers. This frequently fatal disease is caused by a bacterium called meningococcus. We recommend the vaccine if you're going to sub-Saharan Africa, Nepal, or Northern India, especially if you'll be in close contact with locals or if you'll be there during the dry season (December to June). The vaccine is expensive but fairly effective; immunity typically lasts for three years.

• Typhoid fever is also spread by contaminated food and water. Consider immunization if you're traveling to Africa, Asia, or Central and South America—especially rural and tropical areas—and will spend at least six weeks there. An oral typhoid vaccine, Vivotif (one capsule every other day for four doses), is just as effective as injectable vaccine, with fewer (if any) side effects, and lasts five years. Even with vaccination, however, take strict precautions against contaminated food and water (see "Safe water supplies," page 270, and "Safe food," page 272).

• Yellow fever, transmitted by mosquitoes, is reported in Africa, South America, and South and Southeast Asia—especially rural or forest areas within about 15 degrees of the equator. Consider immunization if you're traveling to those areas.

Vaccination isn't required to reenter the U.S., but the Public Health Service still strongly recommends it for those traveling to yellow-fever areas. Even with vaccination, travelers should guard against mosquito bites in yellow-fever areas (see "Insects," page 274).

• In addition, adult travelers should be sure they've had a tetanus-diphtheria shot within the past 10 years. If they're over

Staying healthy **269**

age 65, they should also consider getting a flu shot and perhaps a pneumonia shot as well. Travelers born in or after 1957 should also consider getting a second dose of measles vaccine before traveling abroad.

INSURANCE COVERAGE

No matter where you travel, some emergency services may already be covered by your existing health insurance (make a point to check with your carrier before a trip). Beyond that, medical-emergency coverage is available to pay for services to travelers who become ill or suffer a serious accident anywhere in the world. For more information on medical-emergency insurance, see Chapter 22.

TRAVEL HEALTH PLANNING

Beyond immunizations, you can take other steps to safeguard your health.

A MEDICAL RECORD. Consider carrying a brief medical record to provide information a physician might need in an emergency. Your physician can help you create a form, or you can photocopy the sample on page 281. Also take along copies of current prescriptions, and, if pertinent, a copy of your most recent electrocardiogram.

If you have a medical condition that could endanger your life in an emergency, you may also want to wear a warning for emergency personnel. For a one-time, $35 membership fee (annual renewals are $15), the nonprofit Medic Alert Foundation International provides a special necklace or bracelet engraved with your medical condition and a 24-hour toll-free telephone number for access to your medical history and the names of your physicians and close relatives. Call 800 763-3428 for more information.

270 TRAVEL SAVVY

MEDICAL SUPPLIES. It can be risky to buy unfamiliar drugs abroad, where the safety standards for pharmaceutical products may not be as rigorous as American ones. In many countries, medicines sold over the counter—including some that are available only by prescription in the U.S.—may have serious side effects.

Refuse any unfamiliar remedies that friends or pharmacists urge on you during your travels. Instead, take your own medications and supplies, as listed on page 282 under "Packing your medical kit."

TRAVEL ADVISORY. Another resource for planning a health-conscious trip is the U.S. Department of State's travel-advisory service. It identifies countries and areas where war, civil strife, health alerts, or other problems might affect travel plans. For more information, see Chapter 21.

ONCE YOU ARRIVE

Immunization can never guarantee 100 percent protection against typhoid fever or other intestinal diseases—several of which can result in diarrhea or worse. In each case, the best defense is to avoid food and drink that might be contaminated.

The main culprits are untreated water, unpasteurized dairy products, unpeeled raw fruits and vegetables, uncooked foods, and cooked foods that are improperly handled (by unclean hands, in contaminated utensils, or by inadequate cooking, storing, or serving). Good personal hygiene, including frequent hand-washing, is essential.

Health hazards vary with the territory. The U.S. Public Health Service considers most developing countries of Africa, Asia, Latin America, and the Middle East to be high-risk areas, and most of Southern Europe and a few Caribbean islands to pose intermediate risks.

SAFE WATER SUPPLIES. Since contaminated water is a common

Staying healthy **271**

source of infection, prudent travelers will pay close attention to the water they ingest, whether as a liquid, as ice cubes, or as an aid to brushing their teeth and even the water they bathe in.

FOR DRINKING. The drinking water is usually safe in large cities. But in rural regions, it may be contaminated by bacteria, viruses, or parasites. If chlorinated tap water is not available, or if local conditions are questionable, stick to other beverages or purify the water yourself.

Generally, carbonated drinks (canned or bottled), beer, and wine are safe. So are citrus fruit juices, either bottled or made from frozen concentrate with purified water (water that has been boiled or treated; see below). Glasses and cups may be contaminated, so drink from disposable paper containers or directly from the can or bottle, after wiping it clean. Noncarbonated, bottled fluids aren't necessarily safe; it depends on how and where the drink was bottled. Use ice cubes only if they're made from purified water.

If you must drink or brush your teeth with suspect water, treat it first. Boil the water for one minute (three minutes at altitudes above 6,500 feet) and let it cool. Or treat the water chemically with iodine or tetraglycine hydroperiodide tablets (Globaline, Potable-Agua), both available at pharmacies and camping stores. (Chlorine may be used as well, though it's less reliable than the two other chemicals.) While chemical treatment may prove more convenient and practical than boiling, however, it's less reliable. Be especially wary of cloudy water: If possible, boil it.

FOR SWIMMING. Swimming or bathing in contaminated water can lead to skin, eye, ear, and intestinal infections. Fresh water— particularly warm, dirty water—is the most hazardous, especially in the tropics. Chlorinated pools are usually safe. So is salt water, though some beaches are contaminated by streams, sewage outlets, or animal feces. Inquire locally before you test the waters.

TRAVEL SAVVY

Schistosomiasis is a disease that occurs sporadically throughout the tropics. It's acquired by swimming or bathing in freshwater streams, ponds, or lakes containing snails that harbor the infectious form (called cercariae) of the schistosoma parasite. The cercariae can penetrate intact skin and cause an itchy eruption known as swimmer's itch. They then enter the bloodstream and can lodge in the liver or other organs, where they become adult worms, inflicting serious damage on the liver, intestines, or urinary tract.

While schistosomiasis can be treated with drugs, it's obviously better to avoid swimming in suspect water. If you do come in contact with contaminated or doubtful water, strip immediately and towel off vigorously to prevent the cercariae from penetrating the skin as the water evaporates.

SAFE FOOD

Where hygiene and sanitation are poor, view every food source with suspicion.

MEAT, FRUIT, AND VEGETABLES. If you think food handling may be questionable or refrigeration lacking, avoid cold cuts and potato or egg salads. Order any meat, poultry, fish, or shellfish dishes thoroughly cooked and served piping hot.

In tropical areas, don't eat raw fruit unless it has an unbroken skin that you can peel yourself (after washing it with purified water). Otherwise, only freshly prepared, thoroughly cooked foods are safe. Be especially wary of salads and leafy vegetables.

MILK AND DAIRY PRODUCTS. In large European cities, milk and other dairy products labeled as pasteurized can usually be considered safe. Outside the urban centers, however, dairy hygiene may not be as strict as in the U.S. or Canada. Where sanitation, food handling, or refrigeration is a problem, avoid raw egg mixtures, cream, milk (even if pasteurized), and milk-containing

Staying healthy **273**

foods such as cream sauces and certain pastries. Avoid ice cream, frozen desserts, whipped-cream confections, and other dairy products.

In risky regions, canned, evaporated, or condensed milk is safe only if used straight or reconstituted with boiled water. Consider bringing powdered milk to mix with boiled water.

To be free of contamination, cheese must either be made from pasteurized milk or be cured for at least 60 days. In Europe, most cheeses are cured for at least that long to improve flavor. Fresh and special native cheeses similar to our cream cheese, which are not cured, are best avoided unless you're sure they came from pasteurized milk.

For infants who aren't being breast-fed, the safest and most practical food is formula that's ready to use.

TRAVELER'S DIARRHEA

Of the millions of people who travel to developing countries, about one-third get traveler's diarrhea at least once during their stay. It's usually caused by a pathogenic variant of a common bacterium that normally lives in the intestine. You can help prevent traveler's diarrhea by scrupulously observing the precautions against contaminated food and drink discussed previously.

Symptoms of traveler's diarrhea include frequent watery bowel movements and abdominal cramps, sometimes accompanied by weakness, muscle aches, dizziness, and loss of appetite. Severe chills, high fever, nausea, vomiting, bloody stools, and dehydration usually indicate something more serious. In that case, seek medical care promptly. (Infants, toddlers, and older people in particular may become dehydrated rapidly.)

Prevent dehydration by drinking lots of fluids. Canned soup and fruit juices help offset losses of sodium and potassium in the stool. Avoid alcohol and caffeine.

274 TRAVEL SAVVY

As uncomfortable as it is, traveler's diarrhea is rarely life-threatening. Most cases last only one to three days. But recurrences are possible, so before heading to a high- or intermediate-risk area, ask your doctor to prescribe an antidiarrheal product (loperamide or Imodium A-D, say) for mild traveler's diarrhea and an antibiotic, in case a more severe case develops.

Bismuth subsalycilate (for instance, Pepto-Bismol) can prevent diarrhea in travelers who take two tablets four times a day. It does, however, turn the tongue and stools black, and it can cause mild ringing in the ears. No one should take it for more than three weeks; people who are allergic to aspirin or who take anti-clotting drugs (Coumadin, Ticlid or Plavix, and aspirin) or who have diabetes or gout should check with their physician before using it.

INSECTS

Insects are most numerous—and most dangerous—in tropical climates. Malaria is the most common insect-borne disease, but there are also yellow fever, dengue fever, Lyme disease, and others.

A country-by-country report on the risk of malaria and other insect-borne diseases can be found in the latest edition of the Centers for Disease Control and Prevention's "Health Information for International Travel," published annually (publication stock #017-023-00195-7). That comprehensive health guide can be purchased for $20 from the Superintendent of Documents, U.S. Government Printing Office, but it's also available via the Internet (see the Resource Guide in the back of the book). Travelers can also purchase "International Travel and Health Guide," $20, an exhaustive 471-page compendium of health information for travelers by Stuart R. Rode, M.D. It's available at bookstores or from the publisher, Travel Medicine (800 848-2793).

Staying healthy **275**

To protect against mosquitoes, flies, fleas, ticks, mites, and other pests, follow these precautions:

• Sleep in an air-conditioned or well-screened bedroom, or under mosquito netting.

• Avoid insect territory from dusk to dawn.

• When you go out, cover your skin, including your feet. Avoid dark colors, which attract some insects. Wear long pants and tuck them into your boots.

• Don't use scented toiletries in insect-infested areas.

• Apply insect repellent to clothing and exposed skin. The most effective insect repellents contain "deet" (diethyltoluamide, or N,N-diethylmeta-toluamide). However, CONSUMER REPORTS' medical consultants advise against using deet-based repellents on children under age 6.

For older children, adolescents, and adults, it's usually unnecessary to use any product that contains more than 30 percent deet on the skin; if needed, higher concentrations can be used on clothing. Spraying clothing with permethrin (Duranon, Permanone) and using permethrin-impregnated mosquito netting can also provide some protection.

• Shower at least daily, and check for lice and ticks.

• Store food in insect-proof containers. Dispose of garbage promptly.

SEXUALLY TRANSMITTED ILLS

With the increased prevalence worldwide of many sexually transmitted diseases (STDs), choosing a new sexual partner while traveling can be risky.

Before AIDS (acquired immune-deficiency syndrome) appeared, techniques for preventing STDs were not often discussed openly, and public awareness of the risks was low. Things have changed. Because there is not yet a cure or a vaccine for AIDS, prevention

TRAVEL SAVVY

276 TRAVEL SAVVY

is the only way to control its spread. Other types of STDs can be successfully treated if detected early, but prevention is always better than treatment.

By observing the safe-sex practices described below, one can reduce the risk of contracting any STD—including syphilis, gonorrhea, chlamydia, herpes simplex II, venereal warts, and hepatitis B, as well as infection with the human immunodeficiency virus (HIV), which causes AIDS.

• Avoid multiple, casual, or anonymous partners, prostitutes, and others who may have had multiple sex partners.

• Avoid sexual contact with a person who has genital warts, discharge, or sores.

• During intercourse (including oral-genital and anal-genital), use latex condoms and a spermicide. Use a water-based lubricant—not petroleum jelly—as a lubricant for the condom. Don't trust contraceptive products available abroad; bring your own.

• Consider vaccination against the hepatitis B virus if you're traveling to an area where it's endemic and you anticipate having sexual contact with residents there.

• If you engage in any high-risk sexual behavior, seek prompt medical advice.

COPING WITH CLIMATE

It doesn't have to rain every day to spoil your vacation; you could ruin it yourself with one long day in the sun. Be prepared to deal with weather extremes.

TOLERATING THE HEAT. The cardinal rule for tolerating oppressive heat is *take it easy.* Overexertion can lead to heat exhaustion or heatstroke.

The warning signs of heat exhaustion include headache, weakness, dizziness, blurred vision, cramps, and sometimes nausea and vomiting. Stop activities, get out of the sun, sip cool water, and lie

Staying healthy **277**

down with your feet elevated until the symptoms subside; if they don't, get professional help.

Heatstroke shares many of those symptoms but is also marked by hot, dry, flushed skin; disorientation; racing pulse; rapid breathing; and high fever. Have the victim lie down in the shade, and place cold, wet towels on the body. Seek medical care immediately.

To protect yourself against the heat:

• Don't exercise during peak heat hours (generally 10 a.m. to 3 p.m.). Avoid the hot sun.

• Wear a broad-brimmed hat and lightweight, light-colored, loose-fitting clothing. Cotton and linen are preferable to synthetics.

• Wear cotton socks and lightweight shoes or open sandals.

• Drink plenty of fluids (but none that contain caffeine or alcohol, which can promote dehydration).

• Shower once or even several times a day (but not in very cold or hot water).

AVOIDING SUNBURN. The sun's rays and dangers are strongest in tropical zones and at high altitudes. But you can overdo it almost anywhere. Fair-skinned people are the most vulnerable. Ultraviolet (UV) rays can also cause skin reactions in people taking certain drugs, including some antibiotics, diuretics, and antihypertension medication.

Sunscreens are the best defense against UV radiation. They contain one or more chemicals that absorb UV radiation before it can harm the skin. Each sunscreen carries a "sun protection factor," or SPF number, which indicates the degree of protection from UV light. An SPF of 15 to 30 effectively blocks most UV rays.

Treat sunburn as you would other burns. First-degree sunburn can be soothed by cloths dipped in cool water, or by a cool bath with baking soda. Hydrocortisone creams and ointments may help decrease the inflammation; moisturizing lotions may also be helpful. Ibuprofen by mouth can be used to calm the inflammatory reaction and for pain relief. A severe sunburn can cause fever, chills, and blistering, and usually warrants professional care.

COLD WEATHER TIPS. Extreme cold presents the twin dangers of frostbite and hypothermia (abnormally low body temperature). Anyone who is underdressed and inadequately prepared for the cold is vulnerable. Older people are especially at risk.

Frostbite results from exposure to subfreezing temperatures; the colder the temperature, the quicker and more severe the frostbite. Frostbitten skin progresses from painful to numb, turns white or bluish, and becomes firm and stiff. Do not rub the skin or thaw it with intense heat. Follow these first-aid measures:

• Gently wrap the frostbitten areas in a blanket, clothing, or newspaper.

• Find shelter immediately, preferably in a hospital. Otherwise, go indoors and start thawing immediately by immersing the frost-bitten parts in tepid (not too warm and never hot) water for up to one hour. Function, feeling, and color should return gradually. Do not touch any blisters that may appear during the warming process.

• Give acetaminophen, aspirin, or ibuprofen for pain. A hot, nonalcoholic beverage may also be useful if the victim is awake.

• After that initial thawing treatment, cover the affected skin with sterile gauze and bring the victim to a hospital.

Hypothermia is a life-threatening condition. It can result from overexposure to cold alone, and not necessarily to below-freezing temperatures. The combination of cold and wet can drastically hasten its onset.

Mental confusion is one of the most ominous symptoms of hypothermia. At the first signs—violent shivering, difficulty in walking, slurred speech—seek warmth and shelter. In a more advanced state, marked by progressive disorientation or even unconsciousness, the victim requires immediate medical help.

To avoid frostbite and hypothermia, dress warmly and stay within reach of shelter in case of emergency. Garments should be layered and loose-fitting to trap insulating pockets of air.

Staying healthy **279**

To protect extremities, wear thin glove liners under fur-lined or down- or synthetic-filled mittens. Shoes or boots should be loose enough to accommodate wool socks over cotton socks with a little room to spare. Wear a hat that covers the ears, a scarf, or even a face mask.

Snow presents two additional risks: sunburn and snow blindness. Sunlight reflected off snow can burn you even more quickly than at a beach, so use sunscreen. Dark sunglasses can prevent snow blindness.

ALTITUDE PROBLEMS. Until you become acclimated to high altitudes, you may experience mountain sickness. Symptoms include headache, nausea, shortness of breath, insomnia, fatigue, poor appetite, and mental confusion. Acetazolamide (Diamox), a prescription drug, can be used to prevent mountain sickness, though people with allergies to sulfa drugs should avoid it. Anyone with a history of heart or lung problems should consult a doctor before traveling to altitudes over 5,000 feet. Above that point, the air's oxygen content may be dangerously low for them.

FINDING MEDICAL CARE

Well-trained physicians and well-equipped hospitals can be found in most large cities worldwide, even in some of the economically underdeveloped countries of Africa, Asia, and Latin America.

Use the following suggestions to help locate medical care abroad:

• In a real emergency, when minutes count, go to the nearest hospital. Transfer to a better-equipped facility is always possible once an acute situation has been stabilized.

• When time is less critical, find a reliable physician by checking with a hospital affiliated with a medical school or operated by the government. Medical specialty societies (French Diabetes Association, for example) may also be able to help.

• In areas where physicians aren't connected with community

TRAVEL SAVVY

EMERGENCY MEDICAL RECORD

This information supplements—but does not replace—the International Certificate of Vaccination, which may be required for entrance into certain countries (see page 263).

Name _____

Address _____

Blood type _____ Rh Factor _____

Date of birth _____

Tetanus and Diphtheria Immunization:

Primary series _____ Date _____

Last booster dose_____ Date _____

I have these medical conditions:

_____

_____

I am allergic to:

I take these drugs (generic name, U.S. trade name, dosage schedule):

_____

_____

_____

My medical insurance plan is: _____

My doctor is: _____

Address: _____

Phone: _____

In an emergency please notify: _____

Address: _____

Phone: _____

Staying healthy **281**

or medical-school hospitals (as in Great Britain), your hotel manager may be able to direct you to a group-practice medical center or, in more remote areas, a general practitioner. If you need a specialist, these physicians can refer you to a qualified (usually hospital-based) consultant.

• If you're sick enough to require a house call, ask your hotel manager for help. Many hotels keep lists of English-speaking physicians willing to make a hotel-room call.

• If you're in a major city, contact the U.S. embassy or consulate. Embassy personnel can refer you to English-speaking physicians who provide service for their staff.

• If there's an American military base nearby, you may be able to get reliable medical care or advice from the physicians assigned there.

• If Peace Corps representatives are nearby, check with them.

• In a remote small town or village, medical facilities may be either scarce or rudimentary, and a sick traveler may be at a loss. The hotel concierge or local police may be able to recommend a qualified practitioner.

• Consider joining the International Association for Medical Assistance to Travelers (IAMAT) before you leave home. That nonprofit organization provides members with a worldwide directory of English-speaking physicians who have agreed to a set fee schedule. IAMAT also distributes a variety of helpful charts and publications on immunizations, tropical diseases, worldwide climatic and sanitary conditions, and many other travel-related health topics.

ONCE YOU'RE HOME

Fever or intestinal problems that develop after you return home even weeks or months later may have had origins abroad. Delayed-onset symptoms can be caused by malaria, schistosomi-

MEDICAL KIT WHAT TO TAKE

The more remote your destination and the longer you'll be there, the more medications and supplies you'll want to take along. Pack all drugs safely away from heat, light, moisture, and children.

Should you need to take any prescription drugs, have your doctor prescribe or record them by their generic names, since brand names vary from country to country, and make sure that the name and strength of each medication are clearly identified on the pharmacy's original label. (Over-the-counter drugs should travel in their original containers.) If you travel with a prescription drug containing a narcotic (such as codeine), carry a copy of the prescription to satisfy customs officials.

Here are some candidates for your traveling medical kit (not all are applicable for every person and destination):

MEDICATIONS

Pain medication
Altitude-sickness medication
Motion-sickness medication
Antacid
Multipurpose antibiotic
Cold remedies

Diarrhea remedy
Hydrocortisone cream
Laxative
Nausea remedy
Sedative
Fungicidal preparation

SUPPLIES

Ace bandage
Adhesive bandages and tape
Rubbing alcohol
Clinical thermometer
Corn pads
Scissors
Tweezers and needle
Facial tissues
Packaged moist towelettes
Flashlight

Condoms/contraceptives
Menstrual pads/tampons
Water heater/electric immersion*
Water purification solutions
    or tablets
Paper coffee filters*
Insect repellent
Snakebite kit
Sunblock

*To aid in purifying water

Staying healthy 283

asis, typhoid fever, hepatitis, sexually transmitted diseases, and certain parasitic infections. Any symptoms that occur up to six or even twelve months after your return should alert you to the possibility of a travel-related illness.

RESOURCE GUIDE

Phone numbers for domestic and foreign airlines, charter airlines, cruise lines, hotels and motels, car-rental companies, and domestic and international travel advisories.

Airlines
Charter and tour operators 285
Domestic 286
Foreign 287
Cruise lines 290
Hotels and motels 291
Rail passes 296
Rental-car companies 296
Travel advisories 297

NAME	PHONE	WEB SITE

CHARTER AIRLINES AND TOUR OPERATORS

NAME	PHONE	WEB SITE
Adventure Tours USA	800 999-9046	*www.adventuretours.com*
Ah Wee World Travel Agency	718 584-2100	
Airhitch	800 326-2009	*airhitch.org*
	888 AIRHITCH (CA)	
Amber Travel	800 262-3701	
DER Travel Services	800 782-2424	*dertravel.com*
Euram Flight Centre	800 555-3872	*flyeuram.com*
	800 848-6789	
Fantasy Holidays	800 645-2555	*fantasyholidays.com*
	516 935-8500	

286 RESOURCE GUIDE

NAME	PHONE	WEB SITE
France Vacations	800 332-5332	france-vacations.com
Funjet Vacations	800 558-3050	funjet.com
GWV International	800 225-5498	
Homeric Tours	800 223-5570	homerictours.com
Hot Spot Tours	800 433-0075 212 421-9090 (NY)	hotspottours.com
Marcus Travel	800 524-0821 201 731-7600 (NJ)	
Martinair	800 627-8462	martinair.com
New Frontiers/Corsair	800 677-0720	newfrontiers.com
Pleasant Holidays	800 242-9244	pleasantholidays.com
Rebel Tours	800 732-3588	rebeltours.com
Sceptre Tours	800 221-0924	sceptretours.com
Skytours Travel Agency of San Francisco	800 246-8687 415 228-8228 (CA)	skytours.com
SunTrips	800 786-8747 408 432-1101	suntrips.com

DOMESTIC AIRLINES

Air Canada	800 776-3000	aircanada.ca/home.html
Air North	800 764-0407 800 661-0407 (Can.)	yukonweb.yk.ca/tourism/airnorth
AirTran	800 825-8538	airtran.com
Alaska Airlines	800 252-7522	alaska-air.com
Aloha Airlines	800 367-5250	aloha-air.com
American Airlines	800 433-7300	americanair.com
American Trans Air (ATA)	800 225-2995	ata.com
America West Airlines	800 235-9292	www.americawest.com
Canadian Airlines	800 426-7000	cdnair.ca/cpi
Continental Airlines	800 525-0280	flycontinental.com
Delta Airlines	800 221-1212	delta-air.com
Eastwind Airlines	800 644-3592	eastwindairlines.com

Resource Guide **287**

NAME	PHONE	WEB SITE
Frontier Airlines	800 432-1359	*frontierairlines.com*
Hawaiian Airlines	800 367-5320	*hawaiianair.com*
	800 882-8811 (HI)	
Horizon Air	800 547-9308	*horizonair.com*
Kiwi International Airlines	800 538-5494	*jetkiwi.com*
Laker Airways	800 432-2294	
LTU International Airways	800 888-0200	*www.ltu.com*
Midway Airlines	800 446-4392	*midwayair.com*
Midwest Express Airlines	800 452-2022	*midwestexpress.com*
Myrtle Beach Jet Express	800 386-2786	*myrtlebeachjetexp.com*
Northwest/KLM	800 225-2525	*nwa.com*
ProAir	800 939-9551	*proair.com*
Reno Air	800 736-6247	*renoair.com*
Southwest	800 435-9792	*iflyswa.com*
Spirit Airlines	800 772-7117	*spiritairlines.com*
Sun Country	800 752-1218	*suncountry.com*
Tower Air	800 348-6937	*towerair.com*
Trans World Airlines (TWA)	800 221-2000	*twa.com*
United Airlines	800 241-6522	*ual.com*
US Airways	800 428-4322	*usairways.com*
Vanguard Airlines	800 826-4827	*flyvanguard.com*
Western Pacific	800 345-0119	*westpac.com*

FOREIGN AIRLINES

NAME	PHONE	WEB SITE
ACES Airlines	800 846-2237	*acescolombia.com*
Aer Lingus	800 223-6537	*aerlingus.ie*
Aerolineas Argentinas	800 333-0276	*aerolineas.com.ar*
AeroMexico	800 237-6639	*aeromexico.com/start.html*
AeroPeru	800 777-7117	*aeroperu-usa.com*
Air Aruba	800 882-7822	*interknowledge.com/air-aruba*
Air Caledonie/Solomon	800 677-4277	*pacificislands.com*

NAME	PHONE	WEB SITE
Air France	800 237-2747	airfrance.com
	800 667-2747 (Can.)	
Air Jamaica	800 523-5585	airjamaica.com
Air Littoral	800 237-2747	pageszoom.com/air-littoral
Air Nauru	310 670-7302	airnauru.com.au
Air New Zealand & Ansett Australia	800 262-1234	airnz.com
	800 663-5494 (Can.)	
Air Niugini	714 752-5440	airniugini.com.pg/
Air Pacific	800 227-4446	airpacific.com
Alitalia Airlines	800 223-5730	alitalia.it/english
ANA - All Nippon Airways	800 235-9262	ana.co.jp/eng/index.html
Ansett Australia	800 366-1300	ansett.com.au
AOM French	800 892-9136	
Asiana Airlines	800 227-4262	asiana.co.kr/english
Austrian Airlines	800 843-0002	aua.com
Austral Lineas Aereas	800 333-0276	austral.com.ar
Avianca	800 284-2622	avianca.com.co
Aviateca	800 327-9832	iflylatinamerica.com/ing
Braathens SAFE	800 548-5960	
British Airways	800 247-9297	british-airways.com
British Midland	800 788-0555	iflybritishmidland.com
Cathay Pacific Airways	800 233-2742	cathay-usa.com
China Airlines (Taiwan)	800 227-5118	china-airlines.com
City Bird Airlines	888 248-9247	citybird.com
Condor German Airlines	800 524-6975	condor.de
Copa	800 359-2672	copaair.com
CSA - Czech Airlines	800 628-6107	csa.cz
Easy Jet	0870-6-000-000 (UK)	easyjet.com
El Al Israel Airlines	800 223-6700	elal.co.il
Emirates	800 777-399	ekgroup.com
EVA Airways	800 695-1188	evaair.com.tw
Finnair	800 950-5000	finnair.fi

Resource Guide **289**

NAME	PHONE	WEB SITE
Garuda Indonesia	800 342-7832	*garuda.co.id*
Gulfstream International	800 992-8532	*flycontinental.com*
Gulf Air	800 553-2824	*gulfairco.com*
Iberia Airlines of Spain	800 772-4642	*iberia.com/ibusa*
Icelandair	800 223-5500	*icelandair.is*
Japan Airlines (JAL)	800 525-3663	*jal.co.jp*
KLM	800 225-2525	*nwa.com*
Korean Air	800 438-5000	*koreanair.com*
Kuwait Airways	800 458-9248	*travelfirst.com/sub/kuwaitair.html*
Lacsa Airlines	800 225-2272	*flylatinamerica.com/ing*
LanChile	800 735-5526	*lanchile.com/english*
Lloyd Aereo Boliviano	800 327-7407	*labairlines.bo.net*
LOT Polish Airlines	800 223-0593	*lot.com/english*
Lufthansa	800 645-3880	*lufthansa.com*
	800 563-5954 (Can.)	
Malaysia Airlines	800 552-9264	*malaysiaair.com*
Mexicana Airlines	800 531-7921	*mexicana.com.mx*
Nica	800 831-6422	*flylatinamerica.com/ing*
Olympic Airways	800 223-1226	*olympicair.com*
Pakistan International Airlines	800 221-2552	*piac.com*
Philippine Airlines	800 435-9725	*philippineair.com*
Polynesian Airlines	310 830-7363	*polynesianairlines.co.nz*
Qantas Airways	800 227-4500	*qantas.com.au*
Royal Jordanian Airline	800 223-0470	*rja.com.jo*
Sabena Belgian World Airlines	800 955-2000	*sabena.com*
SAS	800 221-2350	*sas.se*
Saudi Arabian Airlines	800 472-8342	*saudiairlines.com*
SilkAir	800 742-3333	*singaporeair.com*
Singapore Airlines	800 742-3333	*singaporeair.com*
South African Airways	800 722-9675	*saa.co.za*

NAME	PHONE	WEB SITE
Swissair	800 221-4750	swissair.com
	800 267-9477 (Can.)	
Taca	800 535-8780	flylatinamerica.com/ing
TAP Air Portugal	800 221-7370	tap-airportugal.de
Thai Airways	800 426-5204	thaiair.com
	800 668-8103 (Can.)	
TransBrasil Airlines	800 872-3153	transbrasil.com.br
Turkish Airlines	800 874-8875	turkishairlines.com
Varig Brazilian Airlines	800 468-2744	varig.com.br/english/rghome-p.htm
VASP	800 732-8277	vasp.com.br/iindex.htm
Virgin Atlantic Airways	800 862-8621	fly.virgin.com

CRUISE LINES

American Canadian Caribbean Line	800 556-7450	accl-smallships.com
American Hawaii Cruises	800 765-7450	cruisehawaii.com
Carnival Cruise Lines	800 327-9501	carnival.com
Celebrity Cruises	800 437-3111	celebritycruises.com
Clipper Cruise Line	800 325-0010	clippercruise.com
	314 727-2929 (MO)	
Costa Cruises	800 462-6782	costacruises.com/home.html
Crystal Cruises	800 446-6620	crystalcruises.com
Cunard Line	800 528-6273	cunardline.com
Delta Queen Steamboat Co.	800 458-6789	deltaqueen.com
Discovery Cruises	800 937-4477	discoverycruises.com
Fantasy Cruises & Tours	800 798-7722	fantasycruises.com
Royal Olympic Cruises	800 221-2470	epirotiki.com
Holland America	800 426-0327	hollandamerica.com
Norwegian Cruise Line	800 327-7030	ncl.com
Premier Cruises	800 327-7113	premiercruises.com
Princess Cruises	800 421-0522	princesscruises.com
Renaissance Cruises	800 525-5350	renaissancecruises.com

Resource Guide **291**

NAME	PHONE	WEB SITE
Royal Caribbean International	800 327-6700	*rccl.com*
Seabourn Cruise Line	800 929-9595	*seabourn.com*
Windjammer Barefoot	800 327-2601	*windjammer.com*
Windstar Cruises	800 258-7245	*windstarcruises.com*
World Explorer Cruises	800 854-3835	*wecruise.com*

HOTELS AND MOTELS

Adam's Mark	800 444-2326	*adamsmark.com*
Admiral Benbow Inns	800 451-1986	*admiralbenbow.com*
AmericInn	800 634-3444	*americinn.com*
AmeriSuites	800 833-1516	*amerisuites.com*
Aston Hotels	800 922-7866	*aston-hotels.com*
Baymont	800 428-3438	*baymontinns.com*
Best Inns & Suites	800 237-8466	*bestinns.com*
Best Western	800 528-1234	*bestwestern.com*
Bradford Homesuites	888 486-7829	*bradfordsuites.com*
BridgeStreet Accommodations	800 278-7338	*bridgest.com*
Budgetel Inn	800 428-3438	*budgetel.com*
Budget Host Inns	800 283-4678	*budgethost.com*
Canadian Pacific	800 441-1414	*cphotels.com*
Candlewood Suites	800 946-6200	*candlewoodsuites.com*
Choice Hotels	800 221-2222	*choicehotels.com*
Circus Circus	800 634-3450	*circuscircus.com*
Clarion	800 424-6423	*clarioninns.com*
ClubHouse Inn & Suites	800 258-2466	*clubhouseinn.com*
Club Med	800 258-2633	*clubmed.com*
Coast and WestCoast	800 426-0670	*coasthotels.com*
Colony	800 777-1700	
Comfort Inns & Suites	800 424-6423	*comfortinns.com*
Concorde Hotels	800 888-4747	*concorde-hotels.com*

RESOURCE GUIDE

NAME	PHONE	WEB SITE
Country Hearth Inns	888 443-2784	countryhearth.com
Country Inns & Suites	800 456-4000	countryinns.com
Courtyard by Marriott	800 321-2211	courtyard.com
Cross Country Inn	800 621-1429	
Crossland Economy Studios	800 398-7829	crosslandstudios.com
Crowne Plaza Hotel	800 227-6963	crowneplaza.com
Days Inns	800 329-7466	daysinn.com
Delta Hotels & Resorts	800 877-1133	deltahotels.com/main.htm
Doral Hotels	800 223-6725	arrowwood.com
DoubleTree	800 222-8733	doubletree.com
Downtowner	800 251-1962	reservehost.com
Drury Inn	800 325-8300	drury inn.com
Econo Lodge	800-424-6423	choicehotels.com
Economy Inns of America	800 826-0778	innsofamerica.com
Embassy Suites	800 362-2779	embassysuites.com
Exel Inns of America	800 356-8013	exelinns.com
Extended Stay America	800 398-7829	extstay.com
Fairfield Inn by Marriott	800 228-2800	fairfieldinn.com
Family Inns	800 362-1188	familyinnsofamerica.com
Fiesta Americana	800 343-7821	fiestaamericana.com
Forever Resorts	800 255-5561	foreverresorts.com
Forte Hotels	800 225-5843	forte-hotels.com
Four Points	800 325-3535	fourpoints.com
Four Seasons	800 332-3442	fshr.com
Friendship Inn	800 424-6423	choicehotels.com
Golden Tulip	800 344-1212	goldentulip.com
Grand Heritage Hotels	800 437-4824	grandheritage.com
Guest Quarters Suites by DoubleTree	800 424-2900	doubletree.com
Hampton Inns & Suites	800 426-7866	hamptoninn.com
Harley	800 321-2323	harleyhotels.com
Harrah's	800 427-7247	harrahs.com

NAME	PHONE	WEB SITE
Hawaiian Hotels & Resorts	800 222-5642	hawaiihotels.com
Hawthorn Suites	800 527-1133	hawthorn.com
Heartland Inn	800 334-3277	heartlandinn.com
Helmsley	800 283-3824	helmsleyhotels.com
Hilton	800 445-8667	hilton.com
Holiday Inn	800 465-4329	holiday-inn.com
HomeGate Studios & Suites	888 456-4283	homegate.com
Homewood Suites	800 225-5466	homewood-suites.com
Howard Johnson/HoJo Inn	800 446-4656	hojo.com
Hyatt Hotels and Resorts	800 233-1234	hyatt.com
Inn Points Worldwide/ Independent B&Bs	800 466-6890	innpoints.com
Innkeeper	800 466-5337	
Inns of America	800 826-0778	innsamerica.com
InnSuites	800 842-4242	innsuites.com
Inter-Continental Hotels & Resorts	800 327-0200	interconti.com
ITT Sheraton	800 325-3535	sheraton.com
Jameson Inns	800 526-3766	jamesoninns.com
Keddy's	800 561-7666	keddys.ca
Knights Inns/Arborgate Inn	800 843-5644	knightsinn.com
Kimpton	Call local property	kimptongroup.com
La Quinta	800 531-5900	laquinta.com
Leading Hotels of the World	800 223-6800	lhw.com
Lexington Suites	800 537-8483	lexhotels.com
Loews Hotels	800 235-6397	loewshotels.com
MainStay Suites	800 660-6246	mainstaysuites.com
Manhattan East Suite Hotels	800 637-8483	mesuite.com
Marc Resorts	800 535-0085	marcresorts.com
Marriott	800 228-9290	marriott.com
Masters Economy Inns	800 633-3434	masters-inns.com

NAME	PHONE	WEB SITE
Master Hosts Inn	800 251-1962	masterhosts.com/index.htm
Meridien Hotels & Resorts	800 543-4300	forte-hotels.com
Microtel Inn & Suites	888 771-7171	microtelinn.com
Milner Hotel	800 521-0592	milner-hotels.com
Moat House Hotels	800 641-0300	hotelbook.com
Motel 6	800 466-8356	motel6.com
National 9 Inns	800 524-9999	
Nendels Inns	800 547-0106	
Nikko Hotels International	800 645-5687	nikkohotels.com
Oakwood Corporate Housing	800 888-0808	oakwood.com
Omni Hotels	800 843-6664	omnihotels.com
Outrigger Hotels & Resorts	800 462-6262	outrigger.com
Pan Pacific Hotels & Resorts	800 327-8585	panpacific.com
Park Inn and Plaza	800 437-7275	parkhtls.com
Passport Inn	800 251-1962	reservehost.com
Preferred Hotels	800 323-7500	preferredhotels.com
Prince Hotels	800 542-8686	princehotels.co.jp
Quality Inns Hotels & Suites	800 424-6423	qualityinns.com
Radisson	800 333-3333	radisson.com
Ramada	800 272-6232	ramada.com
Red Carpet Inn	800 251-1962	reservehost.com
Red Roof Inns	800 843-7663	redroof.com
Regal Hotels International	800 222-8888	regal-hotels.com
Renaissance Hotels & Resorts	800 468-3571	renaissancehotels.com
Residence Inn by Marriott	800 331-3131	residenceinn.com
Ritz-Carlton	800 241-3333	ritzcarlton.com/splash.htm
Rodeway Inn	800 424-6423	rodeway.com
Scottish Inns	800 251-1962	reservehost.com

Resource Guide **295**

NAME	PHONE	WEB SITE
Sheraton	800 325-3535	sheraton.com
Shilo Inns & Resorts	800 222-2244	shiloinns.com
Shoney's Inn	800 222-2222	shoneysinn.com
Sierra Suites Hotels	800 474-3772	sierrasuites.com
Signature Inns	800 822-5252	signature-inns.com
Sleep Inn	800 424-6423	sleepinns.com
Small Luxury Hotels of the World	800 525-4800	slh.com
Staybridge Suites by Holiday Inn	800 238-8000	staybridge.com/home.htm
Sofitel, Hotel	800 763-4835	sofitel.com
Sonesta	800 766-3782	sonesta.com
Studio PLUS	800 646-8000	studioplus.com
Suburban Lodges	800 951-7829	suburbanlodge.com
Summerfield Suites Hotels	800 833-4353	summerfieldsuites.com
Super 8	800 800-8000	super8.com
Susse Chalet	800 524-2538	sussechalet.com
Swissotel	800 637-9477	swissotel.com
Thistle Hotels	800 847-4358	thistlehotels.com
Tokyu Hotels	800 428-6598	tokyuhotel.com
Towne Place Suites by Marriott	800 257-3000	towneplace.com
Travelers Inns	800 633-8300	
Travelodge/Thriftlodge	800 578-7878	travelodge.com
Vagabond Inns	800 522-1555	vagabondinns.com
Villager Lodge	800 328-7829	villager.com
Viscount	800 527-9666	viscountsuite.com
Vista International	800 445-8667	hilton.com
Walt Disney World	800 666-2929	disneyworld.com
Wellesley Inns	800 444-8888	wellesleyinns.com
Westin	800 228-3000	westin.com
Westmark	800 544-0970	westmarkhotels.com

NAME	PHONE	WEB SITE
Wilson Hotels	800 945-7667	
Wingate Inns	800 228-1000	*wingateinns.com*
Woodfield Suites	800 338-0008	*woodfieldsuites.com*
Woodfin and Chase Suites	800 237-8811	*woodfinsuites.com*
Wyndham Hotels & Resorts	800 996-3426	*wyndham.com*

RAIL PASSES

NAME	PHONE	WEB SITE
Australian Tourist Com.	847 296-4900	*aussie.net.au*
BritRail Travel Int	888 274-8724	*britrail.com*
CIE Tours International	800 243-8687	
CIT Rail	800 223-7987	
DER Travel Service	800 421-2929	*dertravel.com*
Forsyth Travel Library	800 367-7984	*forsyth.com*
Japan Nat. Tourist Org.	212 757-5640 (NY) 312 222-0874 (Chicago) 213 623-1952 (LA)	*jnto.go.jp*
New Zealand Tourism Board	800 388-5494	*nztb.govt.nz*
Orbis Polish Travel Bureau	800 223-6037	*orbis-usa.com*
Rail Europe	800 438-7245	*raileurope.com*
Rail Pass Express	800 722-7151	
Scandinavian American World Tours	800 545-2204	*travelfile.com/get/scnm.html*
Scantours	800 223-7226	

RENTAL-CAR COMPANIES

NAME	PHONE	WEB SITE
Alamo	800 327-9633	*goalamo.com*
Auto Europe	800 223-5555	*autoeurope.com*
Avis	800 331-1212	*avis.com*
Rob Liddiard Travel	800 272-3299	
Budget	800 527-0700	*budgetrentacar.com*

Resource Guide **297**

NAME	PHONE	WEB SITE
DER Travel Services	800 782-2424	*dertravel.com/dercar.htm*
Dollar	800 800-4000	*dollar.com*
Enterprise	800 325-8007	*pickenterprise.com*
Europcar	800 800-6000	*europcar.com*
European Car Reservations (ECR)	800 535-3303	
Europe by Car	800 223-1516	*europebycar.com*
Hertz	800 654-3131	*hertz.com*
International Travel Services (ITS)	800 521-0643	*its-cars-hotels.com*
Kemwel Holiday Autos	800-678-0678	*kemwel.com*
Kenning	800 227-8990	
National	800 227-7368	*nationalcar.com*
Payless	800 237-2804	*paylesscar.com*
Renault Eurodrive	800 477-7116	*eurodrive.renault.com*
Thrifty	800 367-2277	*thrifty.com*
Town and Country International	800 248-4350 (Eng., Scot., Wales)	*its-cars-hotels.com*
Ugly Duckling	800 843-3825	
Woods Car Rental UK/ British Network	44-1293-658888 (UK)	*woods.co.uk/index.html*

TRAVEL ADVISORIES

Center for Disease Control International Travelers' Hot Line	404 332-4559	*cdc.gov*
International Association for Medicare Assistance to Travelers	716 754-4883	*centex.net\~iamat*
Media Alert Foundation International	800 763-3428	*medicalert.org*
	800 344-3226	

NAME	PHONE	WEBSITE

U.S. Dept. of State
Travel Advisory Service....202 647-5225 ....*travel.state.gov*

U.S. Public Health Service
Vessel Sanitation
Program ....404 332-4565 (fax) .....*cdc.gov/nceh/programs/*
sanit/vsp/scores/scores.htm

World Health Organization
Publications Center ....518 436-9686 ....*who.ch*

INDEX

A

AAA
  hotel discounts, 166-167, 191
AAA Map'n'Go, 153, 154
AARP, 24
  hotel discounts, 167, 173-174, 191
ABC Corporate Services, 168
Access America, 253
Adam's Mark, frequent-stay program, 208-209
Air Canada
  compassionate fares, 101
  frequent-flier program, 82
  senior discounts, 100
  web site, 61
  youth/student fares, 100
Air Courier Association, 20
Airfares. *See also* Consolidators
  back-to-back tickets, 48-49
  bereavement fares, 101, 104-105, 106
  charter airlines, 44, 53-54, 69-70
  children, 100, 104, 105
  coach excursion, 41-42
  commission overrides, 47
  companion tickets, 46-47, 54-55, 101
  compassionate fares, 101, 104-105, 106
  coupon brokers, 53, 68
  discount agencies, 45-46

300 INDEX

Airfares *continued*
   discount coupons, 46
   in Europe, 107-109
   frequent-flier coupons, 50
   hidden-city, 49-50
   hub connections, 45
   infant, 103-104, 105
   internet, 57-63
   low-fare airlines, 44
   nested tickets, 48-49
   net fares, 67
   off-season, 22-23
   online, buying tickets, 59
   premium charters, 53-54
   premium-class bargains, 52-53
   premium-trip awards, 50-51, 71, 74, 76
   sale fares, 42-43
   senior clubs, 99-100
   senior coupons, 98-99
   senior discounts, 98-103, 105
   status fares, 47-48, 97-106
   travel clubs, 20
   visitor fares, 107-108
   youth/student, 100, 103, 105
Airlines. *See* Airfares; Airplane seating; Charter
     flights; Frequent-flier programs
Airplane seating, 89-96
   charters, 86
   location, 89, 93-94
   middle seats, 94
   non-reclining seats, 91-93
AirTran, 53
Alamo, 141, 143-144, 146-149
Alaska Airlines
   compassionate fares, 101

INDEX **301**

senior discounts, 100
web site, 61
Altitude problems, 279
American Airlines
compassionate fares, 101
frequent-flier program, 52, 81
premium seats, 55
senior club, 100
senior coupons, 100
senior discounts, 100
web site, 60
youth/student fares, 100, 103
American Association of Retired Persons. *See*
AARP
American Automobile Association. *See* AAA
American Express Platinum card, 54-55
American Express traveler's checks, 237
American Society of Travel Agents (ASTA), 16, 32-
33, 248
American Trans Air
compassionate fares, 101
senior discounts, 100
web site, 61
America West
compassionate fares, 101
senior coupons, 100
senior discounts, 100
web site, 61
youth/student fares, 100
Americinn, frequent-stay program, 208-209
AmeriSuites, 197, 198-199
frequent-stay program, 208-209
Amtrak, off-season rates, 23
Asia, wholesale agencies and hotels, 216-217
Aston, senior discounts, 172

302 INDEX

ATMs (automatic teller machines), 235-237
ATN, 259
Austria, car rental, 141
Auto Europe, 141-149
AutoNet, 141-149
Avis, 141-149

B

Baggage liability, 241-243, 248
Baymont, frequent-stay program, 208-209
Belgium, car rental, 141
Benelux rail passes, 139
Best Inns & Suites, frequent-stay program, 208-209
Best Western
  frequent-stay program, 206-207
  web site, 170
Bradford Homesuites, 198-199
BridgeStreet Accommodations, 196, 198-199
BritRail Pass, 139
Budget car rental, 141-149
Budget hotels/motels, 189-193, 220
Bulgaria, car rental, 141

C

Campanile, 220
Canada, car rental, 122-124
Canadian Airlines
  compassionate fares, 101
  frequent-flier program, 79, 82
  senior discounts, 100
  web site, 61
Car rentals, 111-126
  additional drivers, 115

INDEX **303**

age restrictions, 136
at airports, 113, 135
in Canada, 122-124
car rental vs. rail travel, Europe, 127-129
charge-card insurance, 116-117, 124
checklist before renting, 114
collision-damage (loss-damage) waiver
    (CDW/LDW), 115-118, 123-124, 125,
    134-135
debit cards, 113
driving-record checks, 121-122
in Europe, 129-137, 141-149
fuel charges, 120
geographic limitations, 119-120, 135-136
highway charges, Europe, 135
liability insurance, 118-119, 122-123, 124
in Mexico, 124-126
mileage, 120
models, 130-132
monthly, 114
one-way drop-off, 120-121, 133
promotions, 111-112
redlining, 120
seasonal rates, 23
senior discounts, 113-114
travel clubs, discounts, 21
upgrades, 115
value-added tax, 134
weekend rates, 112-113
weekly rates, 132
Cathay Pacific
premium seats, 55
web site, 60-61
Cendant, 196

304 INDEX

Centers for Disease Control and Prevention
  "Health Information for International Travel," 274
  International Traveler's hot line, 262
Charter flights, 83-87
  advantages, 84-85
  booking, 87
  disadvantages, 85-86
  fares, 44, 53-54, 69-70
  premium seats, 85
  refunds, 87
Choice (hotels)
  extended stay, 196
  senior discounts, 172
Cholera, 264
CityBird, 53
Climat de France, 220
Clubhouse Inn, frequent-stay program, 208-209
Clubs. *See* Travel clubs
Collision-damage (loss-damage) waiver
    (CDW/LDW), 115-118, 123-124, 125, 134-135
Colony, senior discounts, 172
Commissions, rebating, 18-19
Companion tickets, 46-47, 54-55, 101
Compassionate fares, 101, 104-105, 106
Compass (mapping system), 163
Condor, 53
Condos. *See* Vacation rentals
Consolidators, 65-71
  buying tickets, 70-71
  international fares, 67-68
  limitations, 69-70
  overrides, 67
  overseas, 109
  premium-seat discounts, 68
  risks, 45-46, 69-70

INDEX **305**

Consular information sheets, 234
Continental Airlines
  and back-to-back ticketing, 49
  compassionate fares, 101
  frequent-flier program, 52, 79, 81
  senior club, 102-103
  senior coupons, 99, 100
  senior discounts, 100, 102-103
  web site, 61
  youth/student fares, 100
Corporate rates, 167
Corsair, 53
Coupon brokers, 53, 68
Courier flights, 20
Cross Country
  frequent-stay program, 208-209
  senior discounts, 172
Crossland Economy Studios, 198-199, 200
Cruise Lines International Association, 36
Cruises
  agencies, 35-36
  booking, 36
  cabins, 35, 37
  destinations, 34-35
  discounts, 21, 34-35
  expenses, extra, 37-38
  last-minute bargains, 21, 36-37
  port charges, 38
  sanitation, 33
  single travelers, 25
  travel agencies, 35-36
  travel clubs, 21
CSA, 252-253
Customs guidelines, 243-244
Czech Republic, car rental, 141-142

306 INDEX

D

Days Inn, senior discounts, 174
DeLorme's maps, 153-154
DeLorme Street Atlas U.S.A., 159
Delta Air Lines
  compassionate fares, 101
  frequent-flier program, 78, 79, 81
  senior club, 100
  senior coupons, 100
  senior discounts, 100
  web site, 62
  youth/student fares, 100
Denmark, car rental, 142
DER Car, 141-149
Diarrhea, 273-274
Diners Club, 239
Dining discounts, 20
Disabled travelers, 26
Disney hotels, 174
Door-to-Door Co-Pilot, 163
Doubletree, extended stay, 196, 198-199
Driving permit, international, 124, 136-137
Drury Inn, frequent-stay program, 208-209
Duty-free goods, 243-244

E

Eastern Europe, rail passes, 139
ECR (European Car Reservations), 141-149
Egypt, car rental, 142
El Al, 53, 105
Emergency medical-evacuation insurance (EME),
    245, 247, 250-251, 253
Emergency road service, 21
Encephalitis, 265-266

Encore, 185
Entertainment Publications, 46, 184
ETN, web site, 62-63
Eurail pass, 138
Europass, 128, 138
Europcar, 141-149
Europe
  airfares, 107-109
  car rentals, 129-137, 141-149
  car rental vs. rail travel, 127-129
  city transit passes, 140
  France, hotels, 214, 220
Europe by Car, 141-149
Exel Inn, frequent-stay program, 208-209
Expotel Interactive, 171
Extended Stay America, 196, 198-199
Extended-stay hotels, 195-201

F

Finland, car rental, 142
Food, safe, 272-273
Four Points, senior discounts, 172
France
  car rental, 142-143
  car rental vs. rail travel, 128-129
  hotels, 214, 220
Frequent-flier programs, 73-82
  code shares, 78
  earning miles online, 80
  elite status, 77-79, 81-82
  partners, 78
  preferred seating, 81
  premium-trip awards, 50-51, 71, 74, 76
  upgrades, 51-52, 74, 76, 79, 81

308 INDEX

Frequent-flier programs *continued*
  using credit wisely, 74-76
  value of miles, 73-74, 78
Frequent-stay programs, 203-212
Frostbite, 277-278

G

Germany
  car rental, 143
  car rental vs. rail travel, 128-129
GetAway Travel Club, 185
Global positioning satellites (GPSs), 151, 162-163
Global Refund, 240-241
Granada Inns, 220
Great American Traveler, 185
Greece, car rental, 143

H

Half-price hotel programs, 181-187, 213-216, 224
Hawaiian Hotels & Resorts
  frequent-stay program, 208-209
  senior discounts, 172
Hawthorn Suites, 198-199
Health Care Abroad, 254
Health precautions, 261-268
Heat exhaustion, 276-277
Heatstroke, 276-277
Hepatitis, 265
Hertz, 141-149
Hilton
  frequent-stay program, 206-207
  senior discounts, 174
Holiday Hospitality, 206-207
Holiday Inn, extended stay, 196, 198-199

INDEX **309**

HomeGate Studios & Suites, 198-199
Homestead Village, 198-199
Hotel brokers, 175-176
Hotel discounts
  advance reservations, 166
  booking agencies, 176
  brokers, 175-176
  corporate rates, 167
  frequent-stay programs, 203-212
  half-price programs, 181-187, 213-216, 224
  internet, 168-171
  off-season prices, 23
  overseas, 213-220
  preferred rates, 167-168, 176
  senior discounts, 171-175
  short-notice bargains, 168-169
  travel clubs, 19-20
  wholesale brokers, 176-177
Hotel guides, 178
Hotel reps, 218-219
Hotel Reservations Network (HRN), 20, 171, 183
Hotels. *See also* Hotel discounts; Vacation rentals
  Asia and wholesale agencies, 216-217
  budget, 189-193, 220
  extended-stay, 195-201
  ratings, 177-180
Hotels and Travel Web site, 171
House exchange, 225
Howard Johnson, frequent-stay program, 206-207
Hungary, car rental, 144
Hyatt
  frequent-stay program, 206-207
  senior discounts, 172
  web site, 169
Hypothermia, 278

I

Iceland, car rental, 144

Immunizations, 262-268

Impulse (hotel program), 185-186

Independent B&Bs, Inns, frequent-stay program, 206-207

InnSuites, 198-199

Insects, 274-275

Institute of Certified Travel Agents (ICTA), 16

Insurance

collision-damage (loss damage) waiver (CDW/LDW), 115-118, 123-124, 125, 134-135

liability, 118-119, 122-123, 124

trip-cancellation/trip-interruption insurance (TCI), 33, 87, 245-254

Inter-Continental

money exchange, 239

web site, 169

International Association for Medical Assistance to Travelers, 280

International SOS Assistance, 253

Internet

airfares, 57-63

frequent-flier programs, 80

hotel reservations, 168-171

mapping sites, 161-162

scams, 63

weekend, short-notice fares, 58

Interval International, 229

Ireland, car rental, 144-145

Israel, car rental, 145

Italy

car rental, 145

car rental vs. rail travel, 128-129

ITC-50, 184-185

ITS (International Travel Services), 141-149

K

Kemwel Holiday Autos, 133, 141-149
Kenning, 144, 147, 149
Kiwi, Web site, 61

L

LaQuinta, frequent-stay program, 208-209
LCI, 259
Liability insurance, 118-119, 122-123, 124
Little Chef Lodges, 220
Luxembourg, car rental, 145-146

M

MainStay
  extended stay, 198-199
  senior discounts, 172
Malaria, 266-267
MapBlast!, 161
Mapquest, 151, 161-152
Maps, computer-generated, 151-163
Marc/Hawaii, senior discounts, 172
Marriott, frequent-stay program, 206-207
Marriott Residence Inn, 196, 198-199
Martinair, 53
Masters Economy Inns, frequent-stay program, 208-209
MCI, 259
Medical care, locating abroad, 279-280
Medic Alert Foundation International, 269
Medical records, 269, 280
Medical supplies, 269-270, 282-283
Meridien, frequent-stay program, 208-209

Mexico, car rental, 124-126
Microsoft Automap Road Atlas, 155-156
Microsoft Expedia Streets, 156, 159-160
Microsoft Expedia Trip Planner, 155-157
Midwest Express
  compassionate fares, 101
  senior discounts, 100
  youth/student fares, 100
Motels, budget. *See* Budget hotels/motels

N

National Association of Cruise-Only Agencies, 36
National car rental, 141-149
National Tour Association (NTA), 32-33
Netherlands, car rental, 146
Northwest Airlines
  compassionate fares, 101
  frequent-flier program, 52, 79
  senior coupons, 100
  senior discounts, 100
  web site, 61
Norway, car rental, 146

O

Oakwood Corporate Housing, 196, 198-199
Official Hotel Guide (OHG), 31, 177-180, 216
Off-season travel, 22-24
Omni, frequent-stay program, 208-209
Outrigger
  senior discounts, 172
  web site, 170

P

Package tours, 27-34
  air transportation, 30
  cancellations, 30
  complaints, 30-31, 33-34
  consumer protection, 32-33
  escorted, 28
  fine print, 29-32
  food, 32
  hotels, 31-32, 166
  single travelers, 25
  and trip-cancellation/interruption insurance, 247-
    249, 252
Papeete, 53
Payless (car rental), 145, 149
Plague, 267
Poland, car rental, 146
Poliomyelitis, 267-268
Portugal, car rental, 147
Precision Mapping Streets, 160
Preferred rates, 167-168, 176
ProAir, 53
Promus, 196, 198-199

Q

Quest, 185

R

Radisson
  senior discounts, 172
  web site, 169
Rail passes, 137-139, 296

314 INDEX

Rail travel
  car rental vs. rail travel, Europe, 127-129
  Europe, 127-129
  first class, Europe, 136
  senior discounts, 140
  youth/student discounts, 140
Ramada
  frequent-stay program, 206-207
  senior discounts, 174
Rand McNally StreetFinder, 158-159
Rand McNally TripMaker, 154-155
RCI, 229
Reno Air
  compassionate fares, 101
  first class fares, 52-53
  senior discounts, 100
Residence Inn, 196, 198-199
Road Trips Door-to-Door, 157-158
Romania, car rental, 147

S

Scams on internet, 63
Scanrail passes, 139
Schistosomiasis, 271-272
Select Street Atlas, 160-161
Senior discounts, 24
  airfares, 98-103, 105
  car rentals, 113-114
  hotels, 171-175
  rail travel, 140
Sexually-transmitted disease, 275-276
Sheraton
  frequent-stay program, 206-207
  senior discounts, 172

Shoney, Web site, 169
Sierra Suites, 198-199
Single travelers, 25-26, 249-250
SkyService, 53
Slovakia, car rental, 147
Slovenia, car rental, 147
Sofitel
  frequent-stay program, 208-209
  web site, 170
Southwest Airlines
  companion tickets, 46-47
  senior discounts, 100, 101-102
  web site, 61
Spain, car rental, 147-148
Spinal meningitis, 268
Student discounts. *See* Youth/student discounts
StudioPlus, 198-199
Suburban Lodges of America, 198-199
Summerfield Suites, 198-199
Sunburn, 277
Sunscreens, 277
Susse Chalet, frequent-stay program, 208-209
Sweden, car rental, 148
Swimming, 271-272
Switzerland
  car rental, 148
  rail pass, 139

T

Telephone services, 255-259
  callback services, 258-259
  choosing a card, 256-258, 259
  pay-phone surcharge, 257
  prepaid cards, 259

316 INDEX

THOR24, 168

Thrifty car rental, 142, 145-146, 148-149

Timeshare, 228-229, 231

TML Information Services, 122

Tours. *See* Package tours

Tower Air
  premium class, 53
  web site, 61

Town & Country, 149

TownePlace Suites, 196, 198-199

Trains. *See* Amtrak; Rail travel

Travel advisories, 233-235, 270

Travel agencies, 15-19, 297
  and consolidators, 66
  credentials, 16
  cruises, 35-36
  discount agencies, 66
  hotel reservations, 218
  information sources, 17-18
  rebating agencies, 18-19, 21
  selection criteria, 17-18

Travel Alert program, 21

Travel clubs, 19-22
  airfare discounts, 20
  car rental discounts, 21
  dining discounts, 20
  hotel discounts, 19-20
  vacation rentals, 224

Traveler's checks, 237-239

Travelers (insurance), 253-254

Travelex Cruise & Tour, 253

Travelgraphics, 168

Travel Guard, 249, 253

Travel Interlink, 216-217

Travelodge, frequent-stay program, 206-207

INDEX **317**

Travel warnings, 234-235

Travel Weekly Web site, 170-171

Trip-cancellation/trip-interruption insurance (TCI), 33, 87, 245-254

Triwest, 231

Turkey, car rental, 149

TWA
  children fares, 100
  compassionate fares, 101
  frequent-flier program, 52, 81
  senior coupons, 99, 100
  senior discounts, 100
  web site, 61
  youth coupons, 103

Typhoid fever, 268

U

United Airlines
  compassionate fares, 101
  senior club, 99-100
  senior coupons, 100
  senior discounts, 100
  web site, 59

United Kingdom
  car rental, 149
  car rental vs. rail travel, 128-129

U.S. Airways
  compassionate fares, 101
  frequent-flier program, 79
  senior coupons, 99, 100
  senior discounts, 100
  upgrades, 52
  web site, 61

U.S. Tour Operators Association (USTOA), 32-33, 248

V

VacationLand, 216-217
Vacation rentals, 21, 221-231
  advantages, 221-222
  agencies, 224-225, 226-227
  brochures, 225-226
  disadvantages, 222-223
Vagabond
  frequent-stay program, 208-209
  senior discounts, 172
Value-added tax (VAT), 134, 239-241
Villager Lodge, 196, 198-199
Visa TravelMoney card, 237-238
Visitor airfares, 107-108
VoiceNet, 259

W

Water supplies, 270-271
West Coast, senior discounts, 172
Westin, frequent-stay program, 206-207
Wholesale booking agencies, 216-217, 224
Wholesale brokers, 176-177
Wingate, frequent-stay program, 208-209
Woodfin Suites, 198-199
Woods, 149
Worldwide Assistance, 253

Y

Yellow fever, 263, 268
Youth/student discounts
  airfares, 100, 103, 105
  rail, 140